# Social Work in a Globalizing World

# Social Work in a Globalizing World

Lena Dominelli

polity

First published in 2010 by Polity Press

Polity Press
65 Bridge Street
Cambridge CB2 1UR, UK

Polity Press
350 Main Street
Malden, MA 02148, USA

ISBN-13: 978-0-7456-4088-4
ISBN-13: 978-0-7456-4089-1 (pb)

A catalogue record for this book is available from the British Library.

Typeset in 10 on 12 pt Sabon
by Toppan Best-set Premedia Limited

For further information on Polity, visit our website: www.politybooks.com

# Contents

# Detailed Contents

# Acknowledgements

Writing a book on a complex subject like social work practice is not a strictly individual affair. It requires empirical research, reading from library collections and the internet, and talking to people who have been involved in social work practice, policy and education. I am indebted to many people for their help, most of whom cannot be named as they have contributed anonymously to my understandings of our world. Thank you all: I owe you an enormous debt for the insights you have gifted me. To protect identities, I have used fictitious names and removed any identifying features in all the case studies that I use. Others have contributed in more specific ways, and I thank them specifically for their assistance: Emma Longstaff and Jonathan Skerrett for their support in getting this book published; Nicholas and David for their unstinting love and refusal to let 'my work' get in the way of our relationships; Mom, Maria, Sam, Nic, Rita and Connie for being there with words of encouragement whenever I have needed them and for sharing my vision of working towards a more just world for us all now and in the future. And Dad, for embedding your dream of social justice in my thoughts from childhood, I thank you.

# 1

# Introduction

The world is becoming increasingly complex as the spread of hitherto unknown diseases, disasters both (hu)man-made and natural, poverty, and migratory movements of people pose new challenges for social workers. These co-exist alongside the traditional challenges of dealing with human well-being, child protection, social welfare, older people's needs, disability issues and offending behaviour, among others. Social workers' responses are significant, although sometimes not the best that could be offered. Social work, practised in diverse settings through a multitude of approaches across the world, has at its heart a commitment to serve people. For some, this involves enabling people to achieve their goals. For others, it is about social change within a context of social justice, human rights and citizenship. This gives social work an incredible heterogeneity. Among a diversity of theories, approaches, settings and contexts within which it operates, there are commonalities especially in purpose and methods. These similarities and differences create contested space filled by service users, policy-makers, academics and practitioners according to the worldviews, ideologies and belief systems that underpin their concepts of what social workers should do, with whom, and how.

Questions about its roles and purpose are crucial in (re)configuring the boundaries of what constitutes professional social work. The answers are often controversial. If these are critical of current practice, they can undermine the morale and confidence of social workers in their profession. Attacks on their professionalism, especially those made in the context of cases that have resulted in the non-accidental injury to and sometimes the death of children, are particularly distressing. It is usually not the social workers who have killed the child. But the failure of social workers to prevent their assault or murder by carers ensures that little comfort is gained from such knowledge. Additionally, issues of confidentiality about specific situations mean that social workers rarely engage in public debates in the media about what may have gone wrong. And the many instances of excellent practice in serving others are seldom given space on television, on radio or in newspapers. Hence, the public is unaware of what social workers do, day in and day out, to protect children and other people requiring assistance. Nor does the general public know about practitioners' heroic and innovative interventions in some of the most horrendous situations brought about through natural and (hu)man-made disasters, where they are among the many professionals who provide emergency relief responses.

## A profession worth having

Social work is a profession with roots in caring for others. Since caring is an integral part of the human condition, individuals feel entitled to hold a view about the contours of the profession, its role and its purpose. Many constantly ask whether it is a profession worth having. My answer is 'yes', as emancipatory practice. Emancipatory social work is person-centred, empowering, and critical of power structures and systems of resource distribution that undermine the well-being of the many. It also wants egalitarian changes in these through collective, participatory, democratic action. And it asks awkward questions such as whether individuals should pay taxes for personal social services to ensure appropriate coverage for all, be encouraged to become consumers purchasing what they need in the marketplace, or look for different alternatives. I acknowledge that there is much work to do to realize a democratic, emancipatory vision of social work.

In neo-liberal Britain, the push towards the market has been powerfully articulated through policies that have promoted the expansion of private provision whereby concerns rarely surface about who is excluded. Thus, alternative views about solutions offered by the social market, often considered in great depth among those supporting the 'new' social movements and the anti-globalization movements, exist on the margins of proposals currently propounded in the media. Present-day discourses about who should pay for old-age pensions and why public-sector wages and services should be cut to deal with the latest fiscal crisis favour the market and indicate attempts to silence opposition to market-based framings of the options available to people living in Western countries.

That this does not work is evidenced by market reactions to the high levels of debt in Greece, Spain and Portugal.

I write this book to argue that social work as emancipatory practice is worth having and that it has significant things to say about some of the intractable social problems faced by contemporary societies. I also wish to encourage debate about social work's history, the enormous contributions made by the profession to improving human well-being in diverse contexts and settings, and confidence in its future development as an important, life-enhancing profession. I do so from a social justice, human rights, citizenship-based perspective, while exploring how this approach developed in response both to critiques from various sources about the inadequacies of mainstream practices during specific historical conjunctures and to service users' demands for more emancipatory interventions under their control. The history of emancipatory social work is one of different struggles to bring it into being and to gain its acceptance among service users and ruling elites, who also shaped its potential boundaries. A key emphasis of this book is social work in the UK. However, I describe its evolution in the global context and draw connections as appropriate between developments in different parts of the world – the USA, Canada, New Zealand, Australia, China, and parts of Africa and Latin America – and what happens in the UK.

In undertaking research for this book, I have consulted with a range of people in different regions of the world, examined policy documents and research and writings by others, and also undertaken my own investigations. Although the names and circumstances of individuals have been rendered anonymous, their activities have added to the store of knowledge available to me in developing my thoughts and insights into the environments and contexts in which people are located and practitioners practice. Some have challenged my attempts to answer the question of how social workers can contribute to creating a world that promotes human well-being while acknowledging that people are only one of the many stakeholders on planet earth and that our interdependencies require us never to lose sight of this reality.

As a result, social work, as the profession charged with enhancing people's well-being through formal social institutions that enshrine caring relationships within socially acceptable norms, is in a state of flux and constantly evolving in response to the many challenges it faces. From its inception, its development was linked to its claims to being a profession. While its status remains a matter of controversy, current discourses are associated with the extent of its professional remit and whether certain elements within it are appropriately defined as falling within social work itself, or whether they are more appropriately situated within other related disciplines, such as health, psychiatry, psychology and criminology. Addressing these challenges complicates social work as a dynamic, fluid and constantly changing entity that seeks to adapt to demands from many quarters – legislative diktats, social policies, service users' expectations, professional aspirations, economic demands, social developments, political ideologies as articulated primarily by policy-makers, and research.

I argue that, in rising to the demands made of it in the twenty-first century, social work is being shaped by a number of forces, among them:

- globalization;
- its spread as a global profession recognized in at least eighty-four countries;
- the settings in which it takes place now, and how these link to its own historical past as a profession and its development and strengths in the future;
- the fiscal crises in the state and the market;
- the technological revolution, including that of informatics and the internet, as these collapse time and space and raise new opportunities for practice as well as training – e.g., SWAP (the Higher Education Academy: Social Policy and Social Work Subject Centre, based at the University of Southampton);
- the interdependence of people within and between countries;
- the growing numbers of natural and man-made disasters (including climate change) that open new areas for practice;
- the profession's uncertain and porous borders, which can be encroached upon by other more organized and powerful professions;
- rising demands for its services at both ends of the age spectrum – children and older people – as life chances change;
- contested egalitarian ethics and values;
- its commitment to human rights and social justice;
- spreading examples of good practice from within and outside the profession;
- learning from the past, especially in ending oppressive forms of practice;
- the influence of international organizations representing professional social work internationally – e.g., the International Association of Schools of Social Work (IASSW), the International Council on Social Welfare (ICSW) and the International Federation of Social Workers (IFSW); and
- the profession's persistent optimism and sense of renewal, including the formulation of locality-specific theories and models for practice.

I invite readers to reflect upon these issues and consider their relevance for the work that practitioners undertake in their daily practice; learning about concepts and skills that can renew the profession; moving beyond the most pressing problems in the in-tray of policy-makers and middle-level management while addressing them; strengthening social work education and training; and supporting students to engage with emerging areas for practice.

## The structure of the book

The book is structured around the idea that social work is a meaningful profession across all regions of the world. However, the primary focus of practice is the nation–state that operates within the international arena, and that those living within its borders prefer forms of practice consistent with their specific locality and traditions.

An array of initiatives to engage in mutual exchanges between local and global players in the profession exists alongside those dressed in neo-colonial garb whereby dominant groups impose their views about social work on those in other countries, particularly in the Global South and among aboriginal peoples (Gray et al., 2009). Nonetheless, service delivery in practice remains distinctly heterogeneous and local. The tendency towards locality-specific versions of social work is gathering pace as 'indigenization' becomes an international preoccupation, largely as resistance to the homogenizing trends embedded in social relations driven by profit motives and the desire of entrepreneurs to appropriate other people's labour, material resources, geographic spaces and intellectual property. I lay the foundations of this premise in chapter 2. In chapter 3, I consider the terrain of 'the social' as part of the project of creating the new profession of social work, initially in Europe. I also consider the contradictions that lie at the heart of professional practice – ethical dilemmas that practitioners might encounter while helping people and/or subjecting them to various forms of social control.

The continuing struggle of social work to be accepted as a fully fledged profession forms the core of chapter 4. A number of ideas have been exchanged across the Atlantic to influence social work developments in countries on both sides of the 'Big Pond'. I highlight the ambiguous nature of these exchanges because not all have been adopted with sensitivity to local cultures. Moreover, a concern in many European countries with being taken over by the larger American market, practice opportunities and academy has created tensions concerning local autonomy.

Contemporary emancipatory social work has been formulated as an alternative to mainstream services as a result of pressure, lobbying and practice initiatives instigated by the new social movements. I explore this development in chapter 5 and show how the concepts of social justice and human rights underpin these new forms of practice, including those designated as feminist social work, anti-racist and black perspectives in social work, and the social model of disability. Because these took the part of the underdog, their development often occurred against the bitter opposition of those on the right of the political spectrum – academics, government ministers and corporate entrepreneurs who felt that social workers should be above politics and remain strictly neutral. While these critics were oblivious to their own political rootedness in maintaining the status quo, they argued that, by adopting explicitly political positions and advocating for those who were alienated and disenfranchised, such 'radical' social workers were exceeding their professional powers and ignoring the requirement of the state and other funders for neutrality in relation to their policies for regulating entitlements.

The state's position as a provider of services, right-wing ideologues argued, placed it beyond reproach by professionals, even when many of those using the services deemed them unfit for purpose. Complaints about inadequate services had rendered the state the object of many protests. Matters were exacerbated when social workers engaged in industrial action, either to protect services or to dispute their own pay and working conditions (Simpkin, 1979). Strikes have featured in localities across the UK since the 1970s. These have ranged from a few hours or days to lengthy ones like those that began in Liverpool in 2005 and 2007.

An early example was in Northern Ireland in the 1970s, when social workers and community workers supported the rent and rates strikes mounted by tenants in public housing. Their protests were fuelled by the Debt Payments Act of 1971, which deducted monies from strikers' benefits even though the latter were intended to support their families (Rollston and Smyth, 1982). The first prolonged national strike of social workers in England took place during 1978–9, primarily in local authorities with a high proportion of newly qualified staff. Watson and Lee (1982) claim that this was because these workers were astounded by the disparities they found between the values they had learnt in the academy and those they found being practised on the ground. Their activism resulted in employers disparaging the training of social workers as being too radical and not sufficiently rooted in day-to-day routines. Yet, when asked to provide evidence to back their assertions, the same employers would say that social workers from 'radical' courses such as those from Warwick University at the time were fully capable of 'doing the day job' and often represented their most 'innovative and thoughtful workers' (personal communications).

The values of human dignity and worth are central to people being treated with respect and receiving the services they need. Their violation in both the social and the physical domain lays the foundation for degrading treatment in both spheres. Human, social and environmental degradation are becoming increasingly common despite government rhetoric about equality of opportunity. The elimination of poverty – particularly among children within the UK, and on a global scale for 2.8 billion people – expressed in the commitments agreed at the World Summit for Social Development in Copenhagen in 1995 and the Millennium Development Goals (MDGs) later pronounced at the United Nations, appears to be receding from reach (Correll, 2008).

In 2000, 189 countries signed up to the MDGs, which cover poverty, health and education and the stipulated targets to be reached for each by 2015. With the exception of China's pledge to address rural poverty and the goal of enabling children to access primary education, it is unlikely that the MDGs will be met (Correll, 2008). I examine these issues in chapter 6 and consider the significance of climate change and the pollution of air, water and land as legitimate arenas for social work interventions, particularly those linked to social and community development. Holistic practice in these matters involves social workers engaging with people and contextualizing their present and future growth amid the spiritual, physical and socio-economic environments in which people live. The roles of the International Association of Schools of Social Work (IASSW), the International Council on Social Welfare (ICSW) and the International Federation of Social Workers (IFSW) are important in promoting cross-border solidarity in matters of this kind. Their endeavours are referred to at relevant points throughout the book because they have been crucial in developing the voice of the profession for over eight decades.

The important context of globalization, and understanding its evolution as a combination of activities that integrate localities to the global and the global to the local, is examined in chapter 7. This demonstrates the need for complex understandings of the processes of globalization and their impact on social work practice, service development and delivery. The 'benefits' of globalization are contested, not least by those involved in what have been termed 'anti-globalization movements', which have demanded that economic growth should sustain human beings and the environments in which they live rather than gathering profits for the few. Social workers have been implicated in such activities on both sides of the divide between those who think globalization benefits poor people and those who do not. Additionally, practitioners have had to respond to the internationalization of social problems, migratory movements among both clients and practitioners, increased managerialism, and the bureaucratization of practice that has accompanied neo-liberalism.

I conclude in chapter 8 that social work is a global profession that has a huge agenda in remaking itself for the twenty-first century. Taking on board the challenges of demands for culturally appropriate, locality-specific forms of practice, climate change and the need to conserve fossil fuels, and the development of renewable sources of energy has laid foundations for innovative thinking in the profession. Social workers have a choice – to continue with oppressive forms of practice that impoverish people rather than help them or to become allies in the endeavour to create liberating forms of practice that affirm people's rights and redistribute power, goods and services equitably across the globe. Responses in accordance with the latter possibility is particularly important, as the destructive effects of climate change will weigh most heavily on poor people throughout the world, regardless of the size of their carbon footprint or their engagement in the processes of industrialization. These challenges currently emphasize the interdependencies that exist between peoples and nations and argue all the more for egalitarian forms of practice based on reciprocity, mutuality, human rights and social justice. They also question notions of citizenship located within a specific nation–state. Responses to these concerns suggest the significance of a portable and transnational or global form of citizenship capable of providing entitlement to unstigmatized, universal services to all those in need, regardless of their geographic location, personal attributes or individual ability to pay.

# 2

# Creating the New Profession of Social Work

## Introduction

Social work is a contested discipline and profession with porous borders. It is rooted in notions of formal caring and popular ideologies about informal caring about and for others, primarily in kinship relationships and voluntary self-help groups and professional agencies. An ethic that affirms both a duty to provide care and an entitlement to be cared for as elements of citizenship is an important component of discourses with which social work has to engage (Knjin and Ungerson, 1997).

In this chapter, I examine social work's beginnings and briefly trace its development as a profession concerned primarily with poor people in European nation–states. It then spread to other parts of the globe as part of an imperialist mission that may now include the use of the internet and ongoing attempts to establish reciprocity between countries. Early exchanges across the Atlantic involved the USA via visitors such as Jane Addams, who found forms of practice in Europe that they subsequently transplanted to their home country. Exchanges could also take place in the opposite direction, as occurred later in the case of Alice Salomon, who sought political asylum in North America when fleeing the terrors of Nazism.

More recent exchanges have drawn on individual motivations, often backed by institutional resources, as 'internationalization' becomes a mantra whereby institutions, professions and individuals seek to influence those living in other countries in particular ways. These can vary from those engaged in new forms of colonization to those seeking to resist such pressures and work in alliances with others to create more egalitarian, empowering and reciprocal forms of practice that are culturally appropriate and locality specific. There is not one unitary story about social work, but many. These stories are linked to specific contexts, historical periods, nation–states and individuals. Practice is marked by flux and change as it crosses borders internally and externally. The form it takes depends on whether people seek to 'work with' others or whether they attempt to 'do to' them, and how those others challenge them for presuming that they should be 'done to'.

This chapter will also consider social work's connection with both the local and the global and highlight key issues and dilemmas affecting practice once it moves beyond national borders and transcends social divides. I will introduce readers to international organizations in social work, particularly the International Association of Schools of Social Work (IASSW) and the International Federation of Social Workers (IFSW). I focus on these two because they are the major civil society organizations that represent social work educators and practitioners, respectively, in the international arena and have formal consultative status with the United Nations. Others, including those that have links with these two, such as the Inter-University Consortium on International Social Development (now the International Consortium on Social Development) and the International Conference on Social Work in Health and Mental Health, are smaller and cater for more specialized audiences.

International non-governmental organizations such as the Red Cross, Oxfam and Save the Children are civil society organizations that undertake social work practice on various issues, notably poverty, disasters and health matters. These organizations are not directly involved in training and education in the university sector, and most of their employees identify not with the profession of social work but with aid and relief work. Unlike these organizations, IASSW (www.iassw-aiets.org) and IFSW (www.ifsw.org) do argue that they represent the profession internationally and exist to promote the interests of social work educators and practitioners rather than deliver personal social services to particular groups in need. Additionally, both have collaborated to increase the power and voice of the profession, particularly in international organizations such as the UN. As a result of working together, they have developed an international definition of social work; the global ethics document; and global qualifying standards as *tools* to identify, debate and inform both those areas that social workers across the world hold in common and those expressions of practice that are different.

Despite my engagement for several decades with the global dimensions of social work, this book is not about international social work, however defined. It is primarily about locality-specific social work and how it both shapes and is shaped by the global contexts within which it is located and operates. The starting point for me is the United Kingdom, a key leader in the early development of the profession. However, I use illustrations from other countries to explore specific points, including connections between social work in different countries.

The myriad actors who influence social work theory and practice and the varied contexts within which they operate each merit discussion and consideration, but it is not possible for me to do this at length in the restricted space offered by a short book. As the current state of knowledge in social work is partial, any ensuing narratives about the profession are limited. The privilege of both shaping the world's professional stage and being shaped by it is, theoretically, accorded to all actors regardless of ethnicity, gender, age, class, religious affiliation or ability. Its realization for all in practice is another matter, and it is in the practical domain that the barriers that create inequalities are erected and some are included at the expense of others. The profession's weaknesses also set the challenges that call for responses from those intending to promote egalitarian relationships and social structures. I add my voice to those of the many others involved in the development of an egalitarian and just world.

## The rise and spread of professional social work

Professional social work emerged in nineteenth-century Europe as nation–states began to excavate the terrain of 'the social' and sought to address the uncertainties that rapid industrialization had wrought in people's everyday routines and expectations. Before this, social work had been conducted within the domain of the family as kinship obligations, in neighbourhoods as philanthropic acts of charity or kindness between strangers, and through social institutions, especially those religious foundations that saw providing assistance to those in need as a moral obligation (Walton, 1975; Kendall, 2000). Charitable duties were often rooted in particular types of community where people shared a specific identity, as was the case with religious organizations and voluntary agencies developed to cater for specific service user groups. Delivery of the care offered often fell on women as part of their role within the family and society generally (Wilson, 1977). Such voluntary agencies now co-exist alongside those that constitute the welfare state.

Today, when people refer to 'social work', they are talking about professional social work rather than informal caring. Professional social workers began engaging with and defining the territory that became known as 'the social' in the late nineteenth century (Lorenz, 1994) and asserted that their profession was the one capable of responding to the challenges of addressing the hardships brought about by industrialization. They simultaneously sought to enhance its scientific and professional credentials and to lay claim to high professional status (Heraud, 1981). That goal remains to be achieved, and social work continues to be a profession with a front line dominated by women. Social work as an informal but structured helping profession within social institutions and organizations predates modernity. However, modernity initiated the formation of *professional* social work and, with it, the individualization of both the service user and the way in which help was delivered. It was also invented within the context of the nation–state (Lorenz, 1994), with practice focusing largely on crucial issues of relevance to national preoccupations (Grande, 2004). As a result, social work is complex and fractured along many axes, despite having a dominant or hegemonic form, even where those involved in 'radical' practice exert agency to contest it in a variety of ways. The challenges to hegemonic forms of practice are more diverse in the international domain, where social development goals are intertwined with individual interventions.

Professional social work eventually spread across the world. Today, IASSW's *Directory of Schools of Social Work* indicates that there are around 3,000 schools of social work at tertiary level, and IFSW's website indicates that there are 1.5 million professional social workers practising in at least eighty-four countries. Thus, social work has become a global profession, by which I do not mean a unitary activity that exists in the same form in every country. Rather, I use the term to indicate that, as a profession, it exists in some form, defined as social work, by those living in specific localities, in all regions of the world. Angie Barretta-Herman (2005, 2008) has organized a world census of social work to ascertain some of this diversity in greater detail.

In modern European societies wracked by social divisions and inequalities of many forms – 'race', gender, disability, mental ill health, age and poverty being key – there was an urgent need to deal with the casualties of a harsh industrial system, maintain social order among disaffected groups, and respond to the needs of vulnerable people enduring ill health, family breakdown, rising crime rates and unreliable sources of income – problems that seem familiar today (Beveridge, 1942; Walton, 1975). Migration was another important consideration, as the destitute of Europe or the economic migrants of yesteryear sought better lives in Canada, the United States, Australia, New Zealand, Latin America and Africa. Once overseas, these colonizers often denied the presence of those already there (Grande, 2004), and the land, especially in Australia, was declared *terra nullius* – empty land that belonged to no one and therefore available for settlement by white Europeans, mainly those of British descent, once the UK assumed sovereignty (Briskman, 2007).

Colonization in overseas territories subjected local people, particularly aboriginal and indigenous peoples* already living in these locations, to the dispossession of their lands, resources, cultures and children (Haig-Brown, 1988; Read, 1981; HREOC, 1997). Brutal and coercive colonizing processes became integral to European settlement initiatives as European migration accelerated and produced many instances of local resistance in response (Grande, 2004). Colonization can be considered as external when exploitative relationships involve another country or lands beyond the national territory and internal when people within the nation–state are manipulated to privilege the dominant group. Social work has been implicated in both forms. In its external variation, social workers were involved in turning indigenous people into Europeans (Grande, 2004) and focused on depriving families of their children. In Australia, such children are referred to as the 'stolen generation' (Read, 1981). The profession's role in sending poor white working-class British children overseas to Australia, New Zealand and Canada (Bagnell, 2001) was indicative of social work's role in an internal colonialism that became expressed abroad. Called 'home children' or child migrants, they were assumed to be orphans and were abused horrendously (Humphreys, 1996; Bagnell, 2001).

Many of the systems of social organization prevailing in the colonizers' countries of origin were transplanted into the 'new' lands. Ideas of inferiority and superiority linked to 'race' became especially important, and European settler thinking was dominated by the notion of indigenous people learning about and assimilating into Western ways of living and being (Haig-Brown, 1988). Assimilationist processes set the scene for the exploitation of indigenous peoples and the appropriation of their resources under various systems of colonial rule (Osterhammel, 2005). Although European powers shared notions about white supremacy, they fought each other for control of these overseas territories. Each had different languages, cultures and ways of relating to the local people, but

---

* I am concerned that the term 'indigenous' has been appropriated by a range of people and institutions that do not have aboriginal histories and legacies preceding colonization – e.g., the British National Party in the UK. The BNP claims it represents the 'indigenous' (white) British, which sounds remarkably like arguing for purely white people to populate the British Isles. Additionally, 'indigenous' was used by imperial rulers and settlers to colonize people different from them and to argue that the latter were 'backward' and 'less civilized' and therefore 'subject' to intervention in the name of improving their capacity to become full members of the human race. I prefer the term 'locality-specific practice' to indicate the same aims as those intended by indigenous movements, but use their term when referring to their discourses.

assimilation and a determination to erase local people's claims to autonomous rights and resources featured in all. Resistance to these practices has survived five centuries of oppression and is now reflected in calls for the indigenization and the development of self-identified systems of welfare by aboriginal peoples in North America, Latin America, Australia and New Zealand (Crisjohn et al., 2006).

The 'agreements' reached with local people were varied and problematic (Siggins, 2005). In British Columbia, for example, the colonizers dispensed with myths that involved symbolic recognition of aboriginal rights and simply assumed control without bothering to make the token treaties or payments for lands and resources that prevailed in other parts of Canada. Settlers simply acquired aboriginal lands through an imposed legal process (Tennant, 1990). In other parts of North America, some form of treaty was used to mark relationships between the local indigenous peoples and the ruling elites, although these involved little payment for the resources that were part of the 'land grab' (Grande, 2004). As recently as 1993 in the USA, a dispute over payments for territories appropriated through these treaties resulted in the Indian Land Trust being accused of depriving Native Americans of $US1.37 billion by not paying compensation as agreed when the Indian Land Trust was formed. This case was finally resolved in December 2009 (ibid.: 77).

The white European elites fought each other and sought alliances with indigenous people in various wars. Native people were valued as guides and cannon fodder, but generally were not trusted to run their own lands (Siggins, 2005). This outlook was eventually institutionalized in what were called 'reserves', of often poor quality land, where 'native' people were consigned to live. In Canada, the reserves were governed by the federal government through the Indian Act 1876, which imposed on indigenous men a colonized identity defined by the white European rulers while removing any claims to it from indigenous women who moved off the reservations set aside for 'Indians' or married white Europeans. By denying indigenous women their right to either a self-defined or a colonized identity, this Act introduced and then reinforced patriarchal relations in communities that had never been so structured. And it left indigenous women fighting additional and protracted battles to resume their status as original inhabitants of the land and reclaim identities that had been removed from them (ibid.).

The white settlers created societies that drew on forms of social organization from their countries of origin and modified them to suit their local circumstances. Although democracy was an important ideology, it was riven by a number of social divisions that characterized it in their home countries, where gender, class, age and 'race' were particularly relevant. Communities were organized to differentiate people's entitlements to rights along many social divisions, both within their own grouping and in relation to those they considered 'outsiders'. While there were examples of acceptance or accommodation, these divides were usually contested by those so colonized, and resistance through everyday life practices or overt rebellion was commonplace (Siggins, 2005). Indigenous peoples' rejection of white rule in countries outside Europe has been sustained for over 500 years (Chrisjohn et al., 2006).

For many indigenous people, colonization and settlement meant losing their extended families, language and culture as well as their lives (Furniss, 1995; Chrisjohn et al., 2006). Social work became implicated in oppressive activities even before the days of professionalization, largely through missionary activities linked to religious organizations. Christianity was promoted in its various versions and educational establishments were created that sought to cater for the needs of children and young people, often some distance away from their families and villages. In such residential institutions, children were deprived of their cultural and linguistic heritages and given education and care that was to turn them into young Europeans. Brutal sanctions and various forms of abuse were used to discipline them, often with tragic consequences that still impact upon family life today, mainly in the form of substance misuse and intra-community and family violence (Haig-Brown, 1988; Grande, 2004).

Education, health and social services for settlers replicated those available 'back home' and were also in keeping with assimilationist ideas in which one (superior) type of provision was available to settler society and other, lesser ones for the indigenous peoples (Hier and Bolaria, 2006). This binary division of society reached its most extreme form under apartheid in South Africa and the Jim Crow laws in the USA, although the indigenous peoples of North America, New Zealand/ Aotearoa and Australia had to endure their own specific versions of segregation.

There is another story to be told about the indigenous peoples of Europe. In considering the post-Columbus period, social workers should not forget the colonization of peoples such as the Sami, Inuit and Greenlanders. Their treatment raises concerns about assimilationist practices that draw upon colonizing powers other than those of England, France, Spain and Portugal. Internal colonialism within Europe has been practised among the hunter-gathers, like the Sami in Northern Europe and Russia (Rink, 2004), and white working-class people included within the same national group – e.g., the Irish in the United Kingdom (Kee, 2000), the Basques in Spain (Payne, 1975) or the Calabrian peoples of southern Italy (Scarpino, 1992). It also includes the hostility of Eastern Europeans to the Roma, whose nomadic lifestyles have been destroyed through being compelled to lead sedentary lives (Zaviršek, 2008).

Access to the benefits of citizenship, including welfare rights, formed part of the weaponry used to persuade or force people to change their lifestyles and worldviews. Resistance to colonizing practices has survived, and the nomadic peoples of Europe are also telling their stories and having them told. For example, the Roma have organized to lobby the European Parliament to uphold their rights (CEUC, 2000); the Greenlanders have demanded their sovereignty back from Denmark (Fitzhugh and Ward, 2000); and the Sami in the Nordic countries are asking for their caribou lifestyles to be safeguarded and highlighting how climate change has exacerbated an already fragile existence (Rink, 2004).

The diversity and heterogeneity of social work as a global profession (Garber, 2000) is both a strength and a weakness. The dominance of the English language has produced a number of debates about how the profession can refrain from enforcing Western geopolitical interests and economic relations that create new forms of cultural imperialism while working towards securing emancipation and equality for people whose interests, identities, concerns and methods of working often differ substantially. Somehow, the profession has to find the means to be empowering in both the local and the global domain. This is a complicated and difficult undertaking because it requires holistic understandings of the world and the social positioning of individuals and groups within it. There are many layers and levels of realities that require detailed and careful attention if practitioners are to respond to locality-specific demands and initiatives without oppressing those involved in the interactions. Resistance to Western hegemony in the profession is being reflected in initiatives to 'indigenize' social work across the globe (Gray et al., 2009) and in resistance to the neo-imperial social relations that currently accompany globalization. Rooting practice in the local, as do those engaged in indigenizing social work, is also a counteraction to a monopolistic and homogenizing globalization that commenced centuries ago.

## The growth of locality-specific social work

The form and expression that social work assumes in any particular place is locality specific and heterogeneous. Even in the more recent history of the UK, when a dominant bureaucratic form of the welfare state has prevailed, there has been a 'mixed economy of welfare' that has drawn on voluntary agencies and those associated with religious foundations. In contemporary Britain, this diversity has broadened to include private for-profit organizations across a spectrum of provision. Variety features in social work, even in places where the system is presumed to be mono-lithic. For example, in Canada, where British and French settlers sought to impose their views of what constituted appropriate welfare services, indigenous forms, and those of other settlers, co-existed alongside the dominant two to cater for the needs of specific groups.

The stories emanating from formerly colonized peoples tell of immense heroism despite the obstacles and huge odds threatening their survival. Lawrence Hill (2007), for instance, movingly tells of Aminata, a young woman of African origin who, like other people captured through the slave trade, was being transported between Africa, North America and England. She draws on her strengths, knowledge and networking skills to survive and grow. Grande (2004) describes the struggles of indigenous people for sovereignty in the USA, while Gord Bruyere (2009) recounts the struggle for a First Nations education in Canada.

Although its early beginnings in the UK were deeply embedded within the voluntary sector, and spearheaded mainly by middle-class women, social work became the handmaiden of a state that was keen to reduce social disorder and maintain discipline among what were considered the unruly masses in the home-grown working class and the alleged 'aliens' in its midst – a term used to define anyone that came from outside the nation–state, including those from overseas colonies. This focused much of social workers' attention on holding the line between deviancy and normalcy and promoting white middle-class views of both in classifica-tion systems that distinguished between 'deserving' and 'undeserving' claimants (Walton, 1975). This division of people was used to ration resources and also to instil middle-class values in sectors of the popula-tion that had limited regard for them (Dominelli, 1997). Women were important in the early profession across Europe (Hering and Waaldijk, 2003), and the first social work education course was started in the Netherlands in 1896 by Marie Muller-Lulofs (Hamburger et al., n.d.). In the UK, courses at universities in London and Birmingham followed a few years later.

## Philanthropic or charitable social work

Religious institutions have a long history of taking responsibility for meeting what might be termed the welfare needs of people, particularly of children and of adults suffering from physical, mental and social infirmities of various kinds. Christian churches, Jewish synagogues, Islamic mosques and Sikh gudwaras have each had their own traditions of promoting the moral obligation of those living in abundance to give to those in need, in the form of the tithe (in Christianity, one-tenth of one's income contributed voluntarily), the *zakat* (alms) as one of the Five Pillars in Islam, and ideas of *langar* (free food) and *seva* (community service) in Sikhism. The Protestant ethic, for example, emphasized 'good works' on the road to individual salvation through what Max Weber (1978) termed the 'work ethic', which prompted the construction of grandiose civic amenities built by Victorian philanthropists.

Such commitments laid the foundations for the philanthropic approach to social work, which was defined largely as 'helping others'. It inspired both individual and institutional forms of giving, often referred to as charity. Charity was based on goodwill and the idea that people would give voluntarily, especially if they were wealthy, when their contributions to good works were considered part of their duty under *noblesse oblige* (Roberts, 1994). Philanthropic aspirations of reducing inequalities were belied in practice, as an unequal distribution of power and resources prevailed (Thompson, 2002). The inegalitarian social system and the resulting disparities in wealth and power impacted badly upon the capacities of poor people to take action consistent with creating institutions to reflect their specific worldviews. Thus people's ability to comply with society's expectations that they should look after themselves and others varied enormously.

Charitable giving was often rooted in a moralizing tendency that sought to affirm views of goodness and 'acceptable' behaviour. Such acts were normative, consistent with the dominant views held by society, and often punitive, in that they sought to limit claims on goodwill to avoid legitimating a desire to expect handouts rather than working for one's living. However, employment was often in jobs that did not pay enough to sustain a decent quality of life for a family of four (Marx, 1965). This approach is evident today in notions of workfare, which has replaced the idea of entitlement to benefit in countries such as the UK and the USA. Barbara Ehrenreich (2002) paints a moving portrayal of how low-income workers in America today juggle several jobs to support their families and work seventy or eighty hours a week without earning enough to pay basic bills such as rent.

The endeavours of the churches in Western societies were supplemented by those of individuals, including philanthropists, and voluntary organizations that targeted specific groups such as children or young offenders (Walton, 1975). One significant and continuing institutional development that straddled the religious and the voluntary arenas in promoting social work activities in Victorian England was the Salvation Army. Begun by William Booth in East London in 1865, it established a wide range of social services for poor people and has now expanded to encompass 117 countries. An important individual was Thomas Barnardo, who set up the Ragged School for poor children in East London in 1867 and before his death succeeded in opening ninety-six homes for 8,000 children. Practitioners in Barnardo homes now work with 110,000 children, young people and their families each year (www.barnardos.org.uk). While Barnardo himself sought to create safe environments for the children in his establishments, this was often not the reality.

Even in his lifetime, with Barnado's personal overview of arrangements, we know that, once they arrived in their new 'homes', poor white British children who were shipped from the UK to Canada and Australia often suffered abuse of many kinds. They were also forcibly deprived of family contact and friendships in the working-class communities in which they originated. Finding out about their original families and trying to make contact has featured in the stories of many since then (Bagnell, 2001). Several of these children were removed from their families in the UK for the simple reason that they lived in poverty and their parents were considered incapable of raising them. This refrain of improving children's life chances by taking them overseas is mirrored in the motives given today by people who seek approval for international adoptions, including those offering to help orphaned children in disaster situations such as the Asian tsunami of 26 December 2004 and the Haitian earthquake of 12 January 2010 (*World News*, 2010). Not all children dragged into the net lacked parents or kin (Johnson, 2006) and, as occurred in the placing of children of yesteryear, not all are safe. Paedophiles were abducting 'orphaned' children in both disasters.

Other options that contrasted strongly with the stigmatizing provisions inherent in the charitable model of helping people during hard times began to emerge during the Victorian era. British working-class people sought community-based alternatives to charity. These relied on collective action, often expressed through the craft guilds and the trade union movement, and introduced the idea of contributing towards group provision to help during times of individual and family hardship (Calmfors, 2003). Socialists subscribing to Marxist thought believed that capitalism sowed the seeds of its own destruction, would implode from its own contradictions, and would enable the working class to assume control of the state apparatus (Marx, 1965). History has not corroborated this view. Indeed, the financial crises of 2007–8 have revealed the remarkable resilience of capitalist formations to reinvent themselves by uniquely (re)combining the public and private spheres to bring further advantages to those with existing resources and who are committed to the profit-making motive. Thus the banking system has been saved, while the public sector has amassed huge deficits to pay for it and ordinary people have lost their jobs (Sinclair, 2010). Social workers pick up the pieces that unemployment and reduced service provision place on distressed individuals and communities.

## The emergence of state welfare

Meanwhile, Christian socialists such as Henry George (Jones, 1968) affirmed the moralist undertones of philanthropic discourses that demanded good behaviour from the recipients of charitable acts. These discourses held people responsible as individuals for institutional failings, although they endorsed collective solutions to social problems. However, their activities set the scene for secular socialists and, in time, feminists and other social activists in the new social movements to assert entitlements and rights to services instead of charity.

Both the failure of Victorian charitable organizations to deal with the social problems emanating from a rapidly industrializing society that lacked the infrastructure to care for people, particularly those who migrated to urban areas from the rural hinterlands, and a rising tide of secularism undermined individual philanthropic and religious responses to need. White working-class people in the UK who had failed to gain control of the state apparatus continued to rely upon their own forms of welfare through friendly societies, trade union initiatives and cooperatives. And they refused to concede the idea that private philanthropy provided a better way of meeting social need than mutual aid or rights and entitlements provided on the basis of contributions to community well-being (Van Opstal and Gijselinckx, 2008).

There was little general support for state-funded initiatives among the Victorian ruling class. Their resistance was marked by parliament defeating the structural reforms to alleviate poverty and hunger that had been proposed by the Chartists in 1834. Opposition from the Catholic Church, especially under Pope Leo XIII, also thwarted any ambition for state-guaranteed support. There were competing discourses around welfare provision that could be marshalled in support of particular approaches to social work at the very point that the profession was being formed. But those who gained sway among the ruling classes were those who emphasized individual self-reliance. This ideology was brought down to a fine art in the workhouses of the UK and under the aegis of possessive individualism in the USA during the nineteenth and twentieth centuries (Macpherson, 1964). Individual self-reliance was expressed as the epitome of good practice under the auspices of neo-liberalism at the end of the twentieth and beginning of the twenty-first centuries (Dominelli, 1999).

The inadequacy of the Victorian ad hoc philanthropic system to meet the immense and pressing needs of society became even more painfully obvious during various wars and economic recessions, especially the depression of the 1930s. Ultimately, after the Second World War, it became clear that meeting identified needs amid extensive levels of war-based destruction, poverty and destitution were beyond the capacity of charitable giving. Consequently, the modern welfare state in its various guises came into being in the UK and elsewhere in Europe (Krieger, 1963). In Britain, this was enacted when working-class activism and trade unionism combined with the political activism of the Labour government that swept into power in 1945. Ironically, its prime minister, Clement Attlee, had practised social work as a barrister and Fabian and was the author of *The Social Worker*, published in 1920. Eventually, individual and charitable organizational initiatives of the types described above gave way to the welfare state.

The welfare state did not have a 'big bang' moment that brought it into existence; rather, it has grown incrementally over time. For example, in the UK, old-age pensions were introduced by Lloyd George in 1908 through the Old Age Pension Act, and legislation for family allowances came with the Family Allowances Act in 1945 after years of tireless campaigning by people such as Eleanor Rathbone. Health care for poor people was provided by an assortment of religious and other agencies, including the municipal hospitals, until the National Health Service came into being in 1948. Many of these earlier services were means-tested and stigmatizing, family allowances (now child benefit) being a key exception. But even this universal, non-means-tested benefit may become a stigmatizing, means-tested one under the Conservative-dominated coalition government formed after the 2010 general election in the UK (Conservative Manifesto, 2010). The existence of the British welfare state was a precarious one from the beginning, as the Treasury constantly sought to curtail its growth through fiscal measures (Kincaid, 1973). Financial exigencies at its inception were intensified by the USA's demands that Britain repay its war debts (Hogan, 1987, 1991).

The activists in the new social movements eventually shifted notions of welfare entitlements away from the morality of the Christian socialists, who required people to take responsibility for their own well-being, and towards the idea of citizenship, where the state served as the guarantor of people's rights. They also sought to root citizenship-based versions of welfare entitlements in structural understandings of human and social developments among dispossessed groups. Since the 1980s, Thatcherite and Reaganite social policies in the West have reoriented welfare in directions that have undermined civil and human rights in order to curtail public spending as part of the neo-liberal project. The inappropriateness of undermining public goods and services in dealing with serious social problems has been demonstrated in a Canadian study by Mackenzie and Shillington (2009).

## Reframing the entitlement-based welfare state

Cuts in welfare spending have been reaffirmed more recently through legislation aimed at releasing public funds both to provide physical security for citizens as part of the 'war on terror' and to address the financial crisis (Sinclair, 2010). The attack on the financing of welfare rights in response to the current financial crises has raised anew questions about the commitment and the capacity of the Western neo-liberal state to defend people's unconditional entitlement to social services and freedoms (Dominelli, 2004b), despite the commitment of all member states of the United Nations to the Universal Declaration of Human Rights. Consequently, many feminists and socialists have withdrawn their allegiance to the state as the unconditional protector and guarantor of individual and collective rights. Such a realization is not news for neo-conservatives, who have always opposed the advance of either a large or a strong state – reiterated by David Cameron in 2010 in his statements about the 'Great Society' in his bid for the British premiership – for Marxists, who expected the state to 'wither away' under socialism (Engels, [1844] 2009), or for people in the Global South, who have enjoyed neither state-funded welfare rights nor other social benefits for most of their social histories (Vermeer, 1979; Rudra, 2005). I employ the term 'Global South' to refer to nation–states seeking to industrialize and urbanize, which have also been referred to as the 'Third World' (Worsley, 1964), the 'two-thirds world' (Sewpaul and Hölscher, 2004), developing countries and industrializing countries. The Global North denotes those countries that have industrialized to a considerable degree and is composed primarily of the rich nations that are known as 'the West'. These boundaries are becoming increasingly blurred as emerging economies such as China and India begin to overtake Western economies such as Germany and the UK and assert their specific interests in the geopolitical arena (Pramanik, 2000).

The current fiscal crisis is exacerbating the initial underfunding and disinvestment that followed Thatcherite policies (Huber and Stephens, 2001). The reluctance of states adequately to fund welfare provision has been evident during times of fiscal crises elsewhere too – e.g., Nordic countries in the 1980s and 1990s, even if cuts were not as deep and devastating as those in the UK, the USA or Canada (Laxer, 1989).

The overt ideological attack that destroyed the consensus on which the welfare state was predicated was enforced through Margaret Thatcher's commitment to destroy socialism and replace it with a possessive individualism and self-reliance. Her neo-liberal approach favoured market-based welfare provisions of the type much admired in the USA and advanced through multinational corporations intending to profit from people's lack of well-being (Rudra, 2005). As a result, the 1980s and 1990s were characterized by substantial attacks on entitlements to welfare, with the sale of public assets, the introduction of user fees and the promotion of private enterprise in delivering services on behalf of the state (Dominelli and Hoogvelt, 1996; Clarke and Newman, 1997; Huber and Stephens, 2001). Although it was anticipated to bring respite from such developments, the New Labour government of 1997 failed to prevent the further encroachment of privatization in the provision of services associated with the welfare state (Craig, 2001). This trend has continued to the present, with private–public finance initiatives guaranteeing private-sector involvement across all aspects of welfare provision, including the technologies used to monitor activities by both workers and service users/consumers (Dominelli, 2009).

Different typologies have been used to describe welfare states, the most popular one being that of Esping-Andersen (1990), which theorized three typical types of regime – the social democratic (as the best), the conservative corporatist and the Southern Mediterranean (the worst). However, his categorization has been critiqued for not paying attention to gender or 'race' (Dominelli, 1991), and, although subsequent versions of this text have sought to rectify this, his latest work, *The Incomplete Revolution* (Esping-Andersen, 2009), in my opinion still fails to understand the complexities of gender dynamics and relationships. And he remains unable to grasp fully the way in which the social systems of the Mediterranean area operate in synergy to combine family obligations and social networking through religious institutions and state provision in meeting social and welfare needs.

Ostensibly aimed at denying access to state-funded services to those with money, the position of the Tories of excluding wealthy people from state entitlements ignores the empirical reality that their approach produces stigmatized residual services as the norm for poor people and limited public resources being accessed by the middle classes (Mackenzie and Shillington, 2009). Many of these people would not be able to pay totally for their care, as those with chronic health conditions in the USA discover when even those with insurance are refused cover for their treatment. One need look no further than the under-resourced publicly funded social services, the NHS and educational provision in the UK and compare them with the more up-to-date, customer-centred services provided through the market in the USA – but *only to those who can afford to pay for them* – to measure the visible differences between the two approaches (Chan, 2009). This is despite substantial financial investments in the UK services under Labour administrations since 1997, because these have failed either to match rising demands for services or to reverse the chronic under-investment in public services that occurred during the Thatcher years (Whynes, 1994). The failure of both the American and the British residual models to respond to identified or known needs indicates how important it is to have modern, up-to-date, person-centred provision for all residents in a nation–state. The Nordic countries have a much better record of providing unstigmatized, high-quality services that are aimed at all people, regardless of their income.

The idea of citizenship-based entitlement to benefits and services was a crucial contribution of the welfare state for a brief period between the 1950s and the 1970s, when there was a consensus around meeting the needs of all people. William Beveridge in the UK (Beveridge, 1942) and Leonard Marsh in Canada (Marsh, 1943) sought to engage government in eliminating the five giants of want, idleness, squalor, disease and ignorance. The American 'New Deal' under Franklin Delano Roosevelt (Lampton, 1977) was the nearest the USA came to guaranteeing provision for families with dependent children and for older people. The concern to address extreme levels of deprivation and the threat of social disorder and devastation caused by the Second World War, especially in Europe, were picked up by Roosevelt and others at the United Nations and led to agreement around the Universal Declaration of Human Rights (UDHR) signed by all member nations in 1948 (Reichert, 2007). The UDHR covered civil, political and social rights, including the right to welfare, as expressed in Articles 22 to 27. These provisions are significant to social work practice.

The realization of universal citizenship-based services has been difficult, as opposition to raising the required revenues came from those outside government as well as those within it. Even Beveridge's recommendation that personal social services be universal under the publicly funded welfare state regime floundered against the opposition of the Treasury, which refused to fund provisions on this basis (Kincaid, 1973) and instead channelled available resources into debt repayments, including war loans from the USA (Hogan, 1987). Housing endured a similar fate, though health and education did not. However, as I have argued elsewhere, the subsequent introduction of user fees and the relegation of certain services to the private sector in both education and health has undermined their universality in favour of services being bought by those who can afford them (Dominelli, 2004b). The growth of humanism and secularism complemented Beveridge's view of society, as did socialism, in particular Christian socialism (Roy, 2004; Seldman and Murphy, 2004). The ideology of state provision to meet people's needs flourished then, but has weakened since. The demise of universal services through state political and fiscal measures remains a danger in today's economic climate and creates uncertainty in the state's relationship with those who expect it to guarantee their social rights. Social workers have a responsibility to understand this exclusion of poor people and facilitate their endeavours in organizing to acquire the rights to which the UDHR entitles them.

The taxation system is an obvious way of getting rich people to contribute more to the public good and the provision of universal services. However, this option has been rejected by politicians on both sides of the Atlantic. Taxing rich people has become taboo in British and American politics. There was a predictable outcry from those better off when, in the 2009 budget, New Labour introduced a 50 per cent tax on those earning more than £150,000 per annum (Kirkup, 2009). The super-rich have successfully resisted demands to tax their mega-bonuses (Johnston, 2006; Leopold, 2009; Sachs, 2010). Barack Obama skirted the issue by demanding repayment of public loans and controls on derivatives (Babington, 2010). Using taxes to fund welfare provision requires a progressive approach to taxation. Taxation is also a utilitarian and highly efficient basis, as well as a fairer way, of collecting the funds needed to raise standards in the public sector and make services available to all. This idea lies at the core of universal services – pooling resources so that every individual can rely on them at the point of need and, as a citizen, be entitled to unstigmatized services that are funded to be the best possible.

## Contextualizing contemporary professional social work

Social work is an interesting professional and academic discipline because it straddles both the local, which can at times emphasize its parochiality even when addressing international social problems, and the global, which stresses its international dimensions and impact. For these reasons, contextualizing contemporary social work, and engaging with the interstices of practice at the micro-, meso- and macro-levels, contributes to its relevance within and across borders. Attempts to address the ensuing complications have resulted in various theorizations of social work practice, including those that consider it a complex, multidimensional and interdisciplinary entity that operates within a holistic framework. This, some would argue, gives it an all-systems orientation (Pincus and Minahan, 1973). Others envisage practice as networks linking together different levels of activities that address both the structural and the personal elements in a holistic way (Dominelli, 2002a).

The contexts in which contemporary social work operates are multi-faceted and cover the global, the regional, the national and the local. The new information technologies have brought in virtual dimensions focusing on transient affiliations, virtual communities and transnationalism, while the growth of rapid and accessible modes of transportation have collapsed time and space. Coupled with the uneven economic integration of the different nation–states, migratory movements of people, and the spread of organized crime in the form of the arms trade, the drug trade and the trade in human beings, these have given social workers a complex world and difficult problems to address within their practice.

Globalization has brought the world's nation–states closer together, particularly in the economic and cultural spheres, as well as intensified competition between them for scarce resources, and has spread the penalties for not resolving such crucial social issues as climate change, increasing levels of poverty and armed conflicts across all countries, albeit unevenly. Social workers are involved either in picking up the pieces when states fail to tackle these matters effectively or in advocating for alternative ways of addressing them. Like nation–states, social workers are bound by statutes, which now emanate from international agreements and conventions, regional agreements, multilateral agreements, bilateral agreements and in-country legislation. As a profession, social work can be and is active at all these levels. Its engagement beyond the local level is patchy and depends on the confidence of individuals and the strength of national associations as well as the influence carried by practitioners, educators and researchers.

## International social work organizations

There are a number of social work organizations, federations and networks that operate at the international level. These are often called civil society organizations (CSOs) and are varied in their membership, geographic spread and functions. Many CSOs have formed networks – e.g., CoNGO (the Conference of Non-Governmental Organizations) – to strengthen their voice, especially with regard to engaging with international institutions and agencies associated with the UN, such as UNICEF and the UNDP. Some CSOs, e.g., the IASSW and the IFSW, are professional associations; others are voluntary organizations that operate often in disaster stricken areas, e.g., Oxfam, Save the Children and the International Committee of the Red Cross (ICRC). The International Red Cross and Red Crescent societies have bases in particular nation–states, but they came together in 1919 to form the International

Federation of Red Cross and Red Crescent Societies. Each CSO acts independently of the others, although they collaborate around activities linked to the United Nations, in global crises such as natural disasters and armed conflicts, and in pursuing professional interests such as having a voice in key decision-making fora that impact upon the international domain. More than 3,000 CSOs come under CoNGO's umbrella to advance their collective interests at the UN while retaining their specific representation around their particular concerns.

I do not have the space in this book to mention or consider the many organizations that can be found at this level. Many of them are not known outside their limited spheres of activity, but those such as the ICRC, Oxfam, Save the Children, Help the Aged International and World Vision are known well beyond their countries of origin and have formed local branches in the Global South that link up with local NGOs to offer advice, funds and services to various categories of people. Many of the well-known CSOs have originated in the West. However, Red Crescent societies have been founded to address the welfare needs of Muslims and are highly regarded globally. They also work alongside the Red Cross. Interestingly, many of these organizations are practising social work, although they do not necessarily identify with the profession. This can be attributed to both the low status of the profession and its porous professional borders.

While many people welcome the support and interventions offered by NGOs and are grateful for their assistance during times of calamity, there have been a number of critiques of their activities. Chandra Mohanty (1992) has criticized civil society organizations from the Global North that operate overseas for delivering inappropriate aid to countries in the Global South. Their actions often undermine locality-specific civil society organizations which are better able to address local issues, in that they have the knowledge that is needed to make interventions relevant to their particular constituents and to succeed in the implementation of plans for action (Stubbs, 2007). However, organizations internal to a country are disadvantaged in that they cannot compete with external NGOs in terms of materials, finances or personnel. Others have criticized external NGOs for distorting local development (Deacon et al., 1997), having more resources at their disposal than some governments (Duffield, 1996), setting themselves up as 'lords of poverty' – that is, those who profit from the industry that is the aid business (Hancock, 1991) – and encouraging armed conflicts by picking up the humanitarian pieces (Hoogvelt, 2007). These are all matters with which the social workers who are in these organizations need to deal if they are not to be considered part of an alien colonizing force rather than having a contribution to make by working in egalitarian partnerships with local NGOs and people (Razack, 2002).

## Conclusions

Social work developed as a profession to deal with the social problems emanating from the processes of industrialization. It relied heavily on philanthropic initiatives to begin with, but it soon became an outlet for the energies of middle-class women, who were instrumental in challenging definitions of what constituted professional social work, developing its scientific elements and eventually staffing the welfare state. Consequently, social work became a 'handmaiden' of the nation–state, especially in Europe, where it became active in colonizing ventures that sought to spread messages about the superiority of Western culture. Its dependency on state funding also meant that social work was unable to finance its own autonomous development. Its low professional status was rooted in this dependent infrastructure and the societal devaluation of caring labour. This has produced a problem that persists today, despite its greater role in world affairs through consultative status at the UN.

# 3

# Mapping out the Terrain of 'the Social'

## Introduction

The terrain of 'the social' represents that domain or space in which the interstices of the private and public elements of life are configured. It was initiated as one way of providing security in a world beset by the insecurities generated as a result of the industrial revolution, which displaced people from the land to work in factories and subjected them to the discipline and rigours of industrial labour in cities poorly prepared for such a huge influx of humanity (Stedman Jones, 1971). The precariousness of industrial life resulted in the slums in London and other industrial cities of the UK, the urban ghettos leading to living conditions deleterious to human life, including overcrowding, a lack of sanitary facilities and crime (Thompson, 2002). Sadly, we see similar phenomena unfolding before our eyes today in the megacities of the industrializing countries of the Global South. For example, the population of Mexico City, 25 million, is greater in size than that of a number of countries in Western Europe. The lack of forms of development to balance the needs of people and the environment in both rural and urban areas has intensified people's vulnerabilities in a globalizing world.

I explore these developments in this chapter, mapping out how 'the social' was charted as different actors vied with each other for the right to determine the processes whereby the profession of social work developed, and highlighting the different priorities and challenges expounded by various actors, including, from the 1960s, women, black people and disabled people. I also examine key social work values and concepts that facilitate practice at the micro-level, among them power and empathy, bringing in examples from different parts of the world. The British Association of Social Workers (BASW) Code of Ethics from the UK and National Association of Social Workers (NASW) Code of Ethics from the USA will be considered within the context of the IASSW–IFSW ethics document as mechanisms for intervening in discourses about the regulation of social workers. Regulatory forms of control have changed over time, as different priorities have been articulated through dynamic interactions among the myriad stakeholders with an interest in social work.

## Valuing the vulnerable contours of 'the social'

Blaikie et al. (2004: 9) define vulnerability 'as a set of characteristics of a group or individuals', thereby focusing on personal characteristics. Hewitt (1997: 143) suggests vulnerability is the 'human ecology of endangerment ... embedded in the social geography of settlements and land uses, and the ... distribution of influence in countries and political organisations'. Hewitt's work identifies how an unbalanced approach to industrialization creates and intensifies vulnerability. Combining both insights, I define vulnerability as a structurally created phenomenon caused by the lack of infrastructure conducive to human well-being, which is intensified by the lack of personal and material resources with which to adapt to debilitating circumstances and events. As a result, vulnerability continues to feature in the lives of people on low incomes and the homeless, in both the Global South and the Global North. Many of those penalized by the failure of the authorities to provide resources and facilities in urban settings are poor people, especially children, carving out a life on the streets. Although social workers have sought to eliminate such conditions in their practice, they have not achieved their mission. The slums remain and the numbers of street children continue to rise. Despite heroic interventions aimed at reversing the deterioration in life chances of disadvantaged street children, the situation of most remain unaltered (Wernham, 2004).

In Victorian Britain, responding to needs engendered by low-paid waged work – for those lucky enough to secure a job – unemployment, slum housing, and rising levels of crime associated with the squalor of London's less affluent quarters required extensive investment in the public domain. These included engineering projects in sanitation, public health and water supplies, as proposed by Edwin Chadwick; transportation, as advocated by Isambard Kingdom Brunel; and social organizations that addressed the needs of people experiencing hardship. Much of the necessary work was conducted through the professions, notably those dealing with 'the social', or the space that exists in the interstices between the private and public domains and aims to address people's needs for security in all aspects of their lives. Administering this terrain led to the creation of new professionals – psychiatrists, psychologists and social workers. Together, they formed what Foucault (1977) termed the 'psy' professions. More recently, in continental Europe, these have been called the 'social professions' because they deal with the domain known as 'the social'.

## Defining 'the social'

Defining 'the social' is difficult because it centres on relations between people and encompasses so much of what happens in society, rendering it complex, multi-layered and all-encompassing. Given its focus on human well-being, there is little that can be left out. It is also contested territory because various professions play different roles and often vie with each other for influence and space. I have defined 'the social' as:

> the site where people interact with each other and their environment. Social workers engage in it by intervening in social problems experienced by individuals, groups or communities with the aim of helping people regain control of their situations. This work can cover any aspect of people's lives from cradle to grave. (Dominelli 2009: 6)

Adams et al. (2009: 5) do not define it as such but argue that 'The social in social work engages with social relationships or interactions between people as they go about their daily lives in the context of the society in which they live.' Both of the above definitions focus on the interstices between the personal and the public spheres as the site for professional interventions and embrace the social policy context and the gamut of social and physical environments that shape the opportunities and barriers people experience in realizing their aspirations. They also speak about social workers' responsibility to be 'critically reflective' in their interventions in 'the social' sphere.

Donzelot (1982) suggests that 'the social' profession of social work was created specifically to police families and thereby links this caring profession to its social control functions of moralizing, normalizing and punishing those who misbehave. This aspect also strengthens social workers' capacity to restructure working-class families more in keeping with middle-class ideologies around the family and their concern to protect children and other vulnerable people. Parton (1991) calls this family surveillance and highlights the importance of social workers using their own knowledge to situate themselves as experts when intervening in instances of families being suspected of failing to care for children. The concern with child care places women as mothers and as workers, their responsibility for caring labour and gendered dynamics under the spotlight and emphasizes women policing women (Dominelli, 2002b). Rose (1996: 328) focuses more emphatically on issues of state governance by suggesting that, while rooted in social relationships, 'the social' occurs in 'bounded territory governed by its own laws'. O'Malley (2004) adds that 'the social' draws upon data collection and information that the nation–state can use to assess and respond to needs as well as to control populations, a point made earlier by Foucault (1979, 1991) when exploring power relations, knowledge and the 'instruments of governmentality'. The modern British welfare state was founded on the Keynesian premises of full employment (Keynes, 1989) – which in actuality meant paid labour and ignored volunteer labour or unpaid housework. Beveridge's (1942) notions of contributory social insurance premiums, and those of political, civic and social citizenship rights as defined by T. H. Marshall (1970), continued to exclude considerable numbers of the citizenry, such as women and children who were dependent on a wage earner – usually a man, playing the role of husband and father.

Relying on arrangements through waged work, these policy-makers intertwined social protection with vulnerability and dependency at the heart of the welfare state and compelled women and children to bear the brunt of an institutionalized dependency on a male breadwinner. As a result, until 1986 a woman who lived with a man was not entitled to claim social security on her own behalf. This configuration of responsibilities and duties also drew upon the tenets of 'pooled risks'. Such risks were shared by citizens who held common identities and aspirations, but were coupled with individual responsibility for contributing to a social system that was managed, administered and controlled by the state. As such, it focused on individual responsibilities in contributing to the greater good and avoided the political imperative of exposing the structural bases of poverty, unemployment and lack of opportunities for individuals to improve their situation. 'The social' is, therefore, a socially constructed entity.

Another significant contribution to this structuring of the welfare state, and of 'the social' embedded within it, was that of carving out 'the social' as the space between the public and the private spheres. This is no mean feat in Western societies based on the primacy of the nuclear family, whose privacy is defended against all comers. This is evident in the saying 'an Englishman's (sic) home is his castle'. It was also a site that feminists were particularly active in opening up under the slogan 'the personal is political' when they made known the dangers of physical and sexual abuse against women and children that occurred within the so-called safe domain of the family (Gordon, 1988; Butler, 1990). The contradictions that this solution entails are especially evident in child protection and welfare work, where social workers are mandated to intervene in suspected cases of neglect and abuse. But, in conducting an investigation into any allegations, they have to ensure that they respect adults' rights to privacy. Guarantees of anonymity protect the identity of someone who reports abuse, even if these turn out to be erroneous, and the alleged perpetrator has rights that must be observed at all times. If the rights of the child are infringed, as some argue they are – e.g., when the child rather than the perpetrator is removed from the home – this is seen as a lesser evil than violating the rights of adults. Thus, the arena of 'the social' is a problematic and contested one, where one set of values and ethics can clash with another and require social workers to exercise the wisdom of Solomon in making difficult decisions.

## Creating the contested terrain of 'the social'

Social workers, as those given the task of meeting the needs of poor people, became one of the groups assigned to the 'psy' professions. They were obliged not only to respond to need within tightly defined boundaries set by lawmakers and the social mores of the time, but also to ensure the maintenance of the moral and legal order of the day as stipulated by their employers and funders. Some practitioners focused initially on issues of poverty, poor housing and immigration, thus drawing into their remit white working-class people living in poverty, 'deviants' and different ethnic groups. Over time these included Jews and black and other minority ethnic groups. As the numbers of claimants rose, gatekeeping and other rationing devices were introduced. One of the earliest of these, and very much in evidence today, is that of classifying people into the 'deserving' and the 'undeserving' poor.

Only those categorized as deserving were given assistance, usually under tough conditions that required recipients to behave in certain stipulated ways. To link assistance to behaviour that maintained the established social order, social workers, in practice, extended the notion of the deserving and the undeserving client from that prevailing under the Elizabethan Poor Law of 1601 and reinforced through the New Poor Law Amendment Act of 1834. The requirements of adherence to social norms and conduct in accordance with socially defined criteria in order to receive services is recognized as comprising the care and control functions of social work. In that capacity, social work in the UK had been given a historically significant role – that of controlling the white British working class (Corrigan and Leonard, 1978) and other black and minority ethnic groups (Dominelli, 1988; Ahmad, 1990).

In the contemporary period, since the attack on the World Trade Center in the USA and the impact of global warming, the insecurities of continued industrialization now encompass the scarcity of fossil fuels, water shortages, air pollution, environmental degradation, climate change and terrorism. Concerns about security have led to heightenened surveillance over populations to maintain security in its widest sense – physical, social, economic and political. Social workers employ surveillance mechanisms in the form of risk assessments that aim to enhance protective factors and minimize harm, and ensure that those who seek assistance also 'look promising' in order to receive services (Callahan et al., 2002). Risk assessments and risk management have become crucial instruments in the modern social worker's armoury and are deeply embedded in systems of classification and measurement (Dominelli, 2004b; Swift and Callahan, 2009). Risk assessments aim to reduce uncertainties in known directions. However, the scientific basis for assuming certainty in risk assessments that are used to govern people's behaviour is very much in doubt (Quinsey, 1995).

Risk reduction, or the concern to minimize harm, has become central in many forms of social work practice where questions about vulnerability and danger have arisen. It is particularly prominent in child protection procedures and work with offenders. A risk assessment is also a key feature of the terrain that has been defined as 'the social'. Identifying those factors that are considered 'protective' – i.e., that safeguard individuals from harm – is an essential part of the risk assessment and management process. Checklists of various kinds are used to help practitioners assess the relevance of such factors. Even when the outcome sought is unpredictable, social workers are expected to provide certainty in their outcomes (Swift and Callahan, 2009). Beck (1992) argues that this preoccupation with risk symbolizes the search for certainty in uncertain times. This has given rise to the 'risk society' and is a feature of modernity.

Modernity defined as the Western industrial system has been projected in negative terms for offering a universal picture of unlimited progress and bounty on the basis of capitalist production, social organization and a homogeneous unified society. Marxists have critiqued capitalism for its exploitative basis, in which those who own and manage the means of production would benefit from the labour of others (Lenin, 1961). A grand narrative of modernity may have lost favour to postmodernity in social work (Leonard, 1997; Payne and Askeland, 2008), but many of the earth's inhabitants – those who are unable to count on having food, clothing and shelter in everyday life (UNDP, 2009) – have yet to enjoy the benefits of industrialization, especially those pertaining to public health, sanitation, running water in the home and electricity, as well as labour-saving devices, the new information technologies and rapid modes of transportation. And, as I (Dominelli, 2004b) and others (Midgley, 1995) have argued, meeting basic needs cannot be discounted from professional interventions. A determination not to forget the goals of modernity in providing housing, health, education and other welfare services for many of the earth's people is evident in the arguments made by indigenous people about removing poverty from their midst (Grande, 2004). It also underpins the position that China and other countries in the Global South take when affirming that, unless the West makes more progress in reducing its own greenhouse gas emissions, they will not sacrifice their industrial development by reducing theirs (Löscher, 2009).

## A 'social profession' for uncertain times

Addressing the problems caused by life's uncertainties and social exclusion, especially in terms of the lack of shelter, food and clothing needed by poor people – including the large numbers of 'ragamuffin' children on the streets of London – was a key motivation behind the attempts by social reformers in Victorian England to renew civic virtues and the commitment to assist those in need (Stedman Jones, 1971). And it also underpinned public health initiatives aimed at improving sanitation, providing clean water and reducing diseases associated with urban decay (Chadwick, 1842). From its inception, social work experienced a care–control dilemma: its aim was to respond to the needs of vulnerable populations while at the same time maintaining the status quo (Bailey and Brake, 1975) and promoting personal resilience. Vulnerability is defined as an individual's lack of capacity to meet their own needs (Jansen, 2008; Gitterman, 2009), a definition that ignores structural vulnerabilities embedded in capitalist social relations. Personal resilience was deemed its antonym. There was little recognition at the time of the divergent interests of some sections of the populace and the ruling elites and the impossibility of resolving contradictions within prevailing socio-economic and political structures. Thus, one aim for social workers was to help poor people adapt to existing social structures rather than changing those structures, and blaming individuals for their plight. Blaming the victim and insisting on the moral renewal of the labouring classes and their conformity to white middle-class norms through hard work was honed to a fine art by the Charity Organization Society (COS), created in London in 1868. It initiated the form of individualized practice that became known as casework (Walton, 1975) and became the defining feature of social work practice for more than a century.

The COS was the amalgamation of a number of small charitable agencies that initially came together as the London Society for Charitable Relief and Repressing Mendacity. It sought to reduce begging and social disorder and also to reassure the British upper classes, who believed that social intervention was needed to quell working-class discontent before it got out of hand and tipped into the revolutionary fervour that had featured strongly in continental Europe earlier, and especially in 1848 (Rapport, 2009). Thus, it emphasized social work's individualizing elements, social control functions and moralizing tendencies as the bases of practice. The COS retained its name until 1946, when it became the Family Welfare Association. Similar organizations were formed elsewhere in Britain, the British Empire and the USA. This resulted in the casework method of working being emulated as one of the three key methods of social work across the globe, the other two being group work and community work (Younghusband, 1978).

The COS sought to develop social work on the basis of individual interventions. One-to-one work or casework provided the foundation for the scientific underpinnings of the profession as it began to borrow theories and methods of practice from other disciplines and professions, particularly psychology and sociology. This, it was hoped, would enhance its status and address the links between individuals and their inability to make the most of the life chances that came their way. Casework was also a distinctly urban phenomenon, created to deal with specific problems and populations, a feature that continues to dominate today. Although in the UK the urban now exceeds the rural population, this was not so then. And despite the problems of urbanization, which is itself a product of industrialization, the trend seems set to continue globally. The UN estimates that the world's population will exceed 9 billion by 2050, when it is expected to be predominantly urban (United Nations, 2005).

## A devalued professionalism

By defining social work in terms of the individualized methodology known as casework, the COS succeeded in securing funds from wealthy benefactors and the state. Key supporters included C. B. P. Bosanquet, who became the first secretary of the COS in 1870 (Walton, 1975). He was followed by Charles Stewart Loch, who was known for his opposition to the passage of legislation regarding old-age pensions and free school meals for children on the grounds that such measures would cause individuals to lose their sense of being responsible for themselves and earning their own living. The ideologies perpetrated by the COS were challenged by those in the Settlement Movement, who focused on what we would today call the structural components of poverty, various forms of discrimination and the lack of opportunities for those living on the margins of society in Britain's urban centres (Smith, 2006).

Moreover, by not challenging its benefactors to think differently about their roles and responsibilities in meeting the pressing needs of individuals, the COS sowed the seeds for social work as a dependent profession (Dominelli, 1997), a status that has adhered to it since then. This dependency is of concern because it has meant that social work has been unable to develop the autonomous governance structures free of political interference that it needs to assert its professional standing and influence. It has been forced to change in accordance with benefactor priorities, government diktat and media whim rather than as a result of carefully considered plans developed among the multiple stakeholders. Nowadays, these would include the general public who access services, together with practitioners, educators and policy-makers. The summary dismissal of Sharon Shoesmith by the then Secretary of State in the Department of Children, Schools and Families, Ed Balls, illustrates this dependency in contemporary society. It was the Secretary of State and not Shoesmith's employer, Haringey Council, who took the initiative in holding her accountable for failing Baby P (*Daily Telegraph*, 2008), who died on 3 August 2007 of multiple injuries deliberately inflicted upon him by his mother, her boyfriend and his brother and prompted a wide-ranging review of social work education and practice (Laming, 2009).

Meanwhile, as the social work profession developed at the turn of the twentieth century, whether it was by Octavia Hill in the UK, Alice Salomon in Germany, Jane Addams in the USA or Helena Radlinska in Poland, the women who embarked on the task of developing its education and training were also trying to establish a different kind of profession – one that gave credence to the needs of people who were socially excluded from society and that sought to involve them in finding solutions to their problems. Among those marginalized by society were the women professionals, as was shown by Salomon's research on women of the period in Germany. This finding led her in 1925 to set up the Germany Academy for Social and Educational Work for Women (Salomon, 2004). Women were excluded from studying in universities in disciplines associated with men throughout the West, including medicine and the law. In Britain, women did not enter these two professions in large numbers until the 1980s. The first group of British women to organize a protest against their exclusion from university education occurred in 1869 in the village of Hitchen and laid the basis for what became Girton College, linked to Cambridge University, in 1871. However, it was not until 1948 that women undergraduates were formally accepted into the university (Robinson, 2009).

As a result, because social work became dominated by women, focused on caring work that was devalued as 'women's work', and remained an open profession with porous borders and training arrangements, it was seen as a lowly profession at best. But it was initially cast primarily as a vocation or calling for otherwise unoccupied, mainly white, middle-class women who could use their skills to 'do good' by showing working-class women, through their own example, how to lead a better life (Walton, 1975). This gave social work its classist bias. Integrating excluded working-class people into middle-class lifestyles without the requisite resources has been a persistent theme in social work practice (Strega et al., 2009). Consequently, questions of power and control and of identity have been key facets of social work's development and have been specifically challenged at different points in its history, both within the profession and outside it, including most recently by anti-oppressive practice and critical theories.

Social work, as a new profession responding to those in need, was organized differently from the traditional professions. Its claim for professional status was denied by Abraham Flexner, whose report devalued its activities as long ago as 1915, when he stated authoritatively that social work was a semi-profession because it lacked its own knowledge base and did not restrict entry into its ranks by prescribed training, as did those of law and medicine (Flexner, [1915] 2001). Unlike social work, these two professions happened to be dominated by men.

At the same time, the terrain of 'the social', as defined in social work by the COS, was contested. Key exponents of a different kind of practice were the numerous individuals who founded the Settlement Movement (Gilchrist and Jeffs, 2001). They highlighted structural issues, notably unemployment, poor housing and the way in which capitalism organized social relations, as the causes of much human hardship and suffering (Lappin, 1965). Although it resembled the COS in emphasizing self-help, the Settlement Movement was committed to educating and helping poor people to organize in their communities to improve their conditions rather than blaming them for their poverty. Employment and housing constituted the spheres that dominated most of the work conducted under the auspices of the Settlement Movement. Its endeavours produced another form of social work – community work – and, alongside it, group work (Friedlander and Apte, 1974). Casework, group work and community work became the three main methods of practice in social work (Younghusband, 1978) and remain as such today globally, except in

England and Wales, where community work has been detached from social work training since the mid-1980s. Crucial in leading to this disengagement was that employers saw community work as supporting radical ideologies that focused on structural inequalities; it could not be relied upon to enforce social control over those requiring services in the ways espoused by the maintenance school of social work (Davies, 1985).

The Settlement Movement in the UK began in the mid-nineteenth century and was based on the idea that those who were better off could assist those who were less well off to develop their own skills and talents in meeting their own needs. It involved students from universities, including Oxford, going into the East End of London to live and work among those residing there and to provide role models, education and the means of social organization necessary to achieve their goals (Walton, 1975). The first Settlement House was called Toynbee Hall, after Arnold Toynbee, an Oxford don, and was created by Samuel and Henrietta Barnett on Commercial Street in Whitechapel in 1884. The idea soon spread throughout the country in such cities as Birmingham and Glasgow. In 1889, Jane Addams, visiting from Chicago, was so impressed by these developments that she established Hull House upon her return to America. Working in the Chicago slums, she also emphasized responsible self-sufficiency and lived in poor neighbourhoods where communities were encouraged to develop the opportunities that would enable them to tackle poverty (Addams, 1914). Addams established a tradition that ultimately attracted Barack Obama, who worked among the poor in Chicago and went on to become the first African American president of the United States. Employment, in Addams's time as now, was deemed key to enabling individuals to move out of poverty. How workplace relations were organized in capitalist societies was not considered an issue that required extensive exploration. Nevertheless, the main block to the realization of poor people's ambitions to better themselves was that the jobs available did not pay workers enough to lead a decent life. Then, as today, the working poor could not meet their aspirations, not because they did not work, but because they were not paid enough when they did (Ehrenreich, 2002), so they remained in a poverty trap from which they were unable to escape. Today, similar low levels of pay and appalling working and living conditions are experienced by workers in the sweatshops of the Global South, which have usually been established by multinational corporations seeking to reduce their labour costs. Many of these workers are women (Wichterich, 2000).

In Britain, the three arms of social work – casework, group work and community work – formed the dominant paradigms of practice until the mid-1980s (Younghusband, 1978). At that time, the then Central

Council for Education and Training removed community work from its repertoire, and this part of the profession went its own way. However, community work remains part of social work in most other parts of the world. Also, social work in England and Wales lost its link to the probation service in 1998, when Jack Straw increased the role of employers and university criminology departments in probation training at the expense of partnerships involving social work departments. Probation is now closer to the prison service and formally recognized as part of the National Offender Management Service (NOMS). In becoming part of NOMS, probation officers focused less on the welfare of prisoners and more on controlling their behaviour and preventing further offending. Probation continues to be part of social work in Scotland and most other parts of the world.

Engaging with 'clients' in ways that acknowledged their right to self-determination and trying to 'fix' the casualties of industrialization also required a set of values and ethics that would address the tension between controlling or policing populations and helping them. These issues were to become more important when social work came to dominate 'the social' in the latter half of the twentieth century. Social movements among client populations critiqued social work practice and labelled it an 'oppressive' profession for taking the side of the ruling elites rather than that of the marginalized groups that required its services (Corrigan and Leonard, 1978; Dominelli, 1997).

In responding to these critiques, clients, practitioners and academics came up with some of the most significant innovations that have impacted upon the profession in terms of client–worker relationships, relationships between workers and their employers, the relationship between professionals and the state, and relationships between the state and its citizens. Their endeavours also led to the creation of alternative resources for clients, new practice methods and theoretical developments, often categorized as empowering or anti-oppressive. But these did not achieve a substantial reordering of clients' relationships with the state within a rights-based citizenship framework other than at a rhetorical level. Nor did they change the structural nature of the inequalities so frequently identified by its critics. Thus social work continued to be rooted in individualized interventions in response to need, dependent on politicians for its legitimacy, and reliant on voluntary agencies and business enterprises to meet gaps in provision left by the state. The expectation that charitable institutions have unlimited purses is threatened by the decline in donations (CBC News, 2008a; Pope, 2008). For example, one collecting agency in the state of Colorado in the USA claimed that its funds had dwindled by 5.4 per cent, or $175 million, per year between 2000 and 2003 (Fillion, 2008). A survey in the UK by the Department for Communities and Local Government highlighted a decline in both charitable giving and volunteering (Travis, 2010). Meanwhile, structural inequalities have been exacerbated, especially since the financial crisis beginning in 2007, by unemployment, mortgage defaults and fuel inequalities as energy costs soar.

A crucial change initiated in the early 1990s has been the introduction of bureaucratic competency-based practice, dominated by bureaucratic procedures, business language and risk assessment. It underpins most statutory social work interventions in the UK and has replaced relational social work. As a result, stigmatized services remain the responsibility of the state, while higher-quality services provided by the private sector are growing apace for those who can afford them (OECD, 2005). The divide between publicly and privately funded provision is less apparent in Europe than in the USA, where the welfare state is evident largely as a remnant of the 'New Deal' drawn up by Franklin Delano Roosevelt during the 1930s, primarily to support dependent children and older people (Lampton, 1977).

### Ethical codes to govern professional behaviour in the 'social professions'

Given that the 'social professions' were responsible for working with many vulnerable individuals, control over their activities was crucial to ensure that there was no abuse of power. Values and ethics, later codified as codes of ethics, became regulatory mechanisms that could be used as 'instruments of governmentality' (Foucault, 1991) to enable professionals to monitor the observance of appropriate standards of practice and impose penalties on those whose behaviour was judged to be inadequate. Codes of ethics, in focusing on an individual professional's behaviour, assist in pathologizing practitioners when many of the problems they encounter in promoting best practice may be structural.

The bureaucratization of practice in the UK through the competency-based approach has diminished the amount of time social workers spend in developing relationships with service users, despite recognition that these are crucial in initiating behavioural change (Folgeraiter, 2004). It also undermined the capacity of professionals to think autonomously outside the box and yielded budget-led rather than needs-led responses to client demands (Dominelli, 1996b, 2004a). Lord Laming found fault with bureaucratic practice in his 2009 inquiry into the death of Baby P. Yet, it was Sharon Shoesmith, the director of Haringey's Children's Services, and the individual social workers who were dismissed after a media onslaught fomented by *The Sun*. The lack of resources to support deprived families with multiple problems, the lack of authority of social workers to challenge the private spaces in which individual families raise children, and the lack of training for the highly skilled work involved in protecting Baby P, which was undertaken by a recently qualified worker, went without media comment.

Interestingly, codes of ethics in the West are often formulated on a countrywide basis. In India, although a code of ethics has been endorsed by the National Association of Professional Social Workers (NAPSWI), many cities, such as Mumbai, have their own. A summary of the codes of ethics for the British Association of Social Workers (BASW), the National Association of Social Workers (NASW) and the NAPSWI show the similarities between them to be striking. All three mention service, social justice, the worth and dignity of the person, integrity and professional competence. The differences were confidentiality (NAPSWI) and the importance of human relationships (NASW). Yet practitioners in all three countries would subscribe to all the above-mentioned elements, although they would interpret them differently according to context and local legislation.

The values articulated in these codes are similar to the values expressed by the IASSW and the IFSW in the joint ethics document that was agreed in Adelaide in 2004. This document was revisited during the 2010 Joint World Congress in Hong Kong and will be considered in further detail for deliberation again during the 2012 Joint World Congress in Stockholm. The IASSW–IFSW ethics document has been criticized for being Western-oriented and ignoring issues such as harmonization as a key purpose of social work in Chinese society (Yip, 2005). While such comments have to be considered seriously, I remain concerned that generalized critiques conducted within the West–non-West binary give rise to the notion that values and ethics are a Western invention and preoccupation, when this is not the case.

Each society has values and ethics whereby behaviour is judged as acceptable or unacceptable. This means it is important to examine in detail the similarities and differences in the criteria used to judge professional behaviour both within and between countries. For example, in a less dichotomous understanding of the issues, the value of harmony between people in Chinese society is not dissimilar to that of maintaining stability, social cohesion or social order in the West. Much more research needs to be undertaken to establish precisely what values and ethics are held in common across the globe by the profession, which ones are different, and what the bases of such differences might be. Establishing these in a systematic way is a suitable research project for the IASSW and the IFSW. Finding the funds to make this study possible should become a priority for both organizations.

Values change as people interact with and learn from one another. These interactions can produce new values, highlight continuities or identify discontinuities as existing values change over time (Dominelli, 2002c). Given the extensive range of interactions between and within countries and among individuals and groups, it is difficult to envisage that any one particular group would today hold more credibility than others, unless what was being proposed spoke to multiple realities and peoples' capacity to think and act for themselves.

## Challenging residual services and claiming universal, unstigmatized services

The people who access services provided by the welfare state or those with whom social workers come into contact are usually poor and marginalized. They are often stigmatized and divided into categories of 'deserving' and 'undeserving' claimants. The former are assessed as worthy of receiving services and are expected to behave in accordance with dominant middle-class norms. Being a 'deserving' client requires an individual to 'look promising' (Callahan et al., 2002) and 'jump through hoops' (Dominelli et al., 2005) set by social workers.

The stigma associated with those who access public services applies to social workers too. Parker (2007) terms this 'stigmatization by association'. This attitude does not help in raising the status either of social work or of those professionals engaged in it. And so the profession remains one of low status and poor pay. There are other reasons for this state of affairs, including the gendered nature of the profession, dominated as it is by women who are performing women's work, albeit primarily at the front line of practice (Coyle, 1989; Dominelli, 1997). The top managerial ranks continue to be dominated by men. In the UK, no more than 20 per cent of senior managers at this level were women, and this continues to be the case (ONS, 2008). Although there are few men in front-line social work, they are the ones who rise quickly through the ranks to assume managerial roles. They also tend to be found in greater numbers in work with children and families than with older people (Howe, 1986; Dominelli, 2002b).

The most significant challenge to the provision of stigmatized services in Britain came from the new social movements of the 1960s and 1970s – the women's movement, the black civil rights movement and the disability movement. These groups challenged the inadequacy of existing mainstream provision, the tendency to blame individuals for requiring public services, and the division into 'deserving' and 'undeserving' clients, with its accompanying moralizing tones. They also demanded that they be allowed to create their own services to cater for their needs as they defined them. They ran these services themselves; experimented with new forms of social relations – e.g., flat authority structures and rotating positions of power – and redefined social relations away from hierarchies and into more egalitarian and empowering directions. These initiatives were not well received by the establishment, which perceived them as a threat to the prevailing norms and traditions in providing and delivering services, because they made explicit the links between the plight of an individual and their social location (Piven and Cloward, 1971). Those who clarified and supported such critiques became the object of public hostility for exposing the underbelly of their allegedly perfect societies. In the USA, women who set up women's health groups, encouraged women to undertake their own physical examinations and look for more 'natural' and less costly interventions were taken to court by the medical profession for 'practising medicine without a license' (Frankfort, 1972). This was even though their interventions were limited to self-examinations and preventative measures or self-help activities that professionals might have been expected to endorse.

In Britain, those who sought to support the development of feminist and anti-racist initiatives were hounded through personal attacks on their integrity, the loss of career progression and, at times, dismissal from their posts. The most infamous of these were the attacks on anti-racist social work in the summer of 1993 (see Appleyard, 1993; Phillips, 1993; Pinker, 1993). In these, significant academic figures in the profession also attacked their colleagues as 'loonie lefties' (Pinker, 1993) for daring to support ordinary people's aspirations for services that they controlled and defined as appropriate for their needs. Fortunately, the coming to power of New Labour changed the rhetoric if not the substance behind these attacks, and it became possible to talk about empowering practice in ways that ultimately brought the term into the mainstream of social work. However, what is now promoted as such is far removed from the ideals of worker- and service user-designed, controlled and owned public services advocated by the new social movements of the 1960s and 1970s. Now, the rhetoric may be empowering, but the actual services delivered are more likely to be:

• less accessible, because they are supplied by either the private or the voluntary sector rather than the state and have to be paid for directly by individuals, who may lack the funds required. Although the state may pay for some services, options may be constrained because the commissioning process over which it presides stipulates what services can be made available, and these cannot be varied. So an individual may find that the facilities they need are not obtainable. This can happen in 'block' contracts, which do not allow for individualized responses unless these have been specified. Contracting out services also makes the state a powerful commissioner and increases the dependency of voluntary or not-for-profit agencies on it for funding (Long and Clark, 1997);

- limited in range, because choice is restricted to what is determined by the private sector or the state rather than the service user;
- delivered at a lower-quality level, because complaints are limited to formal objections if services do not meet prescribed bureaucratic standards rather than users being proactively engaged in creating or designing them.

The relational element is virtually absent from state-based social work in the UK today, as the norm for public-sector social workers is to commission services and manage budgets. Moreover, services are defined by the government under the auspices of 'modernizing' them. Folgeraiter (2004) laments the passage of the relational social worker, which Dominelli (2004b) claims has been replaced by the techno-bureaucrat.

The actual achievements of the new social movements are mixed. They have raised the profile of empowering service provisions; highlighted the oppressive nature of social divisions based on binary dyads that privilege one group over another – particularly those of 'race', ethnicity, gender, age and abilities – and demonstrated how these are evident even in the caring professions; developed and brought into the mainstream some alternative services, particularly those associated with domestic violence, child sexual abuse, ethnically sensitive provision and autonomous services for disabled people; and demanded recognition of both their experiential and empirical expertise. Their endeavours have not changed the dominant social relations in the profession, which still privilege the experts despite their being required to form partnerships with service users, enable private providers to sell services as commodities on the market with limited accountability to either service users or the professionals working with them, and promote commodified caring social relations in arenas that had formally been excluded from the marketplace.

Despite the various setbacks, the one crucial element that has shifted social relations within the profession considerably, and that the new social movements have fought to introduce and continue to back, is the demand that services be provided as of right – as entitlements based on citizenship and the meeting of claims for social justice (Ife, 2001a, 2001b). This outlook has intensified the political nature of social work. Social workers supporting the aims of the new social movements have been prompted to move away from defining the profession in terms of a neutral stance that leaves questions concerning the allocation of power and resources in the hands of politicians or service providers who cannot be held accountable by service users. Neo-liberal thinkers, who advance the idea that practitioners should be apolitical, build powerful lobbies so that their voices are heard above those of anyone else to demand that the state promotes opportunities for profit-making entrepreneurs (Shek-arau, 2007).

While social workers do not control the political system, they can influence it through a collective voice advanced by their professional associations, as individuals through the ballot box, and by supporting the mobilization of people who wish to hold politicians accountable for public services and infrastructures. Additionally, they can be powerful advocates for those who are on the breadline, because they have information about the hardship that the current social configuration and distribution of resources causes poor people. Resisting the pressures to be silent is an important component in redefining 'the social' as a source of ethical care and social work provision and delivery. How the personal social services are formulated and delivered are matters for ordinary people to affirm and control. Social workers can be allies in this enterprise.

## The three 'sister' organizations: IASSW, IFSW and ICSW

The International Association of Schools of Social Work (IASSW), the International Federation of Social Workers (IFSW) and the International Council on Social Welfare (ICSW) had their beginnings in Paris in 1928 at a multi-professional conference organized by Dr Reneé Sands, a Belgian physician, and are referred to as 'sister organizations' because they are linked to social work in various ways (Kendall, 1991). They cater for the interests of the educators, practitioners and policy-makers, respectively. An important aim for the 1928 conference was the exchange of ideas and curricula for social work education to help the fledgling discipline develop appropriate standards. Many nations attended this gathering, where the commitment to continue meeting and exchange materials was made. Because this conference was inspired by its European organizers, it could be viewed as part of an imperialist venture, but this could not have been further from the participants' minds.

People were encouraged to speak in their own mother tongue. Indeed, the idea that the three official languages then used by the UN should be adopted as official languages by all three organizations had its roots in this meeting. English, French and Spanish had the widest geographic spread at the time. That they were also European languages that had spread as a result of imperialism does not detract from the practicality of a response that sought to be inclusive. IASSW has, like the UN, sought to reduce the impact of its European legacy by adopting a language policy. It has subsequently added the three further languages recently adopted by the UN – Arabic, Chinese and Russian – and has also included Japanese, because one of its largest member groupings is from Japan. In 2004 it elected its first president from an African country – Ethiopia – and in 2008 the organization voted in a president from Hong Kong.

The IASSW has been in existence since 1928, though it was originally called the International Committee of Schools of Social Work; Dr Alice Salomon was its first chairperson. The IFSW, previously known as the International Permanent Secretariat of Social Workers, acquired its current name in 1956, when it was revived after a hiatus caused by the Second World War. The ICSW has also undergone name changes but has kept its acronym. All three organizations are committed to the United Nations charters and to upholding human rights and social justice in and through their activities. To this end, in 1947 the IASSW acquired special consultative status with the UN, where it has since been joined by both the IFSW and the ICSW. All three organizations engage in a number of activities in the UN, both separately and together. They present materials for UN summits and take an active role in the NGO activities linked to various summits. The IASSW and the IFSW have jointly participated in Social Work Day at the UN for some years. They also have a joint Commission on Human Rights to support social work educators and practitioners who are falsely imprisoned for upholding human rights. This began in 1996, with Professor Jim Ife as chair for IFSW and Professor Lynne Healy co-chair for IASSW. Each of the three organizations has representatives at the UN's headquarters in various parts of the world, although the most active are at the New York offices, where they also engage in various weekly meetings and chair certain committees that advise the UN on policy. Particularly important in this respect are the areas of mental health, children, older people and social development.

New areas are being added to this repertoire to take account of new circumstances: changes in social problems, people and expertise. Some new areas include attempts to intervene in some of the most serious matters facing the world – poverty, hunger, HIV/AIDS, and disasters. Social workers become involved in their resolution through capacity-building initiatives, training, professional interventions, policy statements, letters, and press releases that support the elimination of social problems and diseases and the sharing of knowledge and technology, so that these matters can be better addressed by those politicians holding the resources necessary to address these issues. Among these actions were disaster relief initiatives – RIPL (Rebuilding People's Lives) for IASSW and FAST (Families and Survivors of Tsunami Project) for IFSW. Additionally, a seminar was organized by all three sister organizations to give a social work perspective on climate change during the UN summit held in December 2009 in Copenhagen, where a policy statement on the subject was announced.

From the late 1960s onwards, the profession began to endorse demands made by the new social movements for improvements in the provision of services and their involvement in determining both what these were and how they could be delivered at the national and the international levels. The British Association of Social Workers and the American National Association of Social Workers began to include the values of equality and social justice in their national codes of ethics when revising their 1980s documents. Organisations such as the IASSW and the IFSW began to work together again in the mid-1990s to strengthen the voice of the profession internationally. Their commitment to egalitarian values, social justice and human rights gave them a coherent approach to criticizing the inegalitarian structures within which social workers had to practise (Sewpaul and Jones, 2004). Key among these initiatives were the issuing of joint statements on crucial matters of the day, including poverty, HIV/AIDS, affordable medicines for low-income countries, collaborating over activities linked to the UN, and redefining social work, the ethics document and the global standards. By the beginning of the twenty-first century these last three had been jointly agreed. Each of these documents had been subjected to wide-ranging and extensive consultation among the membership of both organizations and agreed at their respective general assemblies. The international definition of social work was the first to be agreed as jointly owned, in Copenhagen in 2001; the other two documents were approved as common documents in Adelaide in 2004. By producing these documents, committees drawn from both organizations proved they could work together to strengthen the profession. ICSW has now become a participant in the subsequent revisions.

These documents are not prescriptive, but offer guidelines for consideration and reflection. They are intended to be interrogated reflexively in the context of local circumstances (Sewpaul, 2005). Local groups can ignore them, change them to reflect local circumstances and needs, or demand that they be completely jettisoned (Sewpaul and Jones, 2004). The international definition was accepted by the General Social Care Council in the UK. In New Zealand, educators and practitioners used the global standards to develop their professional response to the government's attempt to impose bureaucratic competency-based social work on an unwilling profession. Several African countries have used the ethics document to help them develop their own locally specific code. All three documents are now being revised after being subjected to further consultations during the 2010 Global Congress in Hong Kong and for the 2012 Global Congress in Stockholm. Both congresses have been jointly organized by the IASSW, the ISFW and the ICSW.

## Conclusions

The development of professional social work has had a chequered and contested history. It has been fairly tempestuous in the UK since the mid-1980s because of the commitment to radical social work and the anti-oppressive practice that grew out of it. Nonetheless, it has emphasized the terrain of 'the social' as the site in which issues of human rights and social justice are enacted in the process of meeting the need for high-quality personal social services. However, achieving this state of affairs has been fraught, and a number of contentious struggles ensued, leading to compromises that did not always facilitate the growth and promotion of citizenship-based social work. The profession continues to struggle for recognition and status, although certain elements are no longer stigmatized. These difficulties are reflected in the terrain of 'the social', which remains contested as the market, the voluntary sector and the state vie for control over service provision and delivery.

In the UK, the state continues to impact upon 'the social' through its funding mechanisms, via legislative control over the 'psy' professions – particularly social work – and by being a key player in enforcing neo-liberal social relations on an unwilling populace, at least if surveys on the public's willingness to fund health, education and the personal social services are to be trusted. Since the Thatcher era, these have consistently demonstrated that the British population overwhelmingly supports the welfare state, particularly those elements associated with health, education and the care of vulnerable individuals. At the same time, the professionals who have been responsible for mediating the spaces between 'the social' as a public sphere and the family as the private arena have failed to articulate the aspirations of those they serve, particularly when it involves the protection and welfare of children. And practitioners have remained silent about the significant role that structural inequalities play in the intractable forms of hardship faced daily by people in need.

# 4

# Professionalization, Practice Methods and Processes of Intervention

## Introduction

The development of social work owes much to its struggle to establish its claim to professional status and identity within the terrain of professions that have been traditionally dominated by men, especially law and medicine. Ironically, although social work is made up largely of women as front-line workers, its management ranks are dominated by men (Howe, 1986; Coyle, 1989; Dominelli, 2002b; Prospects, 2009). As a result of its uncertain status, its position in the professional hierarchy is constantly being subjected to question or undermined (Di Palma et al., 1999; Bent-Goodley and Sarnoff, 2008). Its low status is particularly evident in situations of inter-professional or inter-agency working, in partnerships with stakeholders that involve members of the traditional professions, and in relationship-building in health agencies, which tend to regard the position of those in the medical profession as being above that of social workers, even when they are undertaking similar tasks. Social work's low public regard in the UK is also evident in everyday practice, where its activities are linked primarily to child protection issues, not the rich variety of interventions engaged in by social workers elsewhere, and when the media become incensed at the failure of those in the profession to safeguard children and older adults living in extremely complicated situations.

The lack of clarity about social work's position has made the issue of professionalization a constant theme in its development and has led to confusion among the public as to its role and place in society. It has also meant that social workers are always looking to other disciplines to increase their cache of theoretical knowledge and kudos, which has resulted in a borrowing from other fields that has often undermined the value of those initiatives that can be attributed to the profession itself. These include its practice theories and methods and models of service provision, particularly anti-oppressive theories and empowering practice, where social work educators and practitioners have taken the lead in getting these embedded in courses in the British Academy. There have been advances in all three areas that have provided sources of inspiration to other professions, particularly in the field of health. The processes of intervention that aim to empower clients and redistribute power within the client–worker relationship have been central in the development of empowering forms of social work practice.

In this chapter, I explore the processes of intervention in client–worker relationships and focus on the move from oppressive to anti-oppressive practice, covering issues of age, race, gender, disability, mental ill-health and sexual orientation. In the course of this, I examine the settings and contexts in which new methods have come to the fore – e.g., task-centred social work, which came to Europe from the USA – and various forms of anti-oppressive and empowering practice with selected client groups, including children, older people, migrants and offenders. Structural social work dominates in Canada and anti-oppressive practice in the UK in ways that are not usually evident in the USA. Culturally competent social work among different ethnic groups, especially those of African, Hispanic and Asian origin, are more relevant in the USA. Aboriginal systems of social work are also significant in Australia, New Zealand and Canada, and to some extent in the USA. These raise new challenges for social work, especially in defining new links between spirituality, the physical environment and all of humanity.

## Professionalizing charitable works

Social work professionals care strongly about the people they serve and strive to work with them to the highest possible standards, however these might be defined and contextualized. These standards should be well researched and rooted in evidence that can be scrutinized and assessed. During the Victorian era, as the demand for services to alleviate hardship rose, the limitations of the ad hoc provisions for helping others and the need for trained personnel to undertake this work became increasingly obvious. An awareness of this situation gave a strong impetus to professionalizing philanthropic and charitable work (Agnew, 2004). Professionalization refers to the process of obtaining external recognition of the value of the work being done and the standards to which practitioners are required to perform. Its professional status reflects the standing of social work in the public arena and articulates a statement about the context in which those practising are viewed. Professional social work began to emerge in Europe towards the end of the nineteenth century (Kendall, 2000). To be recognized at that time, professions had to meet established criteria, namely:

- be distinctive – i.e., have a body of knowledge that it called its own;
- have autonomous governance mechanisms to be able to control its practitioners and ensure their performance according to set standards;
- restrict entry to the profession – i.e., control access to its training and the means of socialization into the profession; and
- have a professional association (Flexner, [1915] 2001).

These criteria, Flexner argued, enabled the profession to control entry, enforce standards and apply sanctions against those that violated them. Thus, codes of ethics, registration and licensing procedures, often under the auspices of the profession's own governing body, enabled those responsible to maintain standards through established and publicized procedures that sought to ensure fairness in service delivery and curb abuses of power by practitioners. The profession was thereby empowered to police its own members and ensure that new developments proceeded to promote its interests and safeguard those relying on professional services. But such structures were lacking in the newly formed social work profession, which promoted employment rooted in charitable giving and women's caring, primarily for middle-class women. For the past hundred years women have challenged assumptions about what constitutes a profession, and their responses to the question have been threaded through its historical development in the West. However, these different practices resulted in its being denied admittance to the ranks of the professions (Flexner, [1915] 2001).

Among these differences were being inclusive, so as not to exclude anyone who wished to train in the profession from doing so; attempting to establish flatter relations between workers and people accessing their services, and encouraging client self-determination – a precursor to engaging with service users, an idea evident long before it was popularized by Beresford and Croft (1993). In the West, Flexner's pronouncements became hegemonic and have shifted little in the intervening century. The established professions of law and medicine met these criteria; social work did not (Heraud, 1981), not least because Flexner's definition was developed with the traditional professions in mind. His definition of professionalism perpetuated an organization along elitist and hierarchical lines (Hugman, 1991) in a way that social work still is not. Significantly, the control of professional knowledge by experts becomes easier when it is transferred into a privileged scientific domain rather than remaining readily accessible to lay people. This occurred in medicine when it acquired a 'scientific' basis that made it the purview of men and raised its status. Previously, it had been a task undertaken largely by women drawing on local knowledge and traditions and had been highly devalued (Ehrenreich and English, 1979). Entry to and knowledge within traditional professions have been guarded and controlled by the professionals themselves, and the standards of behaviour, often organized into a code of ethics, were enforced by their peers.

The exclusion of women at the time prevented their being trained in the prestigious professions. It also intensified the dividing line between the accepted professions and the lesser ones such as social work that involved more informal, less scientific person-to-person relationships (Milner, 2002). As social work was concerned with caring, then defined as 'women's work', and as a type of activity that was deemed of lesser importance and as taking from rather than contributing to economic growth, women's attempts to forge a different kind of profession worked against them (Dominelli, 1997).

A further worry now is that professions that comply with Flexner's definition become so powerful that their influence spills over into other areas of public life and policy and may prevent the promulgation of important social policies. For example, the American Medical Association organized to prevent President Roosevelt from enacting a national health service for Americans during the depression (Lampton, 1977). President Obama faced similar organized resistance to his proposals for health care reform, even though it remains based on insurance principles (EPI, 2007), which means insurance companies are likely to have a powerful voice in how health care develops in the long term. Doctors' opposition to the National Health Service in the UK meant that they were allowed both to be salaried workers in the NHS and to conduct private practice, giving rise to a two-tier system that contributed to undermining the availability of universal health care, free to all at the point of need. Governments, can, if they wish, eliminate professional sources of power, as the Bolsheviks did when they abolished the medical organization the Pirogov Society (Field, 1989). Mao likewise ended the Chinese Medical Association (Lampton, 1977). Both these medical associations resisted the social reforms that the respective Communist Party wished to undertake.

The processes of professionalizing social work have taken different trajectories, depending on the nation–states involved and the capacity of

social workers to demonstrate the scientific basis of their practice and raise its status. This includes professionalizing volunteering, which often supplements social work practice (Haski-Leventhal, 2005). Professional trajectories are tied up with regulatory bodies and mechanisms of control and vary substantially from country to country. I do not have space to go into great detail here, but American practitioners have had a longer history of control over entry to the profession – registration and licensing – than the British. The scientific basis of the clinical approaches that dominate the professional social work landscape in the USA is stronger than that of other forms of practice, and it developed regulatory mechanisms early in its history. The regulatory body in the UK is a quango – the General Social Care Council (GSCC) – which approves the inclusion of a qualified worker for registration. The register identifies the duties that a social worker can undertake, enforces ethical standards of behaviour and protects service users. In the USA, the law defines the standards to be reached at each level of qualification. Arrangements vary according to the jurisdiction within which a social worker wishes to practise. This means that each time an individual moves to another jurisdiction, they have to apply for a fresh licence and undergo another registration process. The Association of Social Work Boards (www.aswb.org) was recently formed to overcome the fragmentation of these arrangements and now regulates licensing arrangements across much of the USA.

In the UK, it was not until 2003, with the advent of the qualifying degree in social work, that registration was introduced by the GSCC. Both registration and licensing are aimed at controlling professional behaviour, including misconduct, and the processes whereby allegations are investigated and dealt with. There are few differences in the goals of registering or licensure. Although there are procedural differences between them, both seek to attract qualified social workers into the profession, uphold standards in professional conduct, withdraw permission to practise for those who violate professional norms, and ensure that training continues throughout the career trajectory – known as continuous professional development or CPD. Additionally, both processes seek to ensure that social workers are able to:

- identify and balance need, risks and rights;
- desist from abusive behaviour;
- intervene in situations to assist and protect individuals and communities; and
- observe the profession's code of ethics.

Both registration and licensure ensure that only those who meet the legally set criteria are allowed to practise. In this way, those who are not registered, including people who are qualified, are prevented from being employed as social workers in a form of professional 'closed shop'. This can lead to a protected title, as it has in the UK, for example, where only those who are registered can call themselves 'social workers'. This restricted title, however, does not preclude others with different titles from undertaking social work tasks, e.g., personal advisors in job centres (Dominelli, 2004b).

There are still no licensing arrangements in the UK, although these are being mooted as a result of the review of social work education that began in 2009 (Social Work Task Force, 2009). Moreover, the basic qualification can be obtained at either Bachelor's or Master's level. This practice, I believe, undermines the profession's capacity to develop strong specialisms at post-qualifying levels, which, in my view, should be what a Master's qualification should entail. And the forms of practice rooted, for example, in care management that are currently in the ascendancy in the UK are less well researched than the support for evidence-based practice suggests. The regulatory body that accredits the academy in the USA is a voluntary body called the Council of Social Work Education. In Britain, it is a state-appointed quango, the GSCC. Other countries have different arrangements. For example, while university courses in Australia are accredited by the Australian Association of Social Workers, other countries leave accrediting arrangements to individual universities. In Europe, the European Association of Schools of Social Work attempted to create a regional accreditation body through voluntary subscriptions, but found itself unable to address the diversity and power of the national regulatory bodies already in place. It also failed to carry the confidence of large numbers of educators, who felt that there was no guarantee of its expensive 'accreditation' being widely recognized.

## Managerial control of professional labour

Managers became keen to reconfigure the processes whereby professional labour was controlled and held accountable. They aimed to reduce the capacity of associations and practitioners to set the parameters of the profession and control their own activities. They also sought to diminish the significance of relational social work in the statutory sector. Consequently, professionalization became more complicated as employers tried to assert control over the development of social work and to make practitioners more accountable to managerial imperatives than had been the norm in either clinical social work or the prestigious professions. Clawing back power from social workers and making them less autonomous as professionals has been a key driving force behind the '3Es' (efficiency, economy and effectiveness) promoted by competency-based social work. This aim was also compatible with the objectives of standardizing service delivery and shifting the balance of power from professionals to service users. This concern converged with the objectives espoused by those endorsing empowering practice, albeit the latter did not envisage the bureaucratic approach to the forms of empowerment that unfolded with managerial control. Neo-liberal ideologies seeking to curb professional power facilitated such moves in both practice directives and social policies.

The processes of managing social workers and the professional routines of labour have changed substantially under the aegis of globalization, with a diminution in power among professional associations such as BASW and a rise in managerial and techno-bureaucratic forms of control (Clarke and Newman, 1997). The impact of globalization on social work practice has been considerable, as nation–states have had to respond to market forces and their demands for discipline in the public sector, enhancing competitiveness in the labour process, and increasing managerial control of resources, including personnel. While they resonate elsewhere, in the UK these processes have resulted in social policies that promote globalizing tendencies. These have led to:

- the growth of the market and private provision, which excludes the many users who are unable to pay, an incapacity that limits choice and gives rise to stigmatized public provision as the commitment to universal services is undermined;
- the internationalization of social problems, which heightens interdependencies and insecurities within and across nations and destroys the consensus that existed among members of the general public around notions of solidarity with those worse off;
- the exacerbation of existing structural inequalities, especially poverty, sexism, racism, disablism and ageism, as the people who are encompassed by these social divisions are defined as not pulling their weight in the competitive marketplace or the race to reduce labour costs (Culpitt, 1992);
- new managerialism and performance management, which undermine individually tailored responses to service users' needs and foster standard provisions targeted at those most in need rather than providing the best care for the whole population;
- the bureaucratization and loss of professional control over the labour process and a reduction in the space for autonomous professional decision-making that can respond to individual needs and particular situations;

- the intensification of existing weaknesses in the professional identity of social work, including:
  - fragmented services that confuse and disorient service users, who may not know where to go to secure much needed help;
  - the appropriation of social work tasks by other professionals who carry more public and inter-professional confidence than social workers; and
  - a weak professional voice at the national and international level that impedes attempts to advocate for the strengthening of the status of social work as a valued and desirable profession with important things to say on all of the social problems that affect contemporary societies;
- bureaucratic forms of service–user engagement, such as citizens' charters and formal explicit rights to complain about services – e.g., individual budgets.

At the national level, the state's engagement with the forces of globalization has empowered managers at the expense of practitioners. The new managerialism (Clarke and Newman, 1997) focuses on bureaucratic forms of control, specified performance indicators and targets, and the technological management of the routines of practice through the new information technologies. These developments are consistent with the use of economic realities, precisely defined budgets and contractual arrangements integral to affirming market discipline and the spread of capitalist social relations to every aspect of human life across the globe. At the same time, under neo-liberalism, there is a major crisis in financial arrangements, as there is no longer the capacity to generate ever rising profits for entrepreneurs. Ironically, the neo-liberals, who have resisted the involvement of the state in the economy, went running to it for funds to assist the recovery of financial institutions without acknowledging that they were perpetuating a longstanding historical tradition of the public sector subsidizing the private one (DBERR, 2007). This position also holds for private and voluntary welfare providers, who would be unable to survive without a regular injection of public funds in the form of grants (Barlett and Steele, 1998). Even before the crisis, the private finance initiative and forms of 'contract government' (Greer, 1994) that began in the 1990s engaged the state in commissioning services from private-sector providers through various types of contractual arrangements.

At a wider level, the internationalization of social problems blurs boundaries between nation–states. Problems experienced by one individual or group in one country can require solutions that involve professionals elsewhere. This reality can be used by social workers to make links with practitioners in other countries to resolve concerns such as people trafficking, organized crime and the elimination of major infectious diseases. Such activities require social workers to be able to converse about how they practise and the standards they apply to act professionally and ethically when their actions cross borders.

### The market reshapes 'the social'

Neo-liberals continue to reject demands for greater accountability for bankers and for limitations to be placed on the bonuses that are paid to chief executives, especially those in banking, for failing to grow their company or sector. For these corporate executives, Bank Aid is OK; People Aid is not OK. Yet the funds for Bank Aid are paid out of the public purse (*Metro*, 2008). In 2009 in the UK, this resulted in a public-sector deficit of 11.4 per cent of GDP (£159.2 billion) and a debt of 68.1 per cent of GDP (£950.4 billion) (ONS, 2010). And these executives continue to blame the public sector for not effectively managing its resources and constantly demand cuts in public expenditure to ensure a fiscal survival that works to their advantage. In this scenario, social services, education and health are prime candidates for cuts, the brunt of which will fall on poor, marginalized sectors of the population in both the Global North and the Global South (Whitmore et al., 2008). This reshapes 'the social' in more punitive and individualistic directions. At the same time, current benefit levels are low: £65.45 a week for single persons over twenty-five; £51.85 per week for those under twenty-five, with an earnings disregard of £5 for childless individuals and £20 a week for those with children (Conn, 2010). Getting a job, not the right to welfare, is promoted as the way out of poverty. The state's key role is to assist individuals to find employment. Thus 'the social' becomes fragmented and personalized, with 'the self' repositioned as responsible for their own well-being (and that of the family) while the professional – e.g., the personal advisor in the job centre – gives expert advice.

The growth of the private market has widened the range of facilities provided by voluntary and commercial for-profit and non-profit agencies. Meanwhile the state retains overall control of the budget as a consumer of their services through grants and contracts, and public-sector provision focuses on heavy end services, such as child protection, work with offenders, and mental health (Finn, 2009a, 2009b). Despite this growth, a rise in the status of social work has not followed. Instead, high-profile child protection cases such as those of Victoria Climbié and Baby P have produced a deep crisis that has led to a demoralized profession and caused workers to leave in droves (Social Work Task Force, 2009).

The lack of substantial progress in professionalism of social work is reflected in its continued low status and lack of attraction to men. The Department of Children, Schools and Families (DCSF) in the UK undertook a survey about social work as part of a review of its position in England and Wales during 2009 and found that 88 per cent of respondents felt that 'The social work profession is undervalued, poorly understood and under continuous media attack. This is making it hard for social workers to do their job and hard to attract people into the profession' (www.dcsf.gov.uk/swtf). Disillusionment is evident in high rates of staff turnover, poor working conditions and lack of professional confidence. Practitioners are aware of the poor conditions they endure at work, where:

- inadequate buildings lead to a preoccupation with security and can intimidate or alienate service users;
- caseloads are overwhelmingly high and deprive service users of adequate time to explain their situations, to be heard and to be fully involved in resolving their problems;
- paperwork dominates the labour process at the expense of professional judgement and discussion with experienced managerial staff capable of offering support in dealing with difficult situations or service users;
- disillusionment and high rates of staff turnover are the rule. General vacancy rates of 10 per cent prevailed in British social work during 2006, compared with only 1 per cent among teachers.

In the UK, these concerns have also been highlighted in a survey undertaken in England by the trade union Unison, which numbers 40,000 social workers among its members. The survey found that:

- adult care workers spent too much time doing paperwork instead of working with service users (96 per cent);
- performance indicators had a negative impact on service user outcomes (73 per cent);
- services were less well resourced than they were five years previously (67 per cent);
- average workloads had increased (86 per cent); and
- personalization was anticipated to reduce social work posts (17 per cent) and deskill social workers (15 per cent) (www.communitycare.co.uk/112385).

These findings replicate those published earlier by various authors (Jones and Novak, 1993; Waterson, 1993; Dominelli, 2004a). The use of agencies for recruitment purposes has grown substantially in the intervening years. This growth has occurred because:

- local authorities have frozen posts to accommodate budgets that were never sufficient to meet the increasing demands and additional legal responsibilities placed on practitioners. This will be exacerbated by the inevitable cuts in public expenditure as a result of the budget deficit caused largely by bailing out the financial sector in the 2007–9 financial crisis;
- state social work became increasingly bureaucratic and unattractive, leading many experienced workers to move into the voluntary sector, where relational social work is still possible; and
- social workers found that they could gain flexibility in managing work and other commitments, including child care, elder care, and maintaining a work–life balance, by registering with an agency. This applies also to social work students on qualifying courses, who find they can earn enough to minimize the sums they need to borrow during the period of their studies (personal communication).

While agency staffing offers both employers and users flexibility in the short term, it has a number of limitations. Agency staff may:

- have inadequate qualifications and/or levels of experience;
- need more administrative time to keep track of their movements;
- not provide continuity of service;
- drain scarce resources, as they cost more to employ – not least through the high fees paid to agencies for the services they provide in recruiting and retaining potential staff;
- be less likely to feel loyalty to their employer; and
- raise turnover rates substantially.

These practices are consistent with managerialist imperatives of having a workforce that can be deployed as needed and controlled more easily. However, it can produce tensions around continuity of services for clients and reduce the amount of staff goodwill that grows as commitment to working for the same employer increases.

## Practice methods: contested approaches to working with people

The development of practice theories and methods specific to social work are part of the project of professionalization (Payne, 2005; Coulshed and

Orme, 2006). In the English-speaking world, this has constantly drawn upon cross-country exchanges of people through various study visits, fellowships, studentships, scholarships and bursaries and teaching materials (books, articles, course curricula and, with the internet, ready access to copyright materials, even if many of these have to be purchased). This has meant that paradigms for practice developed in one country have travelled across borders and been adapted and used in other countries. Much of this traffic relies on individual instigation, but institutions such as universities are increasingly drawn into competing with one another for students, research, grants, scholarships and reputations, often expressed in the form of citations, places in league tables and world rankings. This competition exists despite the commitment of many academics to collaborative relationships. And universities have undertaken a growing number of forays into the international arena to establish institutional bases in other countries, some of which have been extremely successful in opening up new areas of study and research – e.g., Harvard's Villa i tatti in Florence, Italy. Some English universities have formed partnership consortia to assist continental European professional universities establish Master's level programmes in social work. For instance, London Metropolitan University and Zuyd University of the Applied Sciences in the Netherlands are part of a network of thirty-seven universities across Europe that deliver the highly regarded MACESS (Masters in Comparative European Social Studies) course.

While social work exchanges since the Second World War have been dominated by the sheer economic and numerical might of American materials, Australia, New Zealand, Canada and the UK have also contributed a share, as we shall see below. The downside of the dominance of English in social work has meant that materials written in this language may have gained unwarranted influence. However, monolingual English speakers cannot access significant developments that have been written in other languages. This has been the case despite French and Spanish being part of the IASSW, IFSW and ICSW's repertoire of official languages, because translations are costly and few are undertaken. The limited range of materials being translated into English also means that the significant developments now being discussed in the UN's other official languages – Russian, Arabic and Chinese – are not readily available. The heritage of social work in countries dominated by the English language is thereby the poorer, and its practitioners and academics remain ignorant of many exciting developments in theory and practice from other countries. Fortunately, more materials are now being translated – e.g., in the *China Journal of Social Work*.

There is an extensive literature in English on social work theories and practice methods. Within the wide range of materials available I highlight a few of those most pertinent to British social work, including those by Coulshed and Orme (2006); Payne (2005); and Dominelli (2004b). Their writings have supported social work students in exploring the contours of theory and practice in the profession and enabled those studying British social work to:

- continue the project of professionalization;
- respond to employers' and managers' concerns to improve the efficient use of resources, including financial resources and skilled personnel;
- utilize best forms of practice formulated in other countries for their own development; and
- make their own contribution to the wealth of materials that social work educators and practitioners have developed globally.

Professionalization has been a constant concern in social work. It received a major impetus when Freudian theories and insights were used to develop psychodynamic, clinical and psychiatric social work, deriving a lot of support from its development in the United States (Agnew, 2004), particularly after the Second World War. The spread of American forms of practice was assisted through funding for scholarships and fellowships, including the American Fulbright programme and various forms of funding secured though Marshall Aid (Leighninger, 1998). These initiatives enabled the best minds to study in the USA and benefit from its extensive range of educational materials. The strengths of clinical and psychiatric approaches to social work were imported into Europe through such means. Their scientific orientation, rooted in Freudian analyses, lent these methods professional rigour, even though their cultural rootedness in Northern European culture was ignored. When European scholars returned to their countries of origin, they became proponents of the systems they had learnt and transferred knowledge acquired in America to others in their homelands. Further transferral of American social work knowledge to Asia occurred after the Korean War and has had a considerable impact there too (Yang, 2009).

## Managerial concerns about practice

The more efficient use of resources and personnel became a critical issue for managers as public expenditure rose and cuts were sought, particularly in the mid-1970s and the 1980s, and they looked across the Atlantic for possible solutions. Task-centred social work was one they picked up. Formulated by Reid and Epstein (1972) on the basis of earlier research conducted in America (Reid and Shyne, 1969), this indicated that interventions lasting longer than eight to twelve weeks diminished in effectiveness as time passed. These findings chimed with the evidence available in the UK. Many interventions employing psychodynamic casework methods had been sitting on social workers' desks for years with little sign of progress having been made. British managers used Reid and Epstein's work to explore the efficacy of practice and introduce changes that imposed time-limited forms of practice. The outcome was to promote task-centred social work and contract social work (Smith and Corden, 1981) as their preferred approaches.

Managers' concerns combined with critiques mounted by radical practitioners, whose voice at the time was most articulately expressed through *Case Con*, a magazine propounding the views of service users and practitioners critical of the then prevailing forms of practice and the policies underpinning them, and radical social work educators, who used Marxist theories (Corrigan and Leonard, 1978) to explore the hidden facets of class bias in the profession. Together, these groups undermined the popularity of psychodynamic casework and contributed to its decline. Eventually, this particular approach was surpassed by other theories – task-centred social work (Reid and Epstein, 1972), contract social work (Smith and Corden, 1981), cognitive behavioural therapies (Sheldon, 1995), community work (Craig and Mayo, 1995), radical social work (Bailey and Brake, 1975) and, eventually, anti-oppressive practice (Dominelli, 2002a) such as feminist social work (Hanmer and Statham, 1988; Dominelli and McLeod, 1989), anti-racist social work (Dominelli, 1988), black perspectives in social work (Ahmad, 1990), postmodern practice (Pease and Fook, 1999), constructionist practice (Parton and O'Byrne, 2000), African-centric social work (Graham, 2002) and critical practice (Fook, 2002).

The borrowing and use of materials developed in one area of the globe in another, with or without local adaption, therefore, is not a new phenomenon. Nor is it restricted to imperialist enterprises. My own trajectory in formulating feminist social work and anti-racist social work benefited from the existence of an English-language literature, including that from the USA, not only because I traversed several borderlands before settling in the UK, but also because I was a fluent speaker of the language from childhood. My knowledge of several other languages and living in different countries also meant that I could access materials from elsewhere. At the same time, I have been amazed by how materials that I have written explicitly for British social work students and practitioners have travelled across borders, in most cases without my knowing about it for years, and been adapted by others for local use and developed in directions that were novel and exciting (personal communications).

The confluence of corporatist managerial concerns and the radical critiques of social work enabled both sides to argue that improving practice lay at the heart of their alternative approaches to the discipline. Managers sought to enforce the 3Es of efficiency, effectiveness and economy to hold practitioners more accountable for the resources they utilized and how they used them (Clarke and Newman, 1997). They found task-centred social work, contract social work, case management and competency-based practice particularly useful in limiting interventions to the period of time during which change in individuals' behaviour was deemed most likely to occur (Coulshed and Orme, 2006). Practitioners availing themselves of these approaches also had the additional advantage of managers making time-limited resources available for use in any individual instance.

Many radical practitioners bought into these managerialist theories because they sought to get workers to engage with those accessing their services and focus on solving problems. Social workers would systematically work out a jointly agreed plan of action with clients and identify tasks and obligations to be met by both parties. Signing a contract that spelt these out was part of the process (Payne, 2005). This element was seen as empowering by such adherents of task-centred social work as Doel and Marsh (1992), because they focused on equality and empowerment. However, others, including Dominelli (1996b), criticized this aspect as tokenistic on the grounds that the top priority was not what service users might want or need, but the constraints set by managers.

Discussions of power and partnership advocated through task-centred approaches can be tokenistic and disingenuous if managerially imposed limitations are generally not made clear to service users or if the worker set the limits within which those discussions occurred. Moreover, agreement may be 'manufactured' in that a service user with complex needs may be excluded from a programme and told to seek assistance elsewhere, or other options are not suggested because a worker thinks that responding to complex needs might exceed the short time-frame inherent in managerialist approaches to practice. These and other constraints that affect the bottom line and impact upon the worker's skills and motivations can come into play and skew the potential to create empowering dynamics in the relationship (Simons and Jankowski, 2007; Zhang et al., 2008).

Radical social work was being developed in the UK at the same time as the adoption of corporate management theories and modes of practice was proceeding apace. Peter Leonard (1975) compiled an anthology on British community work to argue the relevance of alliances between those workers organized in trade unions and those practitioners working on local issues in communities. This endeavour paralleled the collection edited by Roy Bailey and Michael Brake (1975), entitled *Radical Social Work*, which also included class relations and gender issues. Corrigan and Leonard (1978) followed up this analysis with *Social Work under Capitalism*, which identified the middle-class bias in practice and advocated changes in social relations through community-based action supported by alliances with the trade union movement. However, these authors' guidelines for practice were limited. Opposition to their ideas, coupled with their promotion of Marxist ideology, came from both within the academy and among employers. The lack of specific suggestions for practice also discouraged practitioners from engaging with their work in any substantial way.

### Service users' concerns about practice

At the same time, community workers picked up on and raised concerns about the individualizing nature of practice and the neglect of social forces, especially economic ones, in creating social problems and structural inequalities (CDP, 1972). They also argued that social problems had to be solved collectively through the mobilization of groups and communities and by forming alliances with others who supported their goals, including those in the trade union movement. The main exponents of this view became associated with the Community Development Projects (CDPs) of the 1960s and early 1970s (Loney, 1986). Their identification of the decline of local economies as the source of poverty and hardship in twelve deprived areas of the UK, and their activism in doing something about it, aggravated both local and central government, which subsequently closed down the CDPs. Community action of this type has not been funded by British administrations since that time. Instead, forms of community organization have been promoted that do not critique the status quo, but look to improve efficiency in service delivery by avoiding wasteful duplication (Finn, 1985). The state has utilized community organization and community development models in achieving this goal (Dominelli, 2006a).

The demands of women, black activists and disabled people for change in mainstream social policies and professional practice led to the development of services that met their needs and and which they ran themselves. They wanted their expertise and knowledge developed through life experiences to be recognized and called for more egalitarian relationships with the professionals who worked with them. Their endeavours became encapsulated in feminist social work, black perspectives in social work and the social model of disability.

Those practitioners from within the new social movements developed their own provisions as alternatives to mainstream services. These relied primarily on self-help endeavours where people learnt by exploring each other's experiences and were in contrast to those emanating from Marxist analyses. Personal problems could be linked to inadequacies in the social structures of society, showing that it was not simply individuals who were affected, but entire categories of people who shared similar attributes and outcomes. Practices advocated by these activists undermined the idea that an individual's predicament was the result of their own pathologies and deficits. Feminists, civil rights activists and disabled people became prime movers of these changes. In the academy, works such as Paulo Freire's (1972) *The Pedagogy of the Oppressed* emphasized the probing of social problems to expose their structural underpinnings and roots in unequal social relations. Freire's book also suggested that education could be used to engage people in consciousness-raising processes and enable them to learn how to challenge the power relations that kept them oppressed. The writings of Che Guevara (1969), which inspired young people to dream of a different kind of society; and Mao Zedong's *'The Little Red Book'* (1966) also heightened the possibilities of implementing revolutionary change in the existing social order, as did the writings of Karl Marx (1965), Vladimir Lenin (1961), Leon Trotsky (2007), Franz Fanon (1968a, 1968b), and those involved in scholarly critiques of society, including McLuhan (1995), Chomsky (1980), Fromm (1941, 2002), Laing (1969) and Goffman (1961).

In the USA, the American War on Poverty and ideals of the Great Society meant that many young idealists were being attracted to work in deprived neighbourhoods and communities and highlighted the need for structural change (Piven and Cloward, 1971). Their ideas were reflected in the literature, drama and music of the time – John Osborne's *Look Back in Anger*, Federico Fellini's *La dolce vita*, the Beatles' *Abbey Road* and *Sergeant Pepper* albums and Bob Dylan's lyrics, among others. These added to the heady mix that encouraged young people, many of whom were drawn to social work and social policy, to realize their ideals of making life better for poor people throughout the world, including those on their own doorsteps. This was often expressed through forms of direct action, as young people themselves formed local movements such as the Students for a Democratic Society in Canada and the USA. In 1968, student uprisings occurred throughout the world. Many of these protests focused on young people's opposition to American action in Vietnam and the Israeli occupation of Palestinian lands. Other protests had a more local focus – e.g., in France, China, South Africa and North Africa – but with television and newspapers such protests also had worldwide repercussions.

The idea that progress was possible strengthened young people's beliefs in the community as a source of change. Their thoughts were carried into social work and community work practice alongside the analyses and dreams inspired by the feminist movement, the black civil rights movement and the movement of disabled people. Many of these community activists migrated to the academy when opportunities for community action had diminished. In these settings, their research and scholarship has kept alive the aspirations of marginalized people for a better life, especially one controlled and defined by the poor themselves. The theories and models of practice that became radical social work, feminist social work, anti-racist social work, black perspectives in social work, anti-oppressive social work, the social model of disability, postmodern social work, critical social work, constructionist social work, have roots in such activism.

All these movements sought to enshrine people's rights to social services in the notions of human rights and social justice. Action was not limited to the local level: for example, civil society organizations and social movements mobilized to influence the agendas at the UN and sought to get their ideas included in various conventions – the Convention for the Elimination of Discrimination Against Women (CEDAW), the Convention Against Racism and Xenophobia, the Convention for the Rights of the Child, the agreements that arose out of the social development summit in Copenhagen in 1995; the Action Platform for Women that resulted from the Beijing conference in 1995, the Durban World Conference Against Racism in 2000, the summit on ageing in Madrid in 2002 and the Convention on Rights for Disabled People in 2006. All of these involved submissions and lobbying undertaken by many civil society organizations, among them the IASSW, IFSW and ICSW through their consultative status with the UN. Importantly, these initiatives were carried out not as imperialist endeavours, but as attempts to find commonalities that enabled people to seek change and address their differences in culturally appropriate, peaceful, collaborative, locality-specific ways (Ferree and Tripp, 2006).

Other views of social work co-existed alongside these transformative ones, and there were often acrimonious exchanges between supporters of opposing sides. Employers were often pitted against workers, policy-makers against community activists, and academics from one side of the political spectrum against those on the other. However, as the policy-makers had control of the resources allocated to a dependent profession, it often meant that community activists and social workers found themselves at odds with what was required of them. In Britain, this became increasingly evident as the state pursued bureaucratic notions of social work practice and sought to control its workforce through performance management techniques. Although the CDPs' findings were rooted in empirical evidence that exposed the role played by declining local economies in creating deprivation at neighbourhood level, the state rejected this message (Dominelli, 1990, 2006a). The demise of the CDPs was a notable example of the state calling time on radical social work initiatives (Loney, 1986).

### Bureaucratizing practice

Meanwhile, managers tended to focus on the task at hand, and many bitterly resented the time that trainee social workers on courses spent on broader theories trying to understand society, social interactions, culture and other areas that formed the backbone of the alternative ideas being developed by radical critiques of the profession. The concern that social workers are not trained 'to hit the ground running' is echoed today, as the UK engages in yet another bout of restructuring social work training without having learnt much about how earlier bureaucratic approaches failed both service users and professionals. Some of the most far-reaching changes of recent years have instigated even more bureaucratic forms of social work than those envisaged by the then Central Council for Education and Training in Social Work (CCETSW) in the extensively criticized competency-based approach to practice of the 1990s (Dominelli, 1996b).

Competency-based social work has been subjected to critique, not for its demand that practitioners are proficient, skilled and qualified for the job, but for its lack of innovative thrust, being based as it is on inadequate sociological theories linked to functional analyses incapable of dealing with subtle nuances, complexity, conflict and change. Functional theories as articulated by the American sociologist Talcott Parsons (1957) assume that disturbances in a social system are temporary and can be readily solved to bring the system back to equilibrium or stasis. These theories promote competence-based social work with a division of labour that reduces complex tasks into simple discrete actions, which can be translated into checklists that anyone without qualifications can follow. This development can lock women into low-paid ghettos as actions previously undertaken by qualified social workers are passed on to those who are unqualified or less well-qualified. Unqualified practitioners can be paid less than qualified workers and lack opportunities to progress in their careers (Dominelli, 1996b).

Case management, originally pioneered in adult services in the UK, travelled from across the Atlantic, where it was practised as care management (Challis et al., 1987; Brand, 2009). It reinforced bureaucratic forms of social work intervention and encouraged the computerization of case recording and the growth of corporate management techniques, including performance management and quality assurance mechanisms such as total quality control, that relied more on practitioners following procedures and predetermined interventions – endorsing a 'one size suits all' approach over one that utilizes professional judgement and innovation to meet individual need. Case management, with its managerialist accoutrements, gained ascendancy as a form of practice in the UK as a result of the Thatcherite commitment to introducing business methods in a public sector the Conservative government felt was flabby and inefficient. Following the *Griffiths Report* on services for older people (Griffiths, 1988), Thatcher made this sector the springboard for private involvement in the British welfare state. Key to this plan was introducing a purchaser–provider split, which reduced the role of the state to commissioning services from private- and voluntary-sector providers. The central plank of the alleged modernization of the public sector occurred through the importation of private practice in the personal social services, health, education and prison sectors. These were brought across the Atlantic by American entrepreneurs while social policies were changed to legitimate such activities. This approach to changing public professional practice in the social services arena was retained and extended by New Labour under both the Blair and the Brown governments. Critiques of the damage caused to service users, who were non-players in the market-based welfare service economy, were ignored, although concerns began to be voiced from the early 1990s (Dominelli and Hoogvelt, 1996; Clarke and Newman, 1997).

Commodified social work is another form of bureaucratic social work, initiated under the aegis of the new public-sector management that favoured private enterprise and the introduction of business systems and language. It turned service users into consumers, who were encouraged to think of themselves as individuals able to play the market and choose those services they desired. Consumer choice, based on public choice theories (Buchanan, 1968; Mackenzie, 2008), therefore, is an integral element of the theory of commodified social work. However, its practice leaves much to be desired, as choice is an illusion for those without the necessary funds (Dominelli, 2004a).

The intensification of bureaucratic approaches to professional practice can be traced back to the changes initiated by the Laming Review, which followed the murder of Victoria Climbié by her great-aunt and boyfriend while under the care of Haringey Council (Laming, 2003). Ironically, the recent review following the death of Baby P, also under the care of Haringey, was conducted by Lord Laming as well. This review highlighted the bureaucratic nature of contemporary practice. Yet, rather than setting practice in new directions, Laming merely said that the earlier reforms had not been properly implemented (Laming, 2009).

While there is some element of truth in this assertion, Lord Laming's comment fails to take account of the damage inflicted on practice by an over-reliance on bureaucratic forms of assessment and risk management. When being questioned about the death of Baby P, Sharon Shoesmith was able to claim that the inspections carried out by Ofsted had given Haringey's children's services a clean bill of health (Ross, 2008; Butler and Williams, 2010). Haringey had implemented the reforms advised by Laming after the Climbié review, including that of allowing children's services to be led and managed by someone unqualified in social work. Laming's 2009 review failed to consider more fundamental reforms that could address such issues as how to rehabilitate 'carers' who abuse, torture and kill children; support carers to take responsibility for their actions; enable communities to play their role in safeguarding children; implement children's rights; ensure that children can be protected without 24/7 surveillance over carers; build a ladder of training linked to career progression; acquire sufficient resources for the demands made of the service; and tackle structural inequalities in the social order. Undertaking changes in these areas is crucial if social workers are to gain greater practice capabilities and confidence in engaging in relational social work, formulate trusting relationships with service users as resources for changing behaviour, obtain sufficient time to train beyond basic qualifying levels, and be provided with the resources and supervisory support necessary for engaging in best practice. Structural change is needed alongside these initiatives to raise the incomes of families who are unable to acquire a decent standard of living and a valued place in wider society and to deal with the issues of professionalization and resource shortages.

British employers do not have confidence in the training that social workers currently receive, but there is nothing new about this. As far back as the 1970s, when the basis for qualification was the two-year Certificate of Qualification in Social Work (the CQSW), which was attached to a degree course at the instigation of universities rather than by CCETSW, despite its role as the national accreditation body, employers complained that social workers were not being prepared for the job that they were expected to undertake the day after they finished their training (Bailey, 1982). The reasons for this are familiar today – the tensions between education and training, including that of a wider liberal education versus training for specific tasks; different expectations about what can and should be delivered in training at any given level; insufficient time to cover all the material required; government reluctance to fund fully training of sufficient length and depth; and decisions about social work education and training being determined for politically expedient rather than professional or service-based purposes. In the process, much good practice conducted by social workers under the most extreme and difficult circumstances is ignored. Many people forget that social workers handle extremely complex and intractable cases and deal on a daily basis with people whom other professionals have given up on and often achieve positive results (Ferguson et al., 2007).

## Processes of intervention in social work

The processes of intervention in social work concern interactions between people. Payne (2009: 159) defines these processes as 'points of contact'. Processes extend beyond 'points' of contact because these are relevant to all stages of the worker–client relationship, according to Compton and Galaway (2005). I extend the concept by postulating processes as iterative loops of interactions. By focusing on *how* a person behaves to achieve certain ends through specific means, process becomes the way in which those ends are achieved and, in a critical reflective circle, connects the thinking about what is to be done with the action of doing and then reflecting upon what has been done. A process can be likened, therefore, to the thread that joins a string of beads together, with the beads as 'points of connection' in any one intervention. These beads can consist of several strands and do not have to create a circle. Moreover, the strands can be broken, as those wearing necklaces know. A breakage can occur all too easily, in unwanted circumstances and at any point along the thread. Additionally, I consider evaluation as a part of the process that is interwoven throughout an interaction – a thread within the thread, as it were.

The processes of social work or how an interaction is carried out form an important aspect of any intervention, because process provides the means whereby change occurs or is resisted. Processual considerations occur during all the phases of intervention and are negotiated by those taking part in the activity in question. The different elements that comprise the negotiated aspects of process can be identified as follows:

- referral;
- data gathering;
- assessment of the problem;
- preparing and agreeing a plan of action;
- implementing the plan of action;
- reviewing the plan of action;
- evaluating the action process;
- evaluating the outcomes;

- evaluating client performance;
- evaluating practitioner performance; and
- critical reflection upon future direction and action (Dominelli, 2004b: 82; Compton and Galaway, 2005).

At this level of abstraction, the phases of intervention are likely to be recognized by practitioners across the world. They do not prescribe what happens in each part of the process or the relationship between the ends and the means. They simply indicate considerations that can assist decisions about whom to involve in an intervention and where and how this is to be done. Spelling out how such issues are addressed and their actual implementation is driven by locality-specific contexts and determined locally by those who are directly involved. How these processes are conducted is likely to vary considerably in each situation. This is because practitioners have to work carefully with those involved to ensure that they incorporate micro-level, meso-level and macro-level aspects into their practice. These include local legal considerations, policies, procedures and cultural traditions, as well as broader elements like the Universal Declaration of Human Rights or the Convention on the Rights of the Child, which can inspire social workers to advocate for services and resources that are not otherwise available in a particular situation.

Processes can be singular or multiple, circular, linear or (un)broken, or go back and forth as those interacting are constantly shaping and being shaped by each other. Because they are interactive and continuously negotiated, their trajectory depends on the actors, their goals, the context(s) in which they are working and a range of other important factors, including the relevant legislation, organizational policies and procedures. There may be several processes involved at any one time. Once cultural considerations and local traditions are taken into account, some processes may even contradict each other and complicate the interactions considerably. Each party has a crucial role to play in influencing how the processes develop and whether the interaction between them can progress or not. The different roles that each actor plays may complicate the interaction in both favourable and unfavourable ways, depending on their intentions or anticipated outcomes and the relationships that they develop with each other. External factors and players may also impact upon the processes, which might otherwise appear limited to those explicitly involved. For example, this might happen when social workers are processing asylum applications involving people in other countries or whose whereabouts are unknown. The processes of interaction are depicted in figure 4.1.

The nature of the processes involved in an interaction is heavily dependent on the values held by the practitioners and the service users and

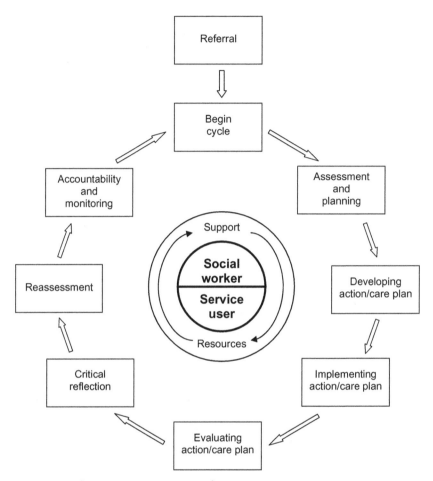

Figure 4.1 The interactive processes of intervention in practice

can be hierarchical or egalitarian. The characteristics that mark out the dynamics of an intervention are often taken for granted, because ethical behaviour in contemporary social work assumes that those who access services are equal partners in any undertaking. However, practitioners who believe that the social worker is the expert would take the lead in the relationship and would work with those seeking to access services in a manner that presumes the professional knows best. Those favouring egalitarian values recognize the experiential knowledge of service users and attempt to include them more in any decision-making process. In egalitarian partnerships, social workers will also seek to identify clients' strengths in order to enable them to initiate changes in their personal behaviour and life circumstances (Saleeby, 2002). If such practitioners assume that empowerment will occur spontaneously rather than through their direct input, they can easily end up reproducing hierarchical relationships and processes and fall into what has been termed 'the false equality trap' (Barker, 1986; Dominelli, 2002b). Additionally, values impact upon how and when sanctions or various forms of control are utilized.

## Conclusions

The struggle to professionalize and acquire a scientific basis to the profession has been a constant motif in social work practice. Despite the many strides it has made in this direction, social work continues to be devalued in relation to more established disciplines. Social workers need to develop further their research base and claim in definitive terms the terrain that they think appropriately belongs to the profession. Also, society in general has to be convinced of the value of caring work and engage both men and women in nurturing relationships that will sustain such activities. Moreover, as a highly fragmented profession that covers a vast range of settings and service user groups, has permeable borders and tries to be inclusive of diversity and difference, social work faces additional complications that have impeded progress in the profession as a whole. These include the absence of a consensus on what constitutes social work, what it should do, who should do it and how it should be done.

Nonetheless, social work does exist as a recognized entity in all regions of the world, and the methods of and models for practice discussed above would be familiar to most social workers practising in those countries. Yet how they are implemented in a particular situation with specific individuals, groups or communities would vary substantially as local contexts and considerations are taken into account. So, while discussions about the processes and phases of intervention can and do cross borders, distinctive aspects that are locality specific can also be identified. Social workers endeavouring to practise in empowering ways would be cognisant both of what they have in common with others and what is different between them. Furthermore, there are different views regarding which processes of intervention are culturally appropriate and relevant – e.g., indigenous forms of social work (Denzin et al., 2008).

The significance of what is done by social workers varies from country to country, with some policy-makers being more supportive of the profession than others. It is unfortunate for social work in the UK that British legislators tend to give the profession less credit than it deserves.

What is required is aptly summed up by the Social Work Task Force, led by Moira Gibb, in a review exploring options for British social work:

> a high quality social work service needs investment, effort, encouragement and high levels of professional expertise ... society needs to attach greater value to the support given to people in the difficult circumstances that social work tries to address. (Social Work Task Force, 2009, p. 34)

# 5

# Social Work, Citizenship, Human Rights and Social Justice

## Introduction

Social work is a heterogeneous global profession enjoying diversity along cultural, economic, political and social dimensions. Each element interacts with the others and finds expression in practice. Social work's position in the professional firmament continues to be contested and its position in each nation–state varies. Should the services provided be rights-based, market-based or residual? In the English-speaking, Anglo-Saxon West, it is in danger of being relegated to a marginal status while strengthening its position in the academy as a research-led discipline. In the UK, social services departments in local authority settings have lost their autonomous status, having been merged within health, education, housing and other departments. This could further endanger the profession's fragile identity.

In this chapter, I examine social workers' struggles to manage the tension between adhering to citizenship-inspired models of practice and their managers' demands for greater bureaucratic control of and rationing over resources. This latter trend intensified considerably under New Labour, despite its commitment to the rhetoric of citizenship and social inclusion. The extension of private provision has created the paradox of policies technically in favour of citizenship rights and entitlement, while managerial control of the labour process and resource allocation has been intensified. The advent of private business practices in the public sector has produced a form of public-sector management termed the 'new managerialism' and imposed greater constraints upon both the workforce and the actual options available to service users. In England and Wales, older people who wish to remain in their own homes and receive social services will have to pay for these, whereas such services are free in Scotland. This is a clear violation of the UK's commitment to Article 23 of the Universal Declaration of Human Rights (UDHR) and divides citizens within a unitary country into eligible and ineligible groups. This position has not been challenged as a denial of human rights under either the European Human Rights Act or the UDHR. But it could be.

## Privatization undermines inclusive notions of citizenship

The Thatcher years in the UK and the Reagan era in the USA marked the aggressive promotion of private-sector intervention in the provision of personal social services, health and education. Engaging private providers undermined inclusive notions of citizenship by replacing entitlement to services with that of people's capacity to pay or behave in accordance with socially accepted norms (Callahan et al., 2002). The policies that governments advanced in these two countries were vigorously pursued abroad under the aegis of what became the World Trade Organization (WTO), which promoted the growth of the private sector in public welfare states. The commodified and residual targeted services that the WTO endorsed replaced publicly funded universal provision locked in the welfare state. In Europe, this move freed the considerable resources located within public welfare to be accessed by private entrepreneurs for the purposes of capital accumulation and profit-making (Dominelli and Hoogvelt, 1996).

Thatcher's and Reagan's strategy involved extensive intrusion into service supply and delivery and the creation of a quasi-market in public services, covering prisons, probation services, personal social services, education and health, according to models of private enterprise with which Americans had long been familiar. One such initiative was the Multilateral Agreement on Investment, successfully defeated by grassroots and other opposition. Another international agreement was the General Agreement on Trades in Services (GATS), which specifically identified social services, health and education as mandatory sites for privatization. Thus, market discipline and corporate management techniques became commonplace in the welfare states of Europe, Australia, New Zealand and Canada, not just the UK and the USA.

Privatization gave rise to the introduction of corporate business practices in the welfare state and commodified citizenship entitlement to services by turning the latter into consumer goods to be purchased in the marketplace. In the public welfare arena, privatization involved lowering wages and diminishing workers' rights in order to reduce costs, curbing the power of trade unions, and curtailing professional autonomy among the workforce. This last included introducing performance management, contract-based interventions, budgets aimed at containing the costs of providing services, and developing business plans to ensure the most effective use of scarce resources. While each of these measures is not objectionable on its own, as a package they became part of what became known as the new public-sector management that led to the bureaucratization of practice. Dominelli (1996b, 2004b) referred to the ensuing professionals it produced as techno-bureaucrats, who spent more time meeting managerial imperatives than working with individuals in need.

Privatization was sold to ordinary members of the public on the grounds that it would enhance the quality of services provided and give individuals greater freedom of choice. This has not occurred for social work clients, the majority of whom are on low incomes. Their inability to play the market by paying market prices meant that they were excluded from exercising choice. This development created the players and non-players inherent in neo-liberal approaches to globalization in the welfare arena. Private provision was retained only as long as profits were maintained. Market fickleness resulted in the withdrawal of services as profits evaporated in a climate of state austerity. This left groups without facilities and intensified vulnerability. For example, cuts in public funding have resulted in one residential home closing every week (PSW, 2008), with negative impacts on older people.

Because managerialist objectives were not focused on enhancing consumer choice by making the market more accessible to those without means, the sector was charged with rationing resources rather than meeting need and with curbing workers' rights to organize. Contradictory tendencies accompanied these changes and, consequently, commodification and consumer choice became mirages that resulted in both practitioners and clients being disillusioned with the modernization of public services led by the marketplace (Dominelli, 2004a). The growth of the quasi-market in the British personal social services also created divisions between managers and front-line workers. A study by Khan and Dominelli (2000) showed that managers felt this development had improved both practice and choice for service users, while the front-line practitioners, regardless of length of employment, considered that the whole enterprise was a scam, with choice technically offered but then taken away because the resources to pay for different options were unavailable (Dominelli, 2004a).

## Problematizing the personalization agenda

Individual budgets and the personalization agenda can be problematic. A recent example involving the disability activist Anna Young exposed the unintended consequences that can follow if service users are given greater control over budgets without being offered sufficient support when things do not work out as planned. Some service users and carers claim that they benefited considerably from privatization (Glendinning et al., 2009). Crucial among these were those providing services for black and minority ethnic groups, who felt that, in contrast to making do with mainstream services, they were now free to develop the services they wanted and needed. The fragmentation of consumers into individual customers had an interesting and worthwhile side effect – that of giving rise to demands for individually based control over the services on offer and influence regarding how these were delivered to individual service users.

British disability activists who wanted to empower themselves initially demanded direct payments, which allowed them some say in what services they received. This has given way to individual budgets, which give them greater control in choosing what services they might spend their money on and which individuals they might employ to assist in their care. As part of the personalization agenda, those receiving individual budgets are obliged to exercise greater responsibility for the choices they make. They are required by law to become employers of their personal care assistants, meaning that they have to pay their wages and deduct income tax, superannuation and national insurance and keep suitable records of their transactions. In this capacity, they become unpaid tax-collectors, held accountable for funds obtained through the public purse. While individual budgets are empowering for service users in terms of giving them the freedom to employ the carers of their choice, having control and flexibility in how their money is spent, there can be complications that have no easy solution. The case of Anna C. Young in box 5.1 is instructive in this regard.

---

*Box 5.1 Case study: Being a responsible employer*

Anna C. Young is a wheelchair user and disability activist who became friends with her personal assistant (PA), whom she began to employ in 2002 when she received direct payments. They worked well together for five years, with the PA undertaking household tasks, scheduling activities and bookkeeping duties as well as correspondence. In 2006, Anna was awarded independent living fund payments, and the PA asked for a pay rise. This was refused, and both the PA and Anna agreed to cut her hours by half in early 2007. During the autumn, the PA stopped working for Anna and in December sent her an email saying she was going to take her to an employment tribunal for constructive dismissal related to the failure to grant a pay rise. The case was heard in July 2009. In August of that year, the tribunal upheld Anna's decision to refuse to increase the PA's remuneration. She now calls her new PA a 'professional assistant', to ensure that the boundaries between friendship and the employer–employee relationship do not become blurred.

Anna's case raises issues about the difficulties that service users may encounter if placed in the position of employer. The support that they can expect in such cases is limited, and it is left largely to the individual to deal with and find their own solutions to the problems that arise.

---

Anna's case indicates that personalization can fail service users by increasing the possibilities of litigation as a result of the blurring of the boundaries between friendship, service provision and employment. Social workers would be able to assist in such circumstances because they are used to supporting people and are familiar with how to handle litigation. They can be challenged by service users and reported to the regulator or sued for poor working practices. The British General Social Care Council has deregistered social workers who have been found guilty of professional misconduct (GSCC, 2009). However, practitioners need time and resources to offer service users such support. This is unlikely to be given in the short term because supporting individual budget holders does not fall into the category of providing basic services.

## Fragility in rights-based services

Private companies acquired old people's homes, children's homes, prisons and immigration detention centres (Finn, 2009a, 2009b) and fragmented service provision. By encouraging private enterprise to provide services, the state has withdrawn from the welfare provider arena, enabled the market to flourish in areas once beyond its domain and established itself at the head of a commissioning regime. Consequently, private providers have cornered a considerable percentage of the welfare market, bringing fragility to the system and making it difficult to turn back the clock in favour of universal public provision, free at the point of need. It also exacerbates the individual vulnerabilities of those who are non-players in the marketplace.

The fragmentation of social work and the political currency of terms such as 'social care' – which many in the international arena would argue is a part of social work in the same way as group work and community work – further complicates the standing of the profession. Internationally, social care as a specialism is consistent with the international definition of social work. The GSCC has accepted this definition without following through on the logic of the relationship between social work and social care. The relationship between them remains problematic (Higham, 2006) in the UK, where many people who access services associate social care with physical care.

In countries such as the USA, practice is driven by clinical approaches to social problems and devalues collective responses to them, especially among powerful opinion-formers espousing neo-conservative values. A recent example was the furore articulated by Republicans against President Barack Obama's modest health-care reforms on the grounds that these constitute 'socialized' medicine and would give bureaucrats the right to determine what kind of health care each person receives (Ward, 2009). While these views parody 'socialism' and social democratic systems of providing health care to national populations, they ignore the enormous amount of money that the present American system spends on bureaucracy rather than services, as well as the exclusion of nearly 50 million people who are not covered under any existing provisions (Ehrenreich, 2002).

Meanwhile, social work in industrializing countries is community work or social development oriented towards dealing with issues such as poverty, economic inequalities and disease (Gray and Mitchell, 2007). These matters demand solutions that do not focus on clinical approaches to practice. Such trends reveal enormous heterogeneity within the profession at both national and international level. Whether or not professional social work in the UK will come of age after 100 years of existence by being formally recognized as a profession will depend both on its ability to deliver the services that are being demanded by an increasingly articulate client base and on its capacity to forge alliances with other professional groupings and develop substantially its research base.

In Britain, modernizing the public sector has a crucial role to play in debates about privatization and citizenship-based services, as do the demands of service users, who no longer wish to see residual services given to them as worthy charitable cases. Both modernization and service-user demands have coalesced around the idea of citizenship as comprising duties and obligations running alongside rights to services. Thus, citizenship and social justice have risen to the fore in discussions about the appropriate kinds of services for those in need. Many of these discourses have been led by the disability movement, which has continued to challenge service providers in two key areas: empowering people to maintain control over the services they access, how these are delivered and by whom; and acquiring a research base that they shape, control and develop (Barnes, 2001). To ensure that these aims are not undermined when they engage with non-disabled people, disabled people ask that those who wish to become allies in their struggles respect their terms and behave in ways consistent with these so that those with disabilities hold the balance of power. The concern to uphold empowering, citizenship-based forms of practice have remained despite the attack that government, the media and members of the public have mounted against those members of the profession who have sought to respond to the pressures of promoting social justice. Although the overt backlash against empowering practice in the UK peaked in the summer of 1993 (see Phillips, 1993), its legacy remains.

Moreover, the focus on citizenship and its redefinition within multiracial societies has returned identity issues and the signifiers of national status back to the limelight. Coupled with increased levels of migration, of both documented (legal) and undocumented (illegal) entrants, these developments have complicated social workers' responses to people within a human rights-based framework, not least because citizens of other countries lose their rights to services once they cross borders. Such movements create ethical dilemmas for practitioners when need is obvious, but legislation authorizes only limited responses as acceptable. This becomes highly problematic in situations where immigration status determines eligibility to the welfare system, e.g., for asylum seekers awaiting deportation, even though their appeals may stretch to years. In 2007, the Asylum and Immigration Tribunal heard 14,935 appeals, of which 72 per cent were dismissed. Those whose applications are rejected are held in detention centres until they are deported. However, the UK had ten detention centres with a total of only 2,500 places, and so the necessary facilities were not available and most people remained in the community. Detention centres – or immigration removal centres, as the Home Office prefers to call them – are run mainly by the private sector. In the UK, those refused asylum cannot access the benefits system, even though they have no job and little income with which to support themselves (Cohen et al., 2004; Vickers, 2009). Those who are given benefits receive £33.39 if aged eighteen to twenty-four or £42.16 if over twenty-five years of age. This is far less even than British citizens receive on benefits. Recourse to charity and family and friends is often unable wholly to provide the help required. Halima Bashir's story, recounted in *Tears in the Desert*, makes the nightmarish plight of asylum seekers wanting refuge in the UK abundantly clear. Their harsh treatment is reflected in other parts of Europe and in Australia, as both these countries follow policies of restricting entry (Briskman, 2007).

Despite government-initiated structural changes in the profession in the UK – ranging from a diminution in the resources to the imposition of greater bureaucratic controls – social workers' commitment to social justice, human rights and citizenship has risen since 1997, when New Labour acquired power. The New Labour government, the enactment of the Human Rights Act 1998, various elements of the European Social Charter, and the country's adherence to international protocols and conventions – e.g., the UN Convention on the Rights of the Child – have deepened the profession's moves in this direction (Beckett, 2001; Buchanan, 2007). International regulations are difficult to enforce unless they are incorporated into national legislation because specific conventions apply only in those countries that ratify them. For example, the USA is alone among industrialized countries in not having ratified the Convention on the Rights of the Child; Somalia is the only other nation to share this position. In contrast, the Convention on the Rights of Persons with Disabilities, agreed in 2006, had been ratified by only twenty countries by 2008.

Current responses to the crises in the banking system indicate that privatization will increase and expenditure for publicly funded services decrease. The strategy of cutting public expenditure will extend the range and spread of private and charitable services. Private providers worry that they will lose out (Timmins, 2010) and figures for those excluded from the market will rise. Reliance on private and charitable providers has proved incapable of meeting needs when a high proportion of the population requires help, as was demonstrated historically during the Great Depression and led to calls for the creation of a welfare state. Even the USA, the country that prided itself as the leader in market-based welfare systems, had to bring in the New Deal to provide for the high numbers of unemployed, homeless and poor people during the recession of the 1930s (Lampton, 1977).

Today's fiscal crisis has diminished contributions and donations made by companies and individuals to the voluntary sector (Fillion, 2008; Freitag, 2009). For example, in Canada and the USA, the United Way, which collects funds for redistribution among charitable agencies, has reported a substantial decline in both corporate and personal giving. Doctors Without Borders faced a huge drop in donations when Lehman

Brothers, one of its major donors, went bankrupt. Oxfam claimed that it faced a 12 per cent fall in donations in 2009 (*Metro*, 2009). These statistics indicate the fragility of charitable approaches to service provision. As long as their needs are not met, people's suffering will continue, the development of their talents will remain thwarted and the struggle simply to survive will dominate their lives.

Social workers can raise issues about the failure of charitable giving to meet demand for support. They can also advocate for the implementation of citizenship-based welfare services and mobilize people to call for change. By incorporating this work into their normal routines, their actions would be consistent with the theories, values and practices of a social justice model of intervention. However, those rooted in bureaucratic responses to practice are unlikely to entertain such possibilities. They would be more likely to deem such interventions as being someone else's responsibility at best and irrelevant to their practice at worst. Many would not advocate for these changes even though they might appreciate the necessity of shifting to a citizenship-based professional mandate.

## Citizenship-based welfare provision

The profession of social work had humble beginnings – in the interstices of family or kin-based care and philanthropic good works conducted by individuals and charitable institutions. State involvement in the UK began with the Elizabethan Poor Law of 1601. It emphasized family responsibility in caring for its members and held the parish in which an individual was born liable for service provision for destitute people. Its punitive approach to services and the link to domicile were retained in the Victorian era, when workhouses were a feature of provisions under the Poor Law Amendment Act of 1834. The legislation on poor relief laid the foundations for viewing social work as a moral and moralizing activity, whereby only the 'deserving' or worthy applicant could expect to receive services. As the services provided were stigmatized and punitive, people sought to avoid rather than take advantage of them. This approach strengthened the view that people should 'care for their own' and take personal responsibility for meeting their own needs. Under neo-liberalism, this insight has been enshrined in the notion of a responsible citizenship linked to the nation–state. Thus, there is remarkable continuity between earlier versions of the Poor Law and the residual services on offer in much of the personal social services today, regardless of who provides them and how they are provided.

Citizenship-based entitlement to services is antithetical to the moralizing ideological perspective that was on the agenda for much of the profession's history (Van Ewijk, 2009). Even the terminology – deviants, the workshy, the lumpen proletariat and, recently, the underclass – used to refer to those in need of assistance was stigmatizing. Avoiding such stigmatization has been a major goal proposed by those who have raised the issues of the significance of power relations and language in shaping services and attitudes towards those seeking to access them. Such endeavours sought to make entitlement to universal, unstigmatized services a right of citizenship (Ife, 2001a). This state of affairs has yet to be achieved anywhere, although the Nordic countries have come the nearest to it (Mishra, 2005).

## Rooting citizenship within the nation–state is exclusionary

Under the social democratic type of regime, high-quality, responsive services would be the norm for all, not just those who can afford to pay for them. However, even in its Nordic variant, citizenship is rooted in nationality. For example EU nationals can be covered anywhere in the Union if they can demonstrate that they are citizens of one of the member states. Other nationals are excluded from services. Hence, a homeless person from Croatia living on the streets of Copenhagen would not be entitled to the assistance a Danish national would receive. This can create moral dilemmas for practitioners who assist homeless people. Those working for Udenfor (www.udenfor.dk), a project targeting homeless people on the streets of Copenhagen, for instance, are very aware of such restraints and work hard to make sure that their street café provides food for anyone in need.

In the UK, struggles for the realization of rights for poor people, whether political rights or social and welfare rights, were lengthy and difficult. Working-class men did not get the vote without lengthy initiatives, including those articulated by the Chartists in 1832. And it was not until 1918, as a result of pressure placed on the system through the suffragette movement, that women were entitled to vote. T. H. Marshall (1970) was a key academic who identified the rights of citizenship as threefold and consisting of political rights, civil rights and social rights, including rights to welfare.

Citizenship based on the nation–state was formulated on the myth of a fixed unitary and homogeneous identity that applied equally to all residents within a particular geographic entity. It was assumed that treating everyone the same would enforce equality. However, it also assumed a situation of full employment. Typically, the white middle-class man enjoyed the fruits of a citizenship formulated on that basis (Dominelli, 1991; Lister, 1997). The politicians that articulated this arrangement ignored the diversity in gender, age, ability, ethnicity and race that existed within the nation–state. Women and children were adversely affected by being positioned as dependent upon men for access to welfare rights. In the UK, until the Social Security Act of 1986 the cohabitation rule prevented women from claiming welfare benefits in their own right if they were married or living with a man. In the USA there was the 'man about the house' rule (Sidel, 1986), which operated in a similar fashion, for those accessing Aid to Families with Dependent Children, which barred women from claiming welfare assistance directly as long as there was an adult male in the household (Dominelli, 1991).

The rights of citizenship were simultaneously deemed crucial to reducing, if not eliminating, marginalization, powerlessness, disenfranchisement and poverty. The social dimension of citizenship was linked, in theory at least, to the economic right to work, although a guaranteed right to employment has not yet been accepted by the British state. The commitment to full employment was accepted not as an individual right, but as one linked to the state of the society's economy, which aimed to keep unemployment to below 4 per cent (Keynes, 1989) – the level anticipated to enable everyone who wanted a job to succeed in finding one. The tie between waged work and welfare entitlement was used initially to enforce women's dependency on men and deny them claimant status in their own right. Assumptions about women engaging in unproductive labour, and their dependence on men for their economic well-being, underpinned the state's willingness to fund public welfare (Beveridge, 1942) and was reflected in the cohabitation restrictions. Also, this structuring of entitlements to benefits ignored the enormous contribution made to the economy by women's unpaid work in the home (Dominelli, 1991). Canada has considered its economic implications since 1971 and valued it at 41 per cent of GDP (Luxton, 1997). The UN and the World Bank later conducted studies that indicated that women's unpaid labour forms a substantial, if unrecognized, part of the economy in many other countries (Hollingsworth and Tyyska, 1988; Chen, 2001).

Marshall predicated a citizen's acquisition of rights as progressive – i.e., the individual accruing more and more rights over time. However, rights were conceptualized in a decontextualized way that paid little attention to power relations or the exclusion of certain categories of people (Dominelli, 1991; Lister, 1997). This formulation ignored the significance of collective rights for citizens who were discriminated against as a group, not just on an individual level. It also downplayed the impact of identity on claims to services and turned citizenship into an issue of personal entitlement to benefits regardless of type. Citizenship based on the nation–state affirms identity and a sense of belonging as being accepted and having a place within a particular polity. Lacking entitlement to rights, they can be excluded from provisions as those who do not belong and have not contributed to the funding of specific services. To be refused assistance when in need, especially if deemed as such through professional assessment, undermines a person's dignity as well as their entitlement to be helped under such international provisions as the 1951 Geneva Convention, the UDHR and, in the UK, the Human Rights Act 1998.

Formulating citizenship on national identities is problematic because it can exclude people on the basis of who they are and not what they do or where they live. This construction presents major challenges for social workers in multicultural societies where non-nationals are excluded from welfare entitlements and citizenship through their immigration status. The precarious situation of non-nationals counters the claims of beneficence made by those who rule liberal democracies and undermines those who believe that their legislation is based on notions of human rights and social justice. This is exemplified in the current exclusion in the UK of asylum seekers from a wide range of welfare and health benefits, or even work, which can place social workers in a moral and ethical dilemma: they may see the need for a service but be unable to deliver it without violating the law. Such quandaries are further complicated by knowing that local people's needs may also be unmet, e.g., where resources are insufficient to respond to those requiring services at other levels.

The predicament of Diane in box 5.2 exposes the difficulties of working in a very stressful area of practice with limited resources. Her

---

## Box 5.2 Case study: Seeking asylum is complicated

Florence was an asylum seeker fleeing the horrors of Darfur, where she had been raped and forced to watch while several members of her family were murdered. The others had escaped, but she did not know where they were, or whether they were alive. She had no money and no friends in the UK and did not know what to do once she had completed her asylum application; she was merely waiting for the reply that would determine if she could stay and begin to rebuild her life. Diane, the social worker who took Florence's life history, felt distressed by what she heard and felt extremely sorry for her. However, the amount of support she could offer was limited by legislation and also by the growing numbers of people she had to deal with. She felt overwhelmed by the task facing her and decided that the best thing she could do under the circumstances was to refer Florence to a voluntary agency that specialized in finding additional sources of help. Diane was acutely aware of the political discussions around asylum seekers, who were configured as 'abusing' the British welfare system. How far off the mark they were! She felt disempowered and wondered if the job she was doing was right for her, but there was no one with whom she could talk about her conflicting emotions and duties. Diane felt she should be able to help everyone, as that had been what motivated her to become a social worker.

concerns highlight the political nature of the work that is being under-taken, even though it has been redefined as a professional dilemma.

In this context, scarcity of resources rather than need has determined what is possible in practice. It would be helpful if governments were to examine their responsibilities in meeting the needs of those who live in their countries and develop policies that respond to the wide range of service users with legitimate claims on social welfare provision. From a social work perspective rooted in human rights and social justice, all those requiring assistance should have their needs met. Doing so requires a shift in discourses about a country's obligations to those who enter its territory, a recognition of the interdependent nature of our world, new directions for social policy and practice, and desisting from creating claimant groups through interventions such as the war in Iraq, which produced huge numbers of refugees, especially in the neighbouring countries of Syria and Jordan. Such scenarios indicate that changing political discourses and priorities are matters to be tackled at the national, regional and international level. Additionally, politicians need to priori-tize an inclusive ethics of care and work with governments bilaterally and multilaterally to divert funds to promoting human well-being. Social work educators, researchers and practitioners can inform these debates and lobby for resources.

Diane herself needed psycho-emotional support to deal with the many emotions raised for her by Florence's case. This, too, was unavailable. Employers should address the issue of supporting workers through the stresses of the job by providing high-quality supervision from managers, peer-support structures and psychological support. Social workers' case-loads should be varied so that no one has to operate as an isolated individual, doing the same type of work until they become unable to deal with the pressures and end up on sick leave or moving out of the profes-sion altogether.

Social workers in the UK are not unique in being placed in such pre-dicaments. Similar restrictions on asylum seekers can be found in other Western countries and can include exclusion from voting rights, even for those born in a particular locale. For example, Germany had for decades refused to consider people of Turkish and Italian origins as eligible for citizenship, even if they had been born in the country (Ehrkamp, 2005). The exclusion of Italians occurred despite both Germany and Italy being members of the EU, because German citizenship required German ances-try or proof of *jus sanguinis* – a blood link. A limited change was intro-duced after the 1999 elections and was enacted on 1 January 2000. At that time, one in ten people living in Germany was of overseas origin and 60 per cent had been living in the country for more than ten years; many were born in Germany (BBC, 1999). Since the 1981 Immigration and Nationality Act, people born in the UK are not permitted to acquire citizenship by virtue of their place of birth. They have to live in the country continuously for ten years and then apply for this status. The 1981 Act ended a 700-year tradition of *sui solis*, whereby anyone born on British soil could claim British nationality; Britain now requires at least one parent to be a British citizen for a child born in the UK to acquire British citizenship automatically (Layton-Henry, 1984).

Nationalistic and dependency approaches to citizenship make it exclusionary and conditional (Dominelli, 1991, 1997). Moreover, the national basis to citizenship contradicts the assumptions made in the UDHR, which root human rights in the individual and place the responsibility of securing the resources required to meet these on the nation–state. However, the UN does not hold enforcement powers to ensure that these obligations are met. As a result, many nation–states claim that they lack the necessary resources and their citizens do not enjoy the human rights to which they are entitled. This failure is especially relevant for those living in low-income countries. The lack of access to care is evident in financially constrained countries experiencing regular catastrophes such as drought or flooding (UNDP, 2009). For example, Ethiopia has suffered drought-induced mass famines since the mid-1980s and been forced to draw upon humanitarian assistance, including that brought together through Band Aid. A similar situation prevails in parts of the country today, as one in ten of its population is at risk of dying of hunger (Meo, 2009). A combination of bad weather conditions, deforestation and degradation of the soil, together with the lack of long-term investment in local development, has contributed to this outcome. Servicing debts financed by Westerners has exacerbated these woes. A similar story could be told in other poor industrializing countries, such as Bangladesh and Mozambique. The campaigns by Jubilee 2000 and the End Poverty Campaign had secured the agreement of rich Western nations at the G8 meeting in Gleneagles in 2005 to cease demanding payments for such debts, double aid funding to Africa and contribute to the long-term development of low-income countries. These pledges have not materialized, although 34 million more children have attended schools in Africa (Hopkins, 2009).

Western liberal democracies have focused on John Rawls's (1973) notion of social justice and human rights. Rawls advocates individually held rights, and thus his ideas deal inadequately with issues of diversity and oppression based on identity traits that have collective dimensions as well as individual ones – e.g., structural inequalities based on gender and ethnicity (Moosa-Mitha, 2002). While Rawls endorses the rights of the autonomous independent citizen who acts without regard to context and power relations, his theories are unable to deal with the interdependence that is integral to a globalizing world. Nor can his views cater for the importance of bonds of reciprocity and solidarity, which again thrive on the connections produced when interdependent individuals interact to promote equality. The concerns of Sen (1999) and Nussbaum (1999, 2000) to enhance capabilities contributes more effectively to initiatives aimed at developing local capacities and understanding connections between the various aspects of a person's life.

### Redefining global citizenship to guarantee human rights for all

Finding ways of ensuring that every person in the world can realize their welfare rights is crucial if individuals are to grow to their full potential. Social workers can both advocate for and work towards its realization. The values of equality, social justice, human rights, reciprocity, solidarity and interdependence can help them achieve this goal by providing a framework within which to act. They can also lobby for nation–states to enter bilateral or multilateral agreements that enable citizenship rights to cross borders with individuals. This has occurred in the EU, where the citizens of one member state are entitled to rights in all other member states. The portability of human rights is an issue that the UN should address as a matter of urgency, given the rising numbers of people who migrate to different parts of the world without necessarily acquiring citizenship in any other country.

Migratory movements raise an important question about citizenship rights. If all of the world's citizens who are technically entitled to human rights can access these in their country of origin, why should these rights be automatically lost when they enter the territory of another nation? If all nation–states could agree on human rights being both inalienable and portable, these could be carried by individuals wherever they go. People needing social services, welfare benefits, health care or education services should be able to access these wherever they are. The issue of who pays for these services could be settled through reciprocal agreements. If an individual has already paid for or otherwise contributed to their entitlements in their country of origin, why should the original state retain the advantage of having received payment for that individual's coverage but not have to honour the supply of services if they go elsewhere? British pensioners have often travelled abroad to countries like Spain, where the costs of living are lower and it is easier to stretch their British pensions to cover basic necessities. This option also alleviates demand for health and social services in the sending countries.

Over time, arrangements that arise on an ad hoc basis can create anomalies, as has occurred for British retirees on the Costa Brava. The financial crisis has reduced the value of the pensions they receive from the UK, as the value of the pound has slumped against the euro. Moreover, as the population ages and makes demands on health care, and health costs rise, the Spaniards are beginning to question the extent of their responsibility in providing services to British pensioners. They are now asserting that this group is making inordinate demands on the Spanish system. This issue is currently under discussion between the two countries, with the Spaniards seeking to curtail the costs to their Exchequer. This stance does not seem unreasonable when these pensioners have not contributed to the Spanish health care system that is providing the services (Harten, 2009). The British Canadian Alliance of Pensioners highlights another anomaly – the position of British pensioners in Canada. They receive their British pensions, but the rates are frozen so that they do not benefit from the increases that are granted to those who remain in the UK, despite holding similar contribution records. This is now subject to bilateral discussion, as the British pensioners in Canada are demanding the entitlements for which they have already paid. Despite these difficulties, such arrangements enable people's welfare rights to be transferred between countries. The existence of multilateral agreements in the EU indicates that such coverage could be extended on an international level to include all countries and all people. But this would require political will, having the appropriate legal frameworks in place, and vesting citizenship rights in the individual as inalienable and portable.

Underpinning this suggestion is the view that each person has rights by virtue of being a citizen of their country of origin. It would also require nation–states to become committed to ensuring that their individual citizens do not lose these rights simply because they enter the territory of another nation–state. Individuals would be obliged to contribute to a social insurance or other contributory scheme in their home country to establish the case that the denial of their rights elsewhere constitutes a breach of contract between the individual and their nation–state of origin. Such recognition would mean that the state of origin would have to agree to pick up the tab for the individual's enjoyment of their welfare rights elsewhere.

If citizenship rights are defined as inalienable and portable, and all countries agree to honour this, the concern to secure coverage for all could be incorporated within the notion of global citizenship. Such action would extend the role of the nation–state in providing for their citizens in a mobile and globalizing world and could enhance its prestige. But there is another issue to be considered in this proposal: ensuring that all people have local coverage to begin with, as proposed by the UDHR. Many low-income countries claim that they lack the resources to provide for people in their own territories, let alone when they travel or move abroad. Thus, it would be incumbent on rich countries to ensure that all states are brought up to the minimum levels of provision already stipulated in the UDHR. This would require them to commit money, people and other resources to establish such a system. This strategy could contribute to the realization of human rights, including social rights, as essential components of the social and human development processes. Their implementation also requires training and the employment of people able to provide these services.

### Environmental rights as citizenship rights

Traditional notions of citizenship ignore another issue that I would argue is becoming increasingly important in this interdependent world, and that is the matter of environmental rights – the right to clean air, safe drinking water, and unpolluted soils and oceans, and the rights to all the earth's resources for future generations. From this perspective, the right to a sustainable physical and social environment is a requirement and a duty in both the present and the future and needs to be fully integrated into concepts of a citizenship-based welfare system. Ungar (2002) has already highlighted the importance of environmental rights to well-being, as have ecofeminists such as Vandana Shiva (2003) and Arhundathi Roy (1999). Shiva also contends that environmental rights include rights to biodiversity, and she critiques multinational corporations for the commercial exploitation of such biological materials as seeds and plants, and farmers' ideas, which she terms biopiracy. Social workers have a role to play in changing policies to ensure that social and environmental rights are upheld. Challenging restrictive definitions of citizenship that disallow claims for help is one way of enabling such change to occur.

### Migration and transnationalism challenge unitary discourses of citizenship

The idea of citizenship being based on the nation–state is being challenged by transnationalism, dual and multiple citizenship status and global citizenship, though none of these notions has prevailed. Migrants are also demanding the safety and affirmation that individuals need to retain psychological and social well-being wherever they go. And they wish to acquire the sense of acceptance and belonging that is associated with citizenship. But the linkage between citizenship and the nation–state means that migrants can currently acquire citizenship and its accompanying benefits only by living in a country for a specified period of time and conforming to certain procedures and rituals, though 'difference' can remain problematic. The language used to endorse such citizenship status is also important. Those wishing to acquire citizenship are considered as 'other' – as 'strangers' or 'aliens'. This endorses stereotypes of 'not belonging' and of being 'unnatural' and colludes with the views of those who dislike immigrants. It is more appropriate to talk about citizenship by acquisition than by naturalization to avoid some of the exclusionary aspects embedded within citizenship discourses (Dominelli, 2009).

Citizenship based on the notion of the unitary nation–state is also being challenged by transnationalism. Transnational individuals have links and associations with several countries simultaneously. These are often based on kinship affiliations and ancestry and claims of support between family members in communities of origin. Expressed as bonding social capital or networks of solidarity, these emphasize the interdependent nature of social relations in a globalizing world, even if they draw primarily on kinship affiliations. These links can be expressed through remittances sent home by migrant workers, whether Jamaicans in the UK, Canada and the USA (Small, 2007), Ethiopians in France and the USA (Abye, 2007), Sri Lankans in the UK or Poles in Western Europe. Their remittances usually form a significant proportion of the foreign exchange earnings of their home country and can play a significant role in the local economy. In some countries, remittances form the largest sector of the economy. This is not always beneficial. Small (2007), for example, argues that such money is used to enhance local consumption rather than build the national economy and local infrastructures. Abye (2007), on the other hand, suggests that, in Ethiopia, expatriates have been crucial in setting up social enterprises and small companies that employ others. Whatever the case, these transnational ties affirm interdependence between and among people, including those from outside the kinship network. Such activities help to promote self-reliance and innovation within a group, alongside the changes presaged for its constituent members.

Additionally, transnational migrants take new ideas and strategies for development into their countries of origin. Abye (2009) argues that these usually become a blend of modern and traditional ideas that demonstrate the resilience of people to change their traditional cultures in transformative ways to create new and different ones. In Ethiopia, returning settlers have created social enterprises, brought in additional forms of capital to establish new initiatives across all sectors of the economy, reinvigorated local customs and traditions, and demanded democratic accountability in governance structures. These initiatives can both accompany or challenge the endeavours of overseas-based NGOs that have assisted in social development processes, often with mixed results. In other countries, e.g., Croatia, research on the role of international NGOs in the social welfare arena has concluded that their interventions have been more negative than anticipated, and has highlighted their failure to appreciate local traditions in welfare support or acknowledge other ways of responding to needs (Stubbs, 2007).

### Asylum seekers as excluded people

Migration discourses present a challenge in both sending and receiving countries to notions of citizenship based on the idea of a homogeneous nation–state. Today, migration discourses in the West coalesce around issues faced by asylum seekers and refugees, especially as many are without the requisite documentation and do not adhere to the correct immigration procedures. According to the UN, there are 42 million people seeking refugee status in the world (Sanders, 2009). Most do not actually end up in Europe or North America but tend to seek protection in neighbouring countries – largely the African states. This is not how Western discourses present the issue. John Major's assertion that six Bosnian families were too many for Britain to absorb as refugees meant that only 1,300 were allowed entry (Bridge, 1992). His stance illustrates the reluctance of Western nations to take in those fleeing persecution if they are 'different' from the majority population, regardless of the numbers involved. Even countries such as Canada that pride themselves on having liberal policies towards migrants react in a similar way. I highlight this problem in box 5.3 by examining discourses articulated in Canadian newspapers during October 2009, when seventy-six men believed to be Tamils escaping persecution from government forces in Sri Lanka were caught entering Canada without the appropriate documentation. Although the specifics of the situation are clearly Canadian, the complex issues posed by the affair resonate in other countries where people smugglers operate. At the same time, trafficking in human beings is a lucrative illegal business (Barne, 1999).

---

### Box 5.3 Case study: Tamil refugees in Canada

A ship named the *Ocean Lady* was apprehended off the coast of Vancouver Island by the Canada Border Services Agency on 16 October 2009 with seventy-six men of suspected Sri Lankan Tamil origins on board. The boat was linked to skipper Abraham Lauhenapessy, also known as Captain Bram, a trafficker of human beings who had been convicted in Indonesia for attempting to smuggle 254 Sri Lankan asylum seekers into Australia's Christmas Island a week earlier. Captain Bram is reputed to have smuggled 1,500 people into Australia since 1999. He charges people $15,000 per person to go to Australia and $45,000 to go to Canada.

Each asylum seeker has to pay these 'transportation' costs, often through bonded labour once they reach their destination. Otherwise, family members in their homeland are subjected to violence until the debt is paid in full. Such exorbitant sums for a voyage in unseaworthy boats to what is often a hostile public reception do not prevent human smuggling being a lucrative business. For example, Lin, an unaccompanied minor in a group of asylum seekers from Fujan province who reached Canada in 1999, was charged $US30,000 for the journey in a decrepit ship. He was incarcerated in a detention centre, but was one of the 133 out of 577 people whose claims for asylum were accepted. He spent six years paying back this 'loan', which with interest amounted to $80,000 (Shore, 2009). Meanwhile, the journeys are treacherous and the risks of dying en route are high (Hume, 2009a, 2009b).

According to Manthorpe (2009), there are 'four human-trafficking gang bosses' who have organized their activities from Indonesia – Captain Bram, Ali Reza and Ali Sadat (both from Pakistan), and Majid Mahmood (from Iran). Most of the people on their boats come from Iraq, Pakistan, Afghanistan and Sri Lanka, all countries suffering from violent conflict. At the end of the summer of 2009, thirty-four boatloads of asylum seekers led to 1,700 people being detained in Australia awaiting the outcome of their applications. The people transported by these gangmasters are not informed of the hostility with which they may be received. They often do not know where they are headed, and gangmasters attempt to disguise their operations by, for example, changing the names of the boats used. The *Ocean Lady*, currently registered in the Seychelles with a mailing address in the Philippines, was previously the Cambodian flagged *Princess Easwary* and before that it was the Japanese *Daiei Maru No 18* (Bell, 2009).

The discourses about the Tamil refugees in the Canadian newspapers ranged from demands that they be deported, because the Tamil Tigers was banned as a terrorist organization in Canada (although this was not the case in a number of other Western countries), to that of letting the law decide who was entitled to stay (Hume, 2009b). One of the seventy-six detainees, Kartheepan Manickavasagarm, was wanted in Sri Lanka on terrorism charges (Bell, 2009). That one refugee was being sought by Interpol fanned the flames of hostility towards the others seeking help, as they were all presumed to be terrorists. None of the allegations has been tested in a court of law, and the Canadian Tamil Congress has suggested that the Sri Lankan government has been known to accuse ethnic Tamils of terrorist activities without foundation. At the same time, American immigration authorities are concerned that refugees to Canada will ultimately flee to the USA, where they can readily blend into already existing communities. Even Lin, who is happily settled in Canada and now applying to bring his parents into the country, claims that he contemplated crossing the border (Shore, 2009).

This account indicates the complex webs that human traffickers weave as they ply their illegal trade. Although refugees count on the 1951 Geneva Convention, which gives those in fear of persecution and violence the right to seek asylum in signatory countries, public discourses in the West tend to ascribe the epithets 'economic migrants', 'welfare abusers', 'criminals' and 'terrorists' to them instead. Like any social issue today, there are diverse views about such situations. Writers such as Stephen Hume (2009a, 2009b), a Canadian citizen of British origins, argues that there is a process of 'compassion and fair treatment' to be followed for those seeking asylum in Canada, and that this should be allowed to run its course. Others deride asylum seekers and wish to impose arbitrary restraints on them. Hume (2009a) points out the varied reasons of different waves of would-be immigrants for seeking political refuge in Canada – people as diverse as the Russians, Finns, Poles, Hungarians, Nigerians, Chinese, Afghans, Pakistanis, Armenians, Indians, Guatemalans, South Africans, Ugandans, Chileans, Mexicans, Vietnamese and Rwandans, as well as people of Sikh origin, the Sioux, the Shawnee, and Americans. Many in the last three groups sought to avoid the destructive effects of the administration of George W. Bush on their societies (Joyner, 2007).

Deportation is not necessarily an easy option. Legal proceedings to enforce the removal of those seeking asylum may be lengthy and tortuous. Australia, for instance, continues to detain those claiming asylum offshore, usually on Christmas Island, while applications are considered (Briskman, 2003). The poor publicity given to such practices caused Prime Minister Kevin Rudd to reduce the time taken to process applications and also to hold talks with Indonesian authorities to see if they would house those wanting refugee status in Australia but travelling through Indonesian waters to reach it (Hume, 2009a). Australian social work practitioners and educators opposed their treatment under legislation initially enacted in 1992 by the then Prime Minister, John Howard, and subsequently made more stringent (Briskman, 2003; ACHSSW, 2006). Their research exposed the inappropriateness of mandatory detention and high levels of mental ill health and post traumatic stress disorder among detainees. This echoed findings made by mental health experts (Barnes, 2009). Some detainees had been incarcerated for years while they waited for their applications to be processed. As around 90 per cent of claims are judged to be genuine, mandatory detention seems particularly cruel and unnecessary.

Canada and Britain also detain people in custodial settings. Private corporations such as Group 4, involved in the security business, are increasingly being used to run such facilities. As a result, governments can deny responsibility for the appalling treatment that can be meted out to inmates, as has occurred in Australia (Briskman and Cemlyn, 2005; Briskman, 2007). In the UK, claimants in detention centres in Campsfield near Oxford (Athwal, 2003) and Yarl's Wood, Bedfordshire (Refugee Council, 2010), found conditions so intolerable that they set fire to the facilites in protest. Yarl's Wood, run by a private security firm, was accused by detainees of having little regard for their human rights and dignity. This allegation was denied by those operating the facility. Canada's campaign group, No One Is Illegal, seeks to ensure that due process is followed for those held under Canadian jurisdiction.

Many asylum seekers who are returned face both legal and illegal punishments, especially if by trying to escape they portray their homeland in a negative light. For example, those returned to Fujan province by the Canadian authorities for attempting to escape China in 2003 were sent to administrative detention in a labour camp and ordered to pay a fine for not having obtained a permit to leave the country. Women who violated the one-child policy were compulsorily sterilized or had their foetuses forcibly aborted (Shore, 2009). A woman whose father had been killed for participating in drug wars in 2002 was deported to Mexico by the Canadian government and murdered by drug gangs there (Greenaway, 2009). Zimbabweans in the UK have made similar claims when their countrymen have been deported and subjected to violence and torture back in their homeland. To assist people in these situations and enable asylum seekers and refugees to secure their rights, social workers and community workers should be able to use the provisions of the 1951 Geneva Convention. In the UK, social workers' roles in this field have been reduced to acting as gatekeepers who minimize claims on national resources (Cohen et al., 2004).

Migration discourses generally highlight difference as a threat, dangerous, risky and to be feared. The assumed 'natural' response is defence, protection and a refusal to engage with it. Such views underpin racist attitudes, which are particularly virulent in white supremacist discourses. Allegations of racist behaviour are strongly resisted by those such as the British National Party (BNP), which declares that 'indigenous' white British people have become strangers in their own country. Its arguments are being heard with increased legitimacy in white working-class areas, where young men in particular feel excluded and disenfranchised. Unemployment and the loss of blue-collar jobs are crucial to this problem. Unemployment in March 2010 stood at 7.8 per cent, a long way off the full employment that New Labour sought to achieve (HRM, 2010). White people's disillusionment resulted in two members of the BNP, one of whom is its leader, Nick Griffin, becoming MEPs in the 2009 elections for the European Parliament. Griffin was also given air time on the BBC's prestigious *Question Time* programme.

Mainstream parties should examine the messages that those voting for the BNP have given out. They are those of a loss of citizenship, of feeling that they have been left out of society, especially from the labour and housing markets. In short, it is about the degradation of 'the social'. Despite rulers' promises of full employment, those in predominantly working-class estates, both black and white, suffer high levels of unemployment as its people bear the brunt of earlier industrial restructuring exercises and the recession. Despite their right to be allocated decent housing, they find themselves located on run-down 'sink estates' and without the prospect of getting a better offer. Despite the hope of better education, they are taught in schools that have an inadequate curriculum, lack equipment and books, and have insufficiently qualified teachers. The BNP's solution to all these problems is to repatriate all foreigners and immigrants to their countries of origin because, it asserts, they have unfairly collared the bulk of the country's housing, education, health, social services and jobs. Yet these claims have been refuted by countless research reports and speeches, including those emanating from the Equality and Human Rights Commission (Phillips, 2008).

But who are the allegedly 'indigenous' British in a country that has experienced over 2,000 years of migration in the form of conquering colonizers, from the Romans to the French under William the Conqueror, as well as other ethnic interactions (BBC, 2010)? There has also been internal migration, whereby the Scottish, English, Irish or Welsh interact and form relationships with those in other parts of the UK. The BNP's message to current immigrants is not vastly different from those given out by mainstream parties, which constantly enact legislation that assumes the majority of those seeking entry to the UK are either illegal or undocumented migrants. Immigrants and migrants make an enormous contribution to the British economy, and some industrial sectors would collapse without their input (Phillips, 2008). The Americans found that entire sectors of their economy had to be shut down on Immigration Day on 1 May 2006 when undocumented migrants sought to prove this point (MSNBC, 2006). There would have been even more sectors involved had documented immigrants joined them.

Citizenship should not be tied to immigration status, but the British government has made such links since the 1971 Immigration Act. The linkage between citizenship and nationality was formally recognized in the Immigration and Nationality Act 1981 and determined one's immigration status. This Act disallowed automatic citizenship to those born in the UK and placed Britain on par with less progressive nation–states in continental Europe, such as Germany, which had traditionally refused to accept birth on its territory as entitlement to citizenship. The blood basis to claiming citizenship has been affirmed in discourses about indigeneity that exclude immigrants, regardless of their period of residence in the UK, from being considered 'real' members of the national polity and are being fiercely promoted by the BNP. The latter's claims about being the 'indigenous' people of a particular geographic space exposes the contested nature of the term. However, that contestation reveals how readily the word can be appropriated by white supremacists to distort and undermine historical realities whereby populations and cultures are created and re-created through interactions with those different from them. The BNP's claims are firmly rooted in the idea of having a fixed, homogeneous identity and having blood ties to a particular territory or geographic space that have existed for generations. Ironically, this basis for affirming identity is analogous to that used by aboriginal peoples to reclaim their rights and status in Canada, the USA and elsewhere (see Grande, 2004). These stances also reveal that ideologies can both include and exclude others.

## Citizenship, human rights and social work

Practitioners can utilize such international instruments as the UDHR to enhance citizenship rights. Knowledge of human rights legislation and conventions is an important part of social workers' repertoire of skills (Ife, 2001a, 2001b). The UDHR, initially promulgated in 1948, has been ratified by all members of the UN despite criticisms of its individualistic and Western conceptualization. The IASSW participated in discussions about its content from very early on. Social workers' insights were thus included in its measures. It is crucial that social workers use the articles contained in human rights legislation to advocate for people and deliver services. Articles 22 to 27, for example, are about the provision of important services, ranging from food and shelter to education, health and social services. These focus on economic, social and cultural rights, including social security, an adequate standard of living, health, education, fair remuneration for work, and maintaining one's culture and family life. Susan George exhorts social workers to use Article 23 in poverty eradication strategies:

> Everyone has the right to a standard of living adequate for ... health and wellbeing ... including food, clothing, housing and medical care and necessary social services and the right to security in the event of unemployment, sickness, disability, widowhood, old age or other lack of livelihood. (George, 2003: 17)

Ungar (2002) argues that human rights are now inseparable from environmental rights and focuses on the provisions of Article 23 as particularly helpful to social workers in upholding both environmental and welfare rights.

## Conclusions

The commitment of social work to services based on a combination of citizenship, human rights and social justice is fairly recent, although elements of this have been around for the past fifty years. This terrain is disputed, and much remains to be done if practices rooted in these values are to be developed further and extended to acknowledge both the interdependency of people in a globalizing world and the importance of including environmental rights to protect the interests of present and future generations.

Globalization requires a rethink of the notion of citizenship. As people become increasingly mobile, the loss of citizenship rights simply because an individual has moved to another country becomes increasingly untenable. Such movements raise the question of why, since they are individually based, these rights are not inalienable and portable. Additionally, globalization promotes the professional worker as a migrant when seeking new job opportunities and through exchanges aiming to expose people to different ideas about their practice. These are all forces that undermine monolithic views about professional work, citizenship, and one-sided international interactions where one party gives and the other takes. People are increasingly engaging others on the basis of demanding reciprocity and mutuality in such interaction.

# 6

# Human, Social and Environmental Degradation

## Introduction

Human, social and environmental degradation, preventing people from leading a decent quality of life, are interlinked conditions. The welfare state and social policies aimed at protecting people from a range of vulnerabilities, ranging from personal illnesses to structural unemployment, have failed to achieve equitable and sustainable forms of social development. Some argue that the policies and structures for doing so are inadequate. Others suggest that the entire system of capitalist globalization is incapable of responding to human needs in an inclusive, non-exploitative manner (Hoogvelt, 2001, 2007) and is better suited to holding individuals responsible for their plight.

In this chapter, I focus on these issues and examine the role that social work educators and practitioners have played, and can play, in raising macro-level issues, including climate change, that impact upon local practice. I demonstrate that citizenship, human rights and social justice are crucial underpinnings of a holistic practice that recognizes the interconnectedness between the social problems in different countries and that hopes to reverse the deleterious impact of human, social and environmental degradation on the lives of people and the planet. Crucial to this achievement is an understanding of the interdependence between countries and the internationalization of social problems, both of which have intensified under globalization.

# New agendas for social work: embedding environmental concerns in practice

Social workers are familiar with the importance of social, geopolitical and economic factors in practice. I also suggest that there are new agendas to be examined in responding to people's expectations about welfare and well-being, environmental considerations among them. My arguments show that social workers have a responsibility to raise concerns about the neglect of the physical environment of their clients, including in so-called sink estates, ghettos and sub-standard accommodation. I emphasize poor people's rights to decent living conditions alongside a consideration of the larger environmental issues, such as industrial pollution and climate change, that face the world community and local polities. These impact most often upon poor people, whose voices are seldom evident in large gatherings of experts in international organizations. Indigenous forms of social work in countries such as the USA, Canada and New Zealand have spearheaded significant understandings of these concerns by arguing that people's spiritual well-being has been linked to their physical and social environments since time immemorial (Green and Thomas, 2007). Indigenous people's worldviews have also inspired new theories and forms of practice that can contribute to the development of innovative approaches to solving problems in the West (Grande, 2004). The exchange of ideas can travel in all directions to enrich all peoples on this earth, not just from the West to the 'others', as Said (1978) indicated. In his seminal text *Orientalism*, he argues that the West exploits the East and sees it as a passive entity which has little to offer human civilization.

In the UK, New Labour did not deliver on its promises of reducing child poverty or helping adults out of poverty through training and waged work, despite its commitment to human rights and social justice and the increase in public expenditure and policies aimed at achieving these objectives. Nor did it succeed in eliminating the divide in health chances between the 'haves' and the 'have nots'. These were key components of the New Deal packages it brought into being. New Labour's commitment to eradicating global poverty is another arena in which it failed to deliver. A concerted effort on this front at the international level is being made through the Programme on Africa, the latest of several other recent multinational endeavours since 2001 relating to this continent. The most widely publicized initiative was formulated under Britain's leadership of the G8 during 2005. Yet world poverty and the gap between rich and poor continue to rise, both within and between countries. In the USA, despite its being a wealthy country, poverty has continued to grow, especially among the working poor, who suffer the indignity of being unable to earn enough to pay their daily bills even when working a seventy-hour week (Ehrenreich, 2002).

This inadequate record has been exacerbated by the current global financial crisis, which has called into question the capacity of the G8 countries to provide the necessary leadership to resolve the situation, so as not to exclude those large segments of the world's population in the Global South already experiencing hardship, and the contributions of emerging economies, particularly China, India, Brazil and Mexico. These four countries are likely to become the powerhouses of the future, as emerging economies contain 84 per cent of the world's population but hold only 12 per cent of global equity capitalization (Patterson and Cochrane, 2008). Their growth is expected to be phenomenal, and the World Bank anticipates that six of the largest ten economies by 2050 will be drawn from those that are currently 'emerging'. Additionally, a projected 1 billion middle-class consumers in China and India alone are reckoned to hold spending power of about $US1 trillion annually and represent enormous market potential for capitalist corporations. As a result of pressure from such quarters, the G8 has had to adapt and enlarge its scope under the banner of the G20, to incorporate a range of new players, the most significant ones being China and India. While it is still too soon to predict how emerging economies will act upon the world stage, China is already the third largest economy in the world and set to overtake Japan, the second largest, fairly soon, and in time the USA, currently the biggest (Löscher, 2009).

China is now also the largest producer of carbon emissions alongside the USA. Its rising status as a world power will place further obligations on the country but, despite its ascendancy, it has still to address issues of poverty affecting 250 million people, mainly in rural areas, challenges raised by the status of ethnic minorities within its current borders (McDougall, 2009) and environmental degradation in its own territories. This combination of factors makes considering only the internal impact of environmental degradation insufficient. Trade between countries creates interdependence that must also be taken into account (Munasinghe and Swart, 2005). For example, the Asian market has implications for the environment in British Columbia, where materials to fuel China's industrial development might be extracted (Tetrault, 2009).

One proposal is to extract annually for the next twenty-five years 1.5 million tons of rare metallurgical coal used in steelmaking from a 3,100 hectare underground deposit (Tetrault, 2009). The partnership to exploit this resource is the Comox Joint Venture, consisting of the Compliance Coal Corporation of Vancouver, subsidiaries of the Japanese import–export company Itochu Corporation, and the South Korean electronics, telecommunications chemical giant LG. Although environmental impact studies will be carried out by 2010 for the project to be functional by 2012, how can a reliable study that takes account of all factors, including multiple stakeholders who live in different countries and all those with an interest in the extraction, production and distribution of the coal over the lifetime of the project, be conducted in that short period? Can the limited risk assessments currently at humanity's disposal, especially as they are known to be unable to address issues of social justice and tend to be locality specific (Swift and Callahan, 2009), supply credible answers? Or are we bound to repeat the mistakes of the past because people exploited the earth's resources before they had all the information they needed, and all of the earth's people are now paying the price for such unintended negligence, albeit differentially? This situation highlights how the economic drive of tapping into Asian markets interlinks with environmental considerations that cross borders.

In the UK, similar problems around the failure to deliver on the 'green agenda' bedevilled New Labour's commitment to environmental issues, in particular reducing pollution and adhering to the Kyoto Protocol. Critics of the slow progress made globally in the realization of these policies focused on the American government's intransigence on these initiatives under the administration of George W. Bush. A lack of resources further exacerbated this situation in many other countries besides the UK and the USA. The situation may alter if Barack Obama adopts a leadership role in climate change discussions and this carries weight with world leaders in countries with a crucial role to play in the discussions, especially China and India. However, Obama's role in the Copenhagen meeting on climate change in December 2009 (the fifteenth Conference of the Parties to the UN Framework Convention on Climate Change – COP15) does not augur well for the future. He used his arrival to discuss issues with some of the world's heaviest polluters – China, Mexico, Brazil and Indonesia – and proposed an agreement that only five nations signed. As a result, COP15 was declared a failure while the ecological clock ticks on (Schneider, 2009).

Currently, only Sweden has lived up to its international treaty obligations on the climate front (Giddens, 2009). However, the Core Cities initiative, which involves some of the world's largest cities working to reduce their carbon footprint without waiting for their national governments to act (Bulkeley and Betsill, 2003) is providing a blueprint on how urban environments can become less polluting. These issues have also been commented upon by social workers using ecological frameworks to ensure that matters such as economic decline in already stressed areas, lack of employment opportunities, and the sense of loss and trauma associated with change are being addressed, at least at the level of individuals and their localities. If social workers devote more energy to mobilizing people living in these communities, helping them to assert control over their own lives and demand the rights of citizenship in the political, economic and social arenas, they can have a greater impact than they have had on climate change to date.

Less commented upon, but equally noticeable, is the lack of a social work voice in the deliberations on climate change at top government levels. Most social work interventions have taken place in the local arena, primarily through civil society organizations, especially NGOs and anti-globalization protest movements. Social work's voice at the UN, though noticeable in social development, has been silent on climate change. Thus, given its role in picking up the pieces in local, national and international disasters, whether natural or man-made, the profession has not had the influence it deserves on these debates. This situation is being tackled, and representation was evident at Copenhagen on 10 December 2009, when the IASSW, ICSW and IFSW presented an all-day seminar that focused on social workers' views on the subject for the first time.

## Human, social and environmental degradation

In Britain, the election of New Labour politicians in 1997 symbolized for the majority of people who voted for them an opportunity to get rid of the Thatcherite social policies that had had the worst impact on poor people. The history of the past ten years indicates that while there were some gains, such as a commitment to end child poverty – a goal that has yet to be achieved – much of Thatcher's agenda on welfare has remained intact. This included increasing the role of the private sector in service provision; emphasizing consumer choice over the rights of the citizen; enforcing the precepts of the new public-sector management; deregulating business, including financial services, while heavily regulating the public sector; keeping benefit levels under control so that they did not become an incentive for people to avoid looking for work; being insufficiently vigorous in realizing the Kyoto targets regarding climate change; and not meeting the commitment to end poverty in Africa.

These failures contributed further to the human, social and environmental degradation that are experienced by poor people both within the UK and elsewhere. Social workers are involved in addressing such failures, especially in refugee camps in Kenya, Somalia (Sanders, 2009) and Ethiopia (Meo, 2009). Humanitarian aid and emergency food rations are never sufficient for the needs of those affected, with small children suffering the most from the lack of food. Feeding stations are not formed in all villages and people may have to trek miles before reaching the nearest one. Many children, older people, disabled people and sick people die on the way, being too malnourished and ill to walk the distances involved (UNDP, 2008, 2009).

## The market devalues and degrades poor people

Human degradation – the failure of human beings to thrive because society has placed barriers that obstruct their development through the methods it uses to organize social relations – is linked to social and environmental degradation. Social degradation is the lack of civility in the public sphere as people become more self-centred and disinterested in the plight of their fellow human beings and refuse to show solidarity or responsibility in improving their situations. Environmental degradation is the destruction of the environment, especially the physical environment, and is often, though not always, caused by human beings. The construction of shoddy housing for poor people, building on flood plains or close to highways with high levels of pollutants, allowing factories to spew out interminable amounts of carbon dioxide and other toxic materials, constructing ever larger cities that lack the necessary sanitation, housing, jobs, health facilities, education services and transportation networks – all contribute to social and environmental degradation (Abhat et al., 2005). That people have to live in overcrowded and unhealthy environments contributes to human degradation and violates their human rights to safe and healthy social and physical surroundings as identified in the UDHR.

Whose responsibility is it to end this state of affairs? Those on low incomes who can barely afford to feed, clothe or house their children? Those in charge of public policies and the public purse? Private entrepreneurs who profit from paying workers low wages? Can a social compact that brings these three diverse stakeholder groups together solve these problems and realize citizenship goals? In complex, contemporary societies, it is highly likely that extensive partnerships involving many stakeholders can find the solutions to these problems. However, achieving them will require political commitment and goodwill as well as resources. The one argument that can gather the momentum needed to keep this idea going is proposed by the citizens' organization Social Watch, among others. It argues that the world has the technology and resources needed to eradicate poverty and enable all human beings to live in decent environments if there is the political will to share resources and power equitably. The realization of these goals, already enshrined in Articles 22 to 27 of the UDHR (George, 2003), will require a redistribution of resources and wealth between the 'haves' and the 'have nots', both within and between countries. This may prove to be an insurmountable hurdle. Social work practitioners, educators and researchers can play an important role in working with people to advocate for such changes, mobilizing people to promote them, and undertaking research that shows the deleterious impact on human beings if these issues are not addressed locally, nationally and internationally.

Modern, secular liberal democracies have been criticized for losing their souls in a welter of consumer spending, workaholism or the exclusion of a relationship-based social life. Such has been the shift that the notion of 'retail therapy' has gained currency, and going shopping is offered as a cure for every ill that is easier to take than any pill. Yet retail therapy is exclusionary even within its own framework. It is available only to those who have enough money to indulge themselves or who manage to secure substantial loans which ultimately they may be unable to repay. There is the additional argument of the price the earth is paying for this materialism and the loss of scarce resources used to produce unnecessary goods. However, retail therapy divides the world sharply into those who consume an inordinate share of the earth's resources and those that barely have enough to survive. This latter category encompasses 1.8 billion of the earth's inhabitants, around 1 billion of whom cannot afford food on a daily basis (Blair, 2009).

For years, the UN has been compiling the Human Development Index (HDI) and producing reports that show that Western countries generally enjoy higher standards of living, greater longevity, lower infant mortality rates and better health and have a higher proportion of educated people than those living in the Global South (UNDP, 2009). These disparities are even greater when comparing the West with the forty-eight least developed countries, where the bulk of the world's people subsisting on less than $US2 per day reside. The UN has struggled with how to measure deprivation and the human, social and environmental degradation caused by industrialization and low incomes. Since it was proposed by the World Bank in 1980 as a consensus measure in the controversial arena of measuring both absolute and relative poverty, absolute poverty has been agreed at $US1 per day. Poverty underpins social degradation.

Although the $1 per day was deemed to mark the absolute level of poverty, its longevity as a measurement has introduced its own problems. Its real value has dropped substantially since its introduction. Its purchasing power has fluctuated even more dramatically, as prices paid to food producers have dropped while the prices that consumers pay for goods, including food, have risen. This situation has been further aggravated by the global financial crisis that started in 2007. Daily life had become so dire for the nearly 2 billion people living on less than $1 per day that riots took place across the world when food prices rose sharply during 2007–8. The 2009 UN survey on food security, which covers fifty-six countries, indicated that food prices have risen by 19 per cent in forty-seven of these countries since 2007. According to this survey, many of the gains made in reducing food insecurity during the 1980s and 1990s have evaporated, although the overall numbers affected have dropped from one-third of the world's population to about one-fifth. Nonetheless, the proportion of people experiencing food insecurity rose from 15 per cent in 2004 to 20 per cent in 2009 (Blair, 2009). It is difficult to increase agricultural output to offset increases in food prices by producing more in the Global South because the proportion of aid allocated to agriculture now stands at 5 per cent, compared with 20 per cent in 1979. And of the $6.8 billion promised by rich countries to feed people during 2010, only $2.8 billion had become available by mid-year. Yet all nation–states have endorsed the right to food through the UDHR.

Meanwhile, the gap between rich and poor has grown substantially. At the same time, an individual's experience of poverty varies significantly according to gender, 'race' and ethnicity, class, ability and age. Statistics show that wealth has become increasingly polarized, both within and between countries, a feature that has accelerated rapidly in the last few decades. Consequently, during this period, the top 20 per cent of the world's population accumulated 86 per cent of the wealth, while the lowest 20 per cent holds only 1.3 per cent. Differentials between countries in the Global North and the Global South rose considerably, from 2 to 1 in 1800 to 70 to 1 at the turn of the twenty-first century (George 2003: 18–19). By 2005, as economic globalization gathered pace, this ratio had reached more than 100 to 1.

In 2006, while 2.8 billion people lived on less than $2 per day, the richest 946 individuals earned $3.5 trillion between them and the richest man on earth had $58.2 billion (Kroll and Fass, 2007). Gender bias is evident in these figures. Among this elite group, only sixty-three were women, and around 58 per cent were American. The richest woman, the owner of L'Oréal in Paris, had $20.7 billion in 2007. This amount was roughly one-third of that held by the then richest man, the American Warren Buffett, who had $62 billion. Most billionaires, men and women, were white. In 2007, the richest African American woman was Oprah Winfrey, with just over $1 billion (Kroll, 2008). Women from China and Russia are catching up and likely to overtake their European and American sisters in the near future. The richest Chinese woman in 2007 was worth $17.6 billion (ibid.). Poor women are at the bottom of these hierarchies and make up most of the 1.6 billion people who are worse off under globalization in its neo-liberal form. This figure is indicative of more people at the bottom of the pile than under past economic systems.

Since 2006, the rankings between rich men have shifted a little. In 2007, Warren Buffett replaced Bill Gates as the richest man on earth with $US62 billion. Gates with $US58 billion slipped to third place as Carlos Slim Helú of Mexico overtook him with $US60 billion. However, by 2008, Gates was back in number one position, only to be overtaken by Helú as the richest man in 2009. By that time, the amount at their disposal had also decreased, to reflect the more dire general economic situation globally. Helú, the richest man, had $53.5 billion; Gates, now number two, had $53 billion and Warren Buffet, now number three, had $46 billion (Kroll and Miller, 2010). The losers in this roulette game of wealth, on the other hand, are far too numerous to name. They comprise the 2.8 billion people who lived on less than $US2 per day in 2007, and continue to be there. Their experience is not individually identifiable in the statistics in the way that occurs for those at the top of the ladder.

The individuals featuring within the richest group rotate among themselves to a greater extent than those at the bottom of the income hierarchy, and individuals from emerging economies are rapidly catching up with their Western counterparts. Wealthy people hold interlocking industrial and financial empires that straddle the globe – East, West, North and South. The fiscal crisis of 2007 has realigned their composition somewhat. The *Forbes Report* on the richest people in the world in 2008 (Kroll et al., 2009) indicates that wealth in the emerging economies is becoming more unequal while the acquisitions of the wealthiest members rise. For example, in India, the number of billionaires rose from twenty-seven in 2007 to fifty-two in 2008 as the Indian economy grew at the rate of 7 per cent during that time and the stock market increased by 75 per cent (Ramesh, 2009). With a combined wealth of $US276 billion, India's 100 richest people held 25 per cent of the Indian gross domestic product (GDP) between them. India has outstripped China's billionaires whose richest 100 have $US170 billion between them. The man at the top of the tree in India, Mukesh Ambani, was worth $32 billion. The second richest Indian was Lakshmi Mittal, who lives in London and was worth $30 billion. His nearest rival, Anil Ambani, has $17.5 billion. Gender differentiation is also evident in India. The richest woman, Savitri Jindal, saw her wealth rise from $2.9 billion in 2007 to $12 billion in 2008. Energy and steel fuelled the growth in wealth for these individuals. In contrast, the 800 million people that were at the bottom of the income ranking in India were living on 80 rupees, or 30 pence, a day. Meanwhile, in the USA, Bill Gates lost $7 billion as a result of the financial crisis, while Warren Buffett lost $10 billion. Moreover, around 100 individuals in the USA lost their billionaire status (Ramesh, 2009: 17).

These figures indicate the starkness of global inequalities in wealth. The image becomes clearer in light of the fact that the three richest people in the world have more wealth between them than the total gross domestic product of the forty-eight poorest countries. Class differentials have also intensified. An employee on the top rung of the corporate ladder in the West earns 200 to 300 times more than the average employee. This ratio has grown from the figure of forty to sixty times more that prevailed during the 1960s and 1970s, when Western societies were more equal (George, 2003: 19). The global financial crisis has made these inequalities more acute for those at the bottom end of the income and wealth hierarchies.

## Human degradation is gendered

As a result of economic deprivation, poor people endure the daily indignities of lost opportunities and chances denied, women and children being among those hardest hit. Many women deprive themselves to feed their children and husbands. Environmental degradation and global warming also actively affect women by increasing the burden of work in agriculture, making it more difficult for them to feed their families, and forcing them to deal with the effects of natural disasters (Pittaway et al., 2007). Moreover, 50 per cent of the world's population lacks access to basic sanitation facilities. The absence of infrastructure to alleviate some of this hardship adds to the human, social and environmental degradation endured by women and children, who undertake the majority of caring tasks in these conditions. Women and children are disproportionately affected by the lack of sanitation and the absence of running water in or near their homes (WHO and UNICEF Joint Monitoring Programme, 2009).

Many structural limitations are embedded in women's daily lives and, despite their individual strengths and resilience, they cannot overcome these. Thus, gaps in the infrastructure that supports everyday life add enormously to their heavy burden of work. Women's health is particularly vulnerable. For example, each year around 5 million unsafe abortions are conducted in Africa, leading to the deaths of about 34,000 women. These women are too poor to access expensive medical interventions and are not aware of what legal options are available to help them (Holden 2008). Meanwhile, Western powers play politics with women's lives. For example, in 2001 President George W. Bush promoted what became termed the 'global gag rule', which prohibited the allocation of American funds to family planning groups that offered abortions or provided information and/or counselling. Another instance occurred in late 2008, when USAid stopped supplying contraceptives to Ghana, thereby endangering women's reproductive health (ibid.: 7).

Social workers are found working with poor families – in the slums of the Global South and the ghettos of the West – trying to maximize the resources that they can access and helping to mobilize families and communities in self-help initiatives (Sewpaul and Hölscher, 2007). Women are targeted in these endeavours not only by social workers but also by aid donors, whether private individuals, governments or NGOs, in the belief that they will ensure that funds are used for the intended purposes and reach their families, particularly the children. This is ironic, given that around 600 million women throughout the world are still unable to read or write, although addressing illiteracy among women is an important MDG aim. A policy of educating women is expected to 'prepare a strong army to stop poverty, health problems, prevent infection and prepare food hygienically. If you educate girls, they will support other girls. It's a big, big change' (George, 2008).

The price of this policy if it does not succeed is paid by women as individuals and by their children, however personally strong they may be. Also, existing unequal gender relations will remain untouched. If the appropriate safeguards have not been put in place at the local level, women may also be subjected to the increased risk of domestic violence. This is exemplified by Gloria's experience, as recounted in box 6.1. Although she was a resourceful woman, she was from a culture that expected her to be an obedient wife, look after the children, respond to the needs of her extended family and hold her husband in awe. Her position was also seriously affected by the lack of facilities to support women such as her when a marriage deteriorates. As she had no one to turn to for help, this state of affairs exacerbated her vulnerability.

---

*Box 6.1 Case study: Domestic violence in unsupportive environments*

Gloria lived in a small rural village in Africa. She had married at a young age, but bolstered her rudimentary education by attending classes given by a village (woman) elder. She had three small children who were under six years of age. Her husband left her after the birth of their third child because she had refused to have intercourse with him. He blamed this reaction on her 'getting too big for her boots'. Although his allegation was unsubstantiated, he blamed the woman elder for putting into her head the idea that she could refuse his advances. One day, when he was in an angry mood and she refused to comply with his demands for sex, he assaulted her in front of the children, breaking several of her ribs and her nose. He then disappeared. Not long after he had gone, she discovered she had contracted HIV/AIDS, presumably from him as she had had no other sexual partners. Since Gloria had no money for the medicines she needed, the woman elder suggested that she take up a post with an international NGO that was looking for a local woman to educate village women on hygiene and health issues, as she had a good grasp of traditional medicines and had done well in her classes. The NGO would train her, pay her a salary and enable her to buy the medicines she needed.

Gloria was successful in her application and got on well with the African, European and American workers running the project. About a year after her husband had deserted her, she came home to find him in the house, smoking a pipe and drinking. She asked him what he was doing there and he said he had come back to resume his rightful place in his family. Moreover, he was hungry and wanted to eat. He let her know, in no uncertain terms, that he was not pleased with her getting a job and 'enjoying' herself with 'those foreign men' when she was barely civil to him. After Gloria had prepared supper and the children were out playing, she raised the question of what he was planning to do now that he had returned, and told him she needed to work to buy medicine to keep her well so that she could care for the children. He was incensed that she blamed him for contracting HIV/AIDS and said that she picked it up because she was a 'loose' woman who had always flaunted her sexuality around. When she protested her innocence, he beat her up badly. There was no one that Gloria could ask for help, as both her family and that of her husband refused to get involved in their disputes. They thought that she should be less 'lippy', placate him and submit to his wishes in all matters.

## Climate change is a major challenge for contemporary social work practice

Climate change has been inadequately examined in social work circles. It presents one of the most exacting challenges for contemporary practice, whether in research, the academy or the field. Climate change and industrialization are causing hardship in different locations throughout the world. In the Arctic, the Inuit are encountering declining polar bear and whale stocks and the Sami are facing the destruction of their caribou-based lifestyle (Axford and Smol, 2009). The indigenous peoples of Latin America are losing their rainforest as its resources are stripped away by outsiders wanting its minerals, animals and plants to sell in the market-place, and the nomadic peoples of Africa and the Middle East are finding that drought is ending their centuries-old traditions of foraging across borders for food for both their families and their livestock. Experts esti-mate that about 10 million people worldwide have been driven from their homes by rising seas, inordinate amounts of rainfall, desertification and other forms of climate-induced disaster (Sanders, 2009). Norman Myers (2005), of Oxford University, argues that this is the tip of the iceberg. He claims that there will be 25 million climate refugees by 2050, by which time climate-induced population movements or displacements will overtake those caused by war.

Many aspects of climate change require political decisions to be taken at national and international levels, especially in securing agreement to reduce greenhouse gas emissions (IPCC, 2007). However, social workers can promote political initiatives by mobilizing people and resources to discuss the threats that climate change poses to local communities, support the development of alternative, sustainable lifestyles, and lobby to change social policies in life-enhancing directions. Additionally, they can assist people in responding to the devastation caused by extreme weather events, including those caused by climate change – as they have during floods in Bangladesh (Mathbor, 2008), the Bihar Valley (Jha, 2008) or Gloucestershire (GCC, 2007), for example. The case study in box 6.2 describes the dire situation facing people who have become climate refugees on the Kenya–Somalia border and how social workers and community workers can intervene to facilitate dialogue among neighbours in conflict over scarce resources.

---

*Box 6.2  Case study: Climate refugees in Dadaab, Kenya*

Dadaab is a refugee camp on the Kenyan–Somali border built in 1991 to house 90,000 refugees following the collapse of the Siad Barre dictatorship in Somalia. It currently holds three times that number and the total is rising all the time. The camp was originally in a fertile valley that had trees, shrubs and water. It is now virtually barren because drought and the number of people making demands on its resources have exceeded its capacity to provide. This ecological failure endangers the ability of the inhabitants to survive. This is also true for the locals, who once lived on the land surrounding Dadaab as herdspeople.

The camp has run out of space, so graves are being dug up to make way for new huts and latrines. About 10 per cent of those now living in Dadaab have left their drought-stricken smallholdings as dry weather has reduced water supplies to nil. As a result, plants do not grow, crops fail and people and animals are dying of hunger and thirst. Although Dadaab is not intended for Kenyan citizens, those experiencing drought conditions and the loss of their livelihoods have joined the camp and refuse to register their presence. Kenyan climate refugees are estimated to number 4,600. Camp authorities are compelling Kenyans to renounce their Kenyan citizenship if they wish to remain in Dadaab, and those not doing so will be denied access to aid. This response is experienced as illegitimate by the local people, who feel that a particular citizenship (Kenyan) has been imposed on them. Before the nation–state set up its boundaries, their nomadic lifestyle always meant that they crossed the border at will.

Other Kenyan herdspeople, including the Maasai and Borano tribes, are migrating to cities such as Nairobi and joining the slum dwellers there as their herding lifestyle disappears. As proud people, they feel humiliated to be begging for money or to take the low-paid jobs on offer. Such movements are accelerating urbanization, but under the worst possible conditions, as the cities are unable to cope with the demands for housing, sanitation, health care, education and jobs. The people moving into these areas are less likely to be immunized or attend school than if they had remained in the rural areas. The departure of large numbers of people has meant the break-up of rural communities which, although underdeveloped and marginalized, offered less risky ways of surviving than the urban slums (Sanders, 2009).

Social workers in Kenya have become involved in these areas to mediate between conflicting groups and ease ethnic tensions, discuss ways of saving water, promote sustainable development in rural areas, and distribute aid in the camps. For example, the IFSW and IASSW sent social workers into the Mathare Valley to promote peace and reconciliation after violence broke out between conflicting groups in 2006. Hence, Dadaab is one example of a large problem. A longer-term crisis is illustrated in Ayub, Ethiopia, described in box 6.3.

---

*Box 6.3 Case study: Drought in Ayub, Ethiopia*

Droughts in Ethiopia are becoming a regular occurrence, with lack of rain being predicted for three out of every four years. This places enormous pressure on a poor country – the fifth poorest in the world (World Bank, 2008). Even the system of modest welfare payments, schools and clinics that has been created since the 1984 famine is failing to cushion the latest drought (Meo, 2009). Human practices have intensified the problems in the country. For example, the highland area, where the drought is hitting hard, has been deforested for fuel and can no longer provide grazing. The Ethiopian population has doubled since the 1980s, and this has intensified pressure on the territory and its resources. Farmers have subdivided their lands into smaller plots to pass them on to sons, but these are no longer viable for sustaining a family of any size.

The Ethiopian government believes that today's starvation crisis threatens 6.2 million farmers and their families and has asked for international assistance. Aid agencies believe the numbers to be substantially higher, because another 7.2 million farmers depend on a government welfare scheme that tides them over until the harvest is collected. Now, no harvest is expected. The World Food Programme estimates that 125,000 metric tonnes of grain are needed to respond to this appeal (Meo, 2009). Long-term development is sorely needed to resolve this crisis, but this will not happen unless the international community reorders its priorities to support an equitable and sustainable distribution of the world's food and other resources. This means looking for innovative solutions rather than continuing with or following unsustainable Western paths to development.

Social workers can engage local communities in finding solutions to these problems and helping them to implement the plans of action they devise. The plight of 'climate refugees' raises a new group for policy-makers to consider and social workers to support. Because this type of refugee is not covered by the 1951 Geneva Convention, the UN high commissioner for refugees has no legal mandate to compel the international community to address their plight (UNDP, 2008). However, their circumstances may be as dire as those of refugees seeking freedom from persecution, human warfare and violence. The UNHCR could ask for assistance on compassionate grounds. The millions of people in 170 countries who participated in the International Day of Climate Change on 24 October 2009 put their views concerning the urgency of reaching agreement in Copenhagen in December 2009 (Wood, 2009).

Although Copenhagen (COP15) failed to meet these aspirations, if agreement could be reached in subsequent meetings – e.g., COP16 in Cancún Mexico, to be held from 29 November to 10 December 2010 – the numbers of people becoming climate refugees could be drastically reduced. However, initiatives can also be undertaken at a local level. For example, one group of people who have taken on board the message of doing something about climate change in their daily lives consists of some engineering students who decided to promote electrical cars at the 2010 Winter Olympics in Whistler, Canada. They received funding to realize their ambition from their department at the University of British Columbia (Hill, 2009). How can social work students take up a similar challenge in the 2012 Olympics in London and the 2016 games in Rio de Janeiro? Becoming involved at a local level is one way in which social workers can support poor people to gain control over their environment, by providing them with information about climate change and its impact on their lives and also in mobilizing them to engage in such initiatives and change policies that will affect them.

The debates about climate change are difficult for ordinary people to follow and are rooted in controversies about how much is human-induced and how much can be attributed to nature (Giddens, 2009).

Such discourses help to obscure the fact that, whatever the cause, the climate is changing in different ways for different groups of people and will therefore require a multidimensional approach to reduce the likely hardships. Castigating people for being doubters of climate change is unlikely to encourage them to engage in dialogue in search of the knowledge that will enable human beings to live in healthy, sustainable environments.

There is a proliferation of 'facts' and 'counter-facts' that make it difficult for interested people to be certain of what they can best do as individuals to reduce their carbon footprint, and this is a failure that governments, academic institutions in charge of research on the subject, and private corporations who contribute to pollution are responsible for addressing. Critical to this is producing accurate and credible information on the subject. It means that those arguing from different positions have a duty to avoid jargon and the suggestions that action is being taken when the opposite is the case – or, worse still, to argue that they are acting in good faith when they know that the information on which they are basing their judgements is inadequate. Box 6.4 gives one taxpayer's critique of a government plan to reduce carbon emissions. Although the arguments are those of a 'climate change doubter' (Giddens, 2009), the criticisms of the government's approach to the urgent need to do something quickly are valid. That little has been done demonstrates the failure of policy-makers to understand fully the complexity of the issues they are addressing and to draw up proposals in which one part does not undermine their overall objective. The case study highlights views held by Maureen Bader (2009), the director for the British Columbia branch of the Canadian Taxpayers' Federation.

---

*Box 6.4 Case study: The government's carbon offset scheme is a scam*

Gordon Campbell, the premier of British Columbia, has announced government plans to make the public sector carbon neutral by 2011. To achieve this aim he set up the Pacific Carbon Trust (PCT), which charges companies or institutions that produce carbon emissions, and gives money to those who have lowered emissions. Schools and hospitals, for example, are charged $CDN25 for each ton of carbon they emit. The amount that non-emitters receive has not yet been disclosed.

Bader (2009) argues that it would be cheaper for public institutions in BC to sign up to the Chicago Climate Exchange scheme, because they could buy an offset for each ton of carbon they emit for the princely sum of only 14 cents. She is concerned that the government paid out $14 million in 'seed' money to set up the PCT and then another $869,000 to offset the 34,370 tons of carbon emissions it is expected to produce. Additionally, each school or hospital building is required to purchase software to monitor emissions, at the cost of 42 cents per person, hire people to keep track of the emissions and pay for monitoring them.

Bader is also concerned that the government is over-rewarding companies that contribute to developing the technology that will reduce emissions. She cites Shell Oil as having received $856 million from the Canadian federal and Alberta provincial governments for its carbon capture and storage project and as also being paid for reducing its carbon emissions. She concludes that 'well-intentioned, government spending to stop global warming will do nothing to stop global warming, hurt families and children and redistribute tax dollars to businesses. It's time to jump off the global warming bandwagon' (Bader, 2009: A13).

Despite her antipathy to Campbell's proposed solution to climate change, Bader has an important message to convey to policy-makers – namely, that someone is bound to profit from the ways in which carbon trading is being configured, and the taxpayer will be asked to foot the bill. Without losing sight of the commitment to reducing carbon emissions as an important component of the climate change debate, it is important to bear in mind that other greenhouse gases, such as methane, need to be reduced as well.

## Interdependencies and holistic responses to climate change

Bader's (2009) concerns are echoed at the macro-level in relation to disagreements as to who is to pay for reducing carbon emissions and how much should be paid by each country. Existing usage of fossil fuels is dynamic and fluid and requires constant monitoring to assess shifts in each country's carbon footprint. Current divisions focus on the Western industrialized countries, which have contributed the majority of greenhouse gases, those in the former Soviet bloc, and those that are industrializing now and, in the hurry to catch up, are using older, more polluting technologies. The concerns that these divisions portray have to be addressed. However, regardless of the differentiated contributions to greenhouse gases, all countries have a responsibility for moving the debate forward and finding agreement whereby each can undertake action commensurate with its capacity to tackle the issues that have arisen. How this goal will be achieved is not clear. According to the most recent calculations released after the EU discussions in Brussels in October 2009, the developing countries will need $US148 billion a year by 2020 to tackle climate change. The EU suggests that between $35 billion and $80 billion should come from the public purse in Western countries, of which the EU expects to contribute between 20 and 30 per cent (Harrison and Grajewski, 2009). This position was placed on the table in December 2009 at the Copenhagen Summit, where it was hoped that a new agreement would be thrashed out to replace the Kyoto Protocol that expires in 2012, but it failed to gain the necessary support.

Industrialising countries are reluctant to agree to deal with climate change without sufficient funds from the rich countries. China, which has now overtaken the USA as the largest contributor to greenhouse gas pollution, adheres to this position. The argument that there is a historical legacy to be made good is problematic, if relevant. One problem with the splitting of the world into polluters and non-polluters is that pollution knows no borders. Another part of that historical legacy is that claiming ignorance about the impact of burning fossil fuels on the environment is no longer tenable for any country, including emerging economies. Thirdly, the countries most likely to suffer disproportionately from the environmental disasters that will ensue if climate change continues will be the poor states that historically have contributed less to pollution. Doing nothing is not an option for them. And, finally, demographics will shift the calculations fairly swiftly.

While China may currently boast that its per capita footprint is smaller than that of each Westerner, the question is how long this status will last, given its steeply rising pollution levels and the growing numbers of middle-class people living a Western lifestyle. The same question can be asked of any country, but the larger the population, the more resources are needed to provide them with a decent standard of living and the greater the carbon emissions will be if clean technology is not utilized. Escalating levels in one country carry implications for other countries because planet earth is indivisible. Although everyone will be affected, those most likely to suffer from the consequences of climate change are people living on the lowest incomes. There seems to be no way of avoiding these realities in this interdependent world. If nothing is done, we will all be destroyed together. So people are better off collaborating with one another, sharing the clean technologies that already exist and looking for other solutions – social and technological – that can help protect the environment in future. For those in the West, this means eliminating their materialistic and environmentally draining lifestyle. For those in industrializing countries, it means not emulating a Western lifestyle, but working to achieve sustainable human and environmental development. Theoretically, this latter point is something every country can work towards. In this context, China's recent commitment to invest in clean technologies is a welcome sign (Mayeda, 2009).

If the logic of the above arguments does not make the case for altering human behaviour with regard to climate change, what is happening in various parts of the world today is warning enough. There are far too many examples to choose from – hurricanes in the Caribbean, floods in Bihar, Bangladesh and Mozambique, hurricanes in the Philippines, wild-fires in Australia, forest fires in the USA and Canada, and unprecedented and unexpected flooding in Britain in 2007 and 2009. I return to Bader's story, told from the comfort of her home in British Columbia, as it stands in stark contrast to those affected by drought in Dadaab or the highlanders living in Ayub in Ethiopia. The international community should take seriously her concern that the schemes used to incentivize people in tackling climate change do not lead to profit-making opportunities that will not reduce carbon emissions. Action needs to address climate change and the pressures of rapidly rising populations on limited resources.

The provision of welfare benefits to cover people's needs from cradle to grave, the education of women and men in planning their families, the availability of safe contraceptives, and adequate health care to enable all children born to live long and healthy lives can all contribute to achieving the new states of being needed to create a sustainable world fit for everyone. Additionally, the earth's physical environment and its flora and fauna have to be included in this equation. Indigenous peoples have much to offer in this regard.

## Indigenous social work and spirituality

Indigenous people have struggled for centuries to retain their right to live holistically in tune with their environments. By drawing upon traditional knowledge and customs, they have begun to develop welfare systems to address the human, social and environmental degradation they experienced under colonialism and neo-liberalism. Particularly important in this regard have been the activities of the Maori and Pacific Islanders in Aotearoa/New Zealand (Tait-Rolleston and Pehi-Barlow, 2001) and the First Nations peoples of Canada (Green and Thomas, 2007), whose innovations have impacted significantly on wider understandings in social work. The traffic in these developments has not been all one way. For example, the Maori developed the notion of the Family Group Conference (FGC) and distributive justice to deal with the discrimination they experienced when problems encountered by their children and families were addressed by white New Zealanders (*pakeha*), including social workers. The FGCs caught Westerners' imagination and travelled across the world. They are now being used in the Nordic countries, the UK, Canada and the USA, for example (Jackson and Nixon, 1999).

### Indigenous knowledge is holistic in its approaches

Indigenous knowledge is noted for the connections it makes between people and their physical environment and the reverence with which the physical sphere is regarded (Cyr, 2007). All parts of the natural habitat are considered sacred. In many ways, indigenous lifestyles were among the first to offer insights into reducing the 'footprint' that people leave on their environment. This is because they take into account the need to preserve nature's largesse for existing and future generations. In this sense, modern industrial humanity can learn much about how to respect the resources of the earth and its bounty in order to create sustainable environments and forms of development. Indigenous lifestyles also focus on the links across generations, displaying a sense of both regard and obligation – another part of the holistic approach that integrates people, other living things, planet earth and the cosmos to the past, present and future. Humility in view of the limited achievements of mankind gives indigenous people a clear sense of the respect required to relate to others and the world around them. There are interesting examples of local indigenous populations responding with ingenuity and inventiveness to the agendas set by climate change. This is illustrated in the case study in box 6.5.

---

*Box 6.5 Case study: Indigenous approaches to climate change in Misa Rumi, Argentina*

An indigenous llama-herding community in Misa Rumi, Argentina, has given up using firewood to cook and to heat mudbrick homes because this had led to deforestation and soil erosion. With the help of a local NGO, the EcoAndina Foundation, which has been working in the area since 1989, they have installed solar-fired stoves and showers to provide for their daily needs. Solar power is used to heat a school, to fire the communal bakery and to run water pumps that irrigate the villagers' vegetable patches. In the process, the community has reduced carbon emissions without using carbon-offset trading schemes and obviated the need to collect and store firewood – an increasingly scarce commodity – or buy expensive canisters of natural gas. Not collecting the yareta for firewood means that a plant that takes hundreds of years to grow will not be decimated. The EcoAndina Foundation hopes that residents will be able to earn carbon credits for reducing their carbon dioxide emissions, because a single solar-powered cooker can save 2 tons of carbon dioxide a year. When multiplied by the 40,000 people who live in the region, this becomes a considerable amount (Stott, 2009).

Social workers become engaged in such activities as community development workers – explaining compatabilities and disjunctures between the technologies on offer, the problems the people wish to solve, and their traditional lifestyles and customs.

Indigenous worldviews offer sophisticated analyses of the world and the relationship between different phases of human historical development. The circle, as the symbol of unity among and between people and their environments, is central to the indigenous peoples of North America and is passed on down the generations from elders to children. Articulated as the medicine wheel, it links the spiritual with the material, the emotional with the intellectual, and the individual to the collective to provide knowledge as an integrated part of a whole ready for practice.

Gale Cyr (2007: 339–40) translates the understandings of the medicine wheel into a framework for a learning, practice and conflict resolution wheel, which integrates 'information' (of all types) with 'ways of knowing' (knowledge and ideologies), with 'individual and collective experience', and with 'wisdom' to produce forms of practice that help people to heal, resolve conflicts and undertake research – all as important and revered aspects of life. Cyr's creation exposes how European dominance in Canada formed the exploitative economic and social systems that have resulted in the 'development of underdevelopment' among First Nations peoples. The Wheel for Practice that Cyr developed indicates how knowledge of the traditional medicine wheel can be adapted to help develop empowering forms of practice that encompass individuals, groups, communities, knowledge and research. In it, the conflict resolution and mediation strategies that comprise part of social work's repertoire of skills become important parts of the processes of undoing the damage caused by inegalitarian and disrespectful relationships between people. These assist in beginning the healing processes that paves the way for indigenous people to regain control of their lives. This is important in overcoming the untold damage caused by colonialism.

Green and Thomas (2007) indicate the significance of learning in a way that respects both elders and children and builds on the interdependencies that exist between generations. This continues after physical death, when the presence of the spiritual world acquires further meaning (Robinson, 2001). Green and Thomas (2007) highlight the importance of community and healing in empowering individuals to overcome adversity, particularly the harm caused by the residential school system, which seriously undermined First Nations individuals, families and communities. The abuse that occurred within these institutions was perpetrated by a range of individuals and organizations and involved religious leaders, social workers, health professionals and policy-makers alongside the ordinary people who settled in what were once indigenous people's lands in Turtle Island – the First Nations' name for Canada (Haig-Brown, 1988).

## Learning from indigenous peoples

In addressing contemporary concerns, the First Nations are now engaging with issues of climate change and renewable energy generation. For example, the Haida Nation in Haida Gwai (people in what was known as the Queen Charlotte Islands, off the coast of British Columbia) propose to develop a 30 per cent equity share, alongside NaiKun Wind Energy, in an initiative in the Hecate Strait to generate energy in their traditional marine territory (Simpson, 2009). They see this as an opportunity to generate power for 130,000 homes and to accumulate funds that will enable them to invest in developing their lands and resources as they wish and in accordance with their traditions. This approach reflects that followed by other First Nations peoples, including the Haisla on British Columbia's mainland. Social workers interested in community development initiatives have a role to play in explaining such ventures to people from outside the area and in helping communities to become involved as full participants, so that the complete social, physical and economic costs and environmental impact of any project can be determined. In this sense, they become central in tackling the effect of the global on the local and working towards reducing, if not eliminating, human, social and environmental degradation. By assisting in documenting and researching the impact of such initiatives on local communities, they can accumulate evidence that will enable them to contribute to discussions about climate change at the global level.

Worldviews based on the links between people, their ancestors and the environment are shared by the indigenous people of Aotearoa/New Zealand, particularly the Maori. In elaborating their philosophy of life, Tait-Rolleston and Pehi-Barlow (2001) argue that the connections between past, present and future generations of Maori people have enabled them to retain their strengths and survive colonialism and the damage that it continues to inflict upon their lives. These coping strategies are rooted in their links to kinship systems built around the extended family and their place in the wider universe. Like the First Nations in Canada, the aboriginal peoples of Australia (Read, 1981) and the Native Americans in the USA (Grande, 2004), the Maori in New Zealand (Rangihua and Maori Perspectives Committee, 1990) were subjected to cruel and inhumane practices that deprived them of their lands, language, culture and traditional livelihoods as a result of colonial settlers' demands that they become 'civilized'. European settlers enacted policies that sought to compel the local people to assimilate into what they considered their own vastly superior lifestyles (Douglas, 1983). As Britain became the main colonizing power, this worldview was rooted in Anglo-Saxon ways of looking at and doing in the world, and this remains the dominant discourse within which social work practice and endeavours to authenticate other approaches to life occur today.

Tait-Rolleston and Pehi-Barlow (2001) talk about the implications for social work practice of a Maori worldview, in which everything, whether animate or inanimate, is deemed to have a spiritual existence alongside a physical one. Unless human action disrupts the dynamics, each complements and works to nurture the other. These authors show how the *whakapapa* (geneology), *whanuangatanga* (kith and kinship ties), *whanau* (family) and *whenua* (land) are crucial to the people's capacities to survive brutal treatment, including that of the disproportionate numbers of their young men behind bars, and to remove the shackles of colonialism from their society. The Maori consider children to be a blessing that tie the past and future together. The valuing of children in maintaining the links between the generations is common to other indigenous peoples, including First Nations in Canada.

Tait-Rolleston and Pehi-Barlow (2001) show how the Maori have used the *Puao-te-ata-tu (Day Break Report)*, initially published in 1986, to reclaim their heritage and traditional rights assured under the Treaty of Waitangi signed with the English colonizers in 1840. Maori social work favours observation and experimentation in using traditional teachings to reflect upon and develop indigenous methods of learning and practice. As in the First Nations' tradition, the place of elders is central to such work. The Maori created the Family Group Conference method of intervention to use family strengths – in this case referring to a wide extended family – to assist troubled and troubling members of their families and keep them out of the structures of the white New Zealand social security and welfare system, which hindered rather than promoted their individual and collective development (Fulcher, 1999). From these beginnings, the FGC model has travelled to other parts of the globe (Schmidt et al., 2001).

This indigenous approach contrasts starkly with the less visionary and fragmented approaches currently being adopted in the West, although there is no one single picture emerging other than that many of these issues are being ignored. This is somewhat strange, given that developing green technology is a strategic area and ripe for the sort of investments that can earn billions even within the existing global system (Löscher, 2009). Where are the money and technological fixes that can contribute to answering the problems the world faces? Collaboration across borders and sharing knowledge and resources involved in the clean, green technologies offer more possibilities and are often supported by those endorsing 'indigenous' perspectives (Soete, 2010).

The current financial crisis has led to cutbacks in public expenditure, including those underpinning research and development in new areas, but this is not the entire story. There remains a reluctance to invest heavily in clean-tech industries. The figures speak for themselves. Investment in clean-energy technologies in the USA grew sevenfold, to $155 billion, between 2002 and 2008. In the recent stimulus package approved under the Obama administration, $94 billion was earmarked for 'green' spending. China has allocated $218 billion towards the development of green technologies and industries (Mayeda, 2009). A recent UN study of investment in green technologies in thirteen industrial countries placed South Korea, China and Australia in the top three positions respectively. Canada was tenth, while the UK and USA were not even in the top twenty. Yet we ignore the safeguarding of the environment at our peril.

There are plenty of historical examples to learn from. For example, the Rapa Nui civilization of the Easter Islands became virtually extinct from the sixteenth century onwards owing to overpopulation, deforestation and the overexploitation of limited natural resources (Diamond, 1995). The Nazca people of Peru suffered a similar fate when their population escalated and the Rio Ica valley became denuded of huarango trees. This act allowed massive flooding to occur around 500 AD, when huge rainfall precipitated by El Niño swept away everything in its path (Chepstow-Lusty and Beresford-Jones, 2009). The city of Ica was flooded in 2007 by another El Niño event and an earthquake that caused substantial damage to property and the loss of many lives (Muñoz, 2007). Today's rulers in China are trying to control the weather by injecting silver iodide into clouds to produce rain and end a drought in Beijing. In 2009, their efforts produced snow when northerly winds sent temperatures plummeting to minus 2 degrees Centigrade. The Chinese have also seeded clouds to wash away smog (Foster, 2009). Although the success in influencing the weather at the micro-level is a technological achievement, the actual long-term effects and costs to the environment and people – especially their health – of regularly injecting silver iodide into the atmosphere is unknown. Social workers can help people raise concerns about the impact of such actions on human health and well-being and assist in holding policy-makers accountable for the decisions they make. However, social workers cannot engage in these activities naively. They need to be aware of local political alignments and identify the risks entailed in implementing (or not implementing) action plans and develop the skills to work with those in power.

Regardless of the politics that configure social relations in any particular situation, the science suggests that it is imperative that all countries tackle climate change and reduce smog and pollution levels. Otherwise, the general health of the world's population, and even their survival, will be undermined. Social workers pick up the pieces when disasters strike, but they also have a role to play in advocating for preventative measures that people can take to safeguard their lives, livelihoods and environments as occurred in Misa Rumi (see box 6.5).

## Conclusions

The degradation of human beings and the social and physical environment has proceeded apace as a by-product of industrialization and colonization, processes aimed at exploiting the earth's resources for capital accumulation and economic growth that has favoured the few (Marx, 1965). Many people have suffered as a result of this because, whatever benefits accrued under this system, they were not equally distributed. Those who shoulder the worst of the burden have been the poor, including the indigenous people of the world, many of whom, like the Tainos in the Caribbean (Sherlock and Bennet, 2006), were exterminated. Those who survived have continued to respect their traditions and develop new forms of living and being. Their insights carry considerable implications for social work practice (Cyr, 2007).

The growth of secularism in the West has severed the links with a spiritual view of the world for many. However, indigenous people, including those who have been subjected to European colonialism, have succeeded in both preserving their ancient and often sacred traditions and adapting them for survival and growth in the present day. They have also bequeathed important paradigms for social work practice that have been adopted in many parts of the world, as occurred with the idea of the Family Group Conference and the medicine wheel. These models have highlighted the importance of:

- having a holistic approach towards people and the environment;
- facilitating dialogue within and across communities;
- mobilizing people to minimize the impact of human activities on both the local and the global environment;
- undertaking research that promotes sustainable ways of living and being;
- encouraging the formation of life-sustaining and environmentally friendly policies;
- discussing issues with policy-makers and decision-makers to promote consensual decisions that will foster the interests of all those involved; and

- engaging in training that will prepare present and future generations of social workers in ways consistent with the worldview of being responsible for what happens on planet earth.

Incorporating indigenous insights into the roles that social workers play can assist them in safeguarding human life, contributing to sustainable forms of social development and protecting the world's physical environment.

# 7

# Globalizing the Local and Localizing the Global in Practice

## Introduction

The development of social work is currently being contested as the profession moves from its modernist project under the auspices of the welfare state to responding to identity-based theories, including postmodernism and post-structuralism and the challenges of indigenous perspectives to social development (Grande, 2004). This is especially relevant in the many parts of the West, where neo-liberalism and globalization have weakened the earlier social democratic consensus that it was the duty of government to respond to people's needs for assistance and security. This has now been replaced by an individualism that has been configured in decontextualized spaces void of their social underpinnings to capture the ideals of personal self-sufficiency and responsibility for welfare provision. The latter is procured primarily through a market that has commodified care while opening up the welfare state for the purposes of capital accumulation by private entrepreneurs and targeting publicly funded resources only on the most needy. Expressions of solidarity rooted in the traditions of working-class activism and social democracy have been undermined.

Insights from the USA, where the welfare mix has involved private providers for a considerable period, can be useful in understanding developments in post-welfare state situations in other countries. However, from an egalitarian point of view committed to inclusion and the celebration of diversity, the exclusion of many poor people from needed services in education, health and social care in the country that still retains the reputation of being the richest in the world does not suggest a positive outlook for future innovation and development inclusive of all the earth's people. The social exclusion of poor people from health facilities may continue under Obama's health reforms because these are still based on the payment of insurance premiums and subject to the market developed by the private providers. And the system continues to require considerable expenditure on bureaucracy to maintain records. Publicly funded universal services available free at the point of need consume far fewer resources in administrative costs than the current American system (Herdman, 1994; Woolhandler et al., 2003), a reality that is unlikely to change in future.

In this chapter, I consider the implications for practice of wider developments in the social, geopolitical and economic spheres at the points where the local and the global intersect. I argue that social work is being globalized so that many local events and interventions have repercussions beyond their national borders. The profession is simultaneously facing pressures to becoming more globally aware while paying more attention to 'the social' at the local level. Excluded groups are demanding additional control in what happens in their specific localities, while the notion of local place and space is being extended by global forces and contested by local ones. The contestation of place and space includes those who 'migrate' virtually by exploring the internet; those doing so in reality through migration; those who remain to defend their sense of the local – as in the case of indigenous peoples living in colonized territories; those segments of majority populations that feel threatened by newcomers to their lands, as do poor white working-class people in Europe; and those seeking to expel migrant workers in both the Global North and the Global South. The riots and social disorder linked to the ousting of migrant workers from South Africa in 2008 are an indication of this last phenomenon (Munnion, 2008). Hostile reactions to migrants, wherever they may occur, indicate the importance of addressing the issues of scarcity and the equitable distribution of resources within and between countries on a global basis.

Moreover, in this chapter I consider the mobility of social work professionals, within Europe as a result of European enlargement, and in the wider world. Migratory issues linked to labour mobility raise questions about the portability of training from one country to another in a diverse discipline such as social work, the recognition of qualifications across borders, and the thorny issue of who should pay for this training – especially when much of the traffic is often from low-income industrializing countries to high-income industrialized ones. The lack of reciprocity is also shown by the absence of bilateral agreements for receiving countries to repay the training of the individuals concerned in order to allow the countries of origin to train new personnel (Dominelli 2004b). Thus, an opportunity to express mutuality and interdependence is lost.

## An interactive and interdependent local–global nexus

Globalization is a two-edged sword. It has provided amazing opportunities to draw people together in both the virtual and the geographic domains. One possibility is that of raising issues that transcend the economic sphere, especially human rights (Ife, 2001b). Globalization has simultaneously privileged industrialized capitalist growth and initiated a series of crises – environmental, financial, demographic and political – that have had the most damaging effects on the world's poorest people. These have included the loss in the Global North of highly paid blue-collar work; the spread in the Global South of jobs that offer insufficient income to provide a decent standard of living (Wichterich, 2000); increasing health hazards that spread rapidly from one country to another; rising food and energy prices; extensive environmental degradation and resource depletion; and significant numbers of armed conflicts (HSRP, 2009). These elements combined constitute an interactive and interdependent local–global nexus whereby what happens in one location carries implications for another. Addressing the ensuing issues requires collaborative endeavours that recognize the interdependent nature of people and the environment.

Globalization, a contested term with no single meaning (Hirst et al., 2009), can denote the simple economic integration of countries in one global economic system (Cox, 1981; Wallerstein, 2005) or signify the impact of economic global relations on social relationships, from the meta-level of a complete social system to the interstices of everyday life practices (Dominelli, 2004a). The latter meaning attempts to address the complexity and depth of social relations in the economic, cultural, political and social domains and the connectedness between people in different parts of the world.

Despite the absence of an agreed definition of globalization, there is a degree of unanimity around some key features:

- cultural diffusion and rapprochement contradicted by increasingly nationalist tendencies in a number of countries;
- social relations that shape all aspects of life while simultaneously according priority to market mechanisms and discipline;

- migration as a response to environmental degradation, economic hardship and violence;
- a general integration and a widening of economic forces across borders that compete for space alongside economic protectionism and exclusion;
- rapid technological change, which has produced new forms of social exclusion – e.g., the digital divide – and opened up opportunities for exploiting individuals, particularly children, through the use of the internet;
- demographic changes, including increasing population and the rapid ageing of many societies, particularly in the West;
- urban growth and the exacerbation of urban–rural disparities; and
- urbanized centralization, which puts stress on the environment.

For social workers, an analysis of globalization would be incomplete without an examination of how it has influenced service delivery in the personal social services and labour processes. Globalization has impacted extensively on social workers by affecting relationships between practitioners and their clients, internationalizing social problems and changing the nature of the nation–state (Cox, 1981; Dominelli and Hoogvelt, 1996; Clarke and Newman, 1997). In the UK, globalization has affected the profession in several ways:

- promoting a 'new' managerialism, which has forced business practices and market discipline into arenas formerly excluded from market forces and the profit motive;
- disempowering social workers by restricting access to resources that would enable them to meet the needs of specific individuals;
- increasing the techno-bureaucratic nature of practice through performance indicators and efficiency measures for the purpose of covering the greatest number of people and maximizing limited resources;
- shifting service user–worker relationships away from relational to a more distant and bureaucratic form of social work so that practitioners can focus on the state's role in commissioning services delivered by private and voluntary-sector agencies;
- commodifying the relationship between service users and the state by turning them into consumers in a quasi-market while at the same time offering them greater choice and control over their lives through the personalization agenda and individual budgets;
- reducing reliance on publicly funded, citizenship-based universal services and promoting residual ones that target the neediest of the needy;
- encouraging family-based and individual responsibility among people for meeting their own needs, while the state becomes preoccupied

with competitiveness, opening the welfare market to international corporations keen to profit from providing services;

- the internationalization of social problems such as poverty, the drug trade, trafficking in women and children, the arms trade, the pornography trade and organized crime; and
- increasing the impact of migration through demands made by movements of people on services, but also the movement of social workers who train in one country but go to work in another (Dominelli, 2004b; White, 2007).

The complexities that social workers have to address have been intensified by the financial and environmental crises. These will require practitioners to look for new paradigms for practice and prioritize social and community development within an ecological framework that addresses both environmental and human degradation.

Moreover, contemporary analyses of globalization have to incorporate the significance of the emerging economies, especially China, India, Brazil and Mexico. These are introducing further challenges and will, in time, decentre the West's role in shaping global economic development. New models of growth are coming to the fore as each country attempts to maximize its position within the global economic system. Additionally, if current levels of population growth are maintained in each of the emerging countries, there will be further demographic challenges that must be addressed by the world as a whole. The UN has raised the issue of the world's population exceeding 9 billion by 2050 and the importance of working out how, in a context of scarce physical resources, the planet can sustain such a level (United Nations, 2005). Furthermore, indigenous and poor people are resisting the homogenization of their cultures and their relegation to the margins of global decision-making (Grande, 2004). Anti-globalization movements and individuals have created new ideas about how to organize paid work and meet human needs in ways that transcend notions at the core of neo-liberal capitalist social relations. Stiglitz et al. (2009) argued that globalization has to focus on the necessity of including indicators of well-being alongside economic indicators. This view is countered by others, such as Samir Amin (2009), who condemns elitist notions of globalization and argues for a bottom-up approach in the search of new models of development – a view that is endorsed by the anti-globalization movement (see Anti-Globalization, 2010). The insights arising from these alternative visions for society can provide new sources of innovation and hope that social workers can tap into.

The demands of indigenous people have heightened aspirations for new theoretical understandings that take account of their spiritual needs, the reclaiming of their traditional rights and heritages, and their dreams of developing as whole human beings, not simply as consumers in the marketplace (Bruyere, 2009). Their calls for endogamous forms of social work stand in contrast to the homogenizing tendencies of the McDonaldization or Americanization of societies (Ritzer, 2000) that have undermined local forms of social work practice (Dominelli, 1992, 1996a). For example, in Eastern Europe, the traditional skills that local practitioners had called upon to meet welfare needs during the Soviet era, but which had been discounted by Western academics, are now being revalidated. Westerners' assumptions that there existed nothing in these countries to build upon led to the imposition of inappropriate models on transitional societies (Stubbs, 2007) and echo practices that indigenous people experienced during the colonization of their lands. Critiques of globalization highlight neo-liberalism as a bankrupt ideology, despite its claim to produce the greatest good for the greatest number – a claim often epitomized in the phrase the 'trickle down' effect (Giangreco and Moore, 1999; Anti-Globalization 2010). Those seeking to create new theories and forms of practice have to take account of interdependence and reciprocated forms of solidarity, pursue interdisciplinary approaches to research, and replace ideologies that glorify possessive individualism, with its focus on self and family, with those encompassing all people.

## Indigenous practice focuses on the local and engages with the global

Social work practice in Europe was developed within nation–states, with each country focusing on its own concerns. In the days of Empire, locality-specific practices from Europe were transported to other countries to meet the needs of the European settlers rather than those of the local populations (Grande, 2004) and to integrate them into a world economic capitalist system (Wallerstein, 2005). Before the advent of modern communications technology, accessing other people's ideas and models of practice was expensive because it required the physical movement of goods and people across the globe. The creation of IASSW, IFSW and ICSW as early as 1928 gave the profession international remits that focused on conferences and the exchange of materials, staff and students and enabled individuals to cross borders with relative ease. Although these initiatives demanded fund-raising as well as linguistic and communication skills to facilitate participation, those who attended shared the aim of learning from each other. The early egalitarian thrust of these bodies was reflected in the facilitation through solidarity funds of the involvement of individuals from across the world and enabling them to use their own languages. Although a solidarity fund has been retained in each organization to assist those in the Global South to travel to conferences and meetings, linguistic parity did not last as long. Following the depression and the Second World War, the physical movement of social work educators and practitioners came to draw heavily on American personnel and resources. This meant that the English language took precedence – a matter that continues to arouse concern (Dominelli, 2004c). Symbolically, the strength of America's role in international organizations was formally recognized through practices such as the incorporation of IASSW in the state of New York in 1971.

Partly in response to the dominance of Anglo-American theories and models of practice, local scholars in other countries took explicit action to develop their own materials. Although there had always been resistance to the imposition of external models on local initiatives, the 'indigenization' movement became much stronger during the 1970s and 1980s. As a result, indigenous forms of social work practice have built on genuine interests in collaboration. In chapter 5, we saw the impact of Maori models, particularly the Family Group Conferences, and the contributions made by First Nations peoples in Canada in bringing spiritual views of the world back into mainstream practice. In addition, Australian aboriginal teachings draw upon reconciliation processes aimed at healing the damage caused by racism and the 'stolen generations' (Read, 1981). Different models are being developed in Asian countries, where such values as harmony and family relationships hold sway (Yip, 2005).

I want to caution against the view that indigenous cultures are the same, even within a country. And I want to warn against considering the West as a homogeneous entity or that its welfare regimes are all the same, as suggested by Yip (2005) and Webb (2003). In their concern to focus on the local within the context of the global, these authors ignore the enormous variety and heterogeneity that exists at both levels, regardless of the social grouping being considered. The West has significant disparities in wealth among its constituent groups, and this cannot be ignored without excluding the narratives of important segments of the population. These disparities are the result of structural inequalities. The disadvantages of those who do not live in the West are also spread unevenly, and inequalities in wealth and power are evident in most countries (UNDP, 2009). Those who migrate from the Global South to the Global North may find that internal disparities in power and resources exacerbate external structural inequalities. For example, gender, ethnic and age discrimination within families intersects and interacts with various forms of discrimination, intolerance and misunderstandings present in the wider society. Responding to crimes involving these inter-actions can be mishandled by law-enforcement agencies and social workers, as is illustrated in box 7.1, an instance of so-called honour killing (Allen, 2009, Bingham, 2009).

---

### Box 7.1 Case study: 'Honour killing' is a misnomer

Tulay Goren was a teenager killed by her father, Mehmet Goren, on 7 January 1999. She had come to the UK from a small village in southern Turkey to join her parents a couple of years earlier. The trouble started when she got a part-time job in a factory and met her boyfriend, Halil Unal, who was twice her age and a Sunni Muslim, whereas Tulay was an Alevi Muslim. This relationship challenged her family's cultural traditions and so created tension. Her father sought to discipline her and secure her compliance, but she ran away on more than one occasion and went to the police for help. But the police contacted her parents and she was returned home, where she was subjected to further physical and psychological abuse from her father. At one point, Tulay had asked to be taken into care by social services. But she was sent home instead (Bingham, 2009).

Tulay's father held a tight rein over the entire family, keeping them all, including her mother, in check. His failure to get Tulay to obey proved too much, and he killed her to 'cleanse the shame that she had brought into his family'. The father declared that he had to defend the family's honour, or *namus*, as Turkish Kurds call it (Sapsted, 2009). Dr Aisha Gill, senior lecturer in criminology at Roehampton University and expert witness at the trial, said, 'Honour killings are anything but honourable. They are brutal, premeditated acts of violence perpetrated by the very people supposed to protect the victim from harm' (Gill, 2009).

Mehmet Goren evaded capture for nearly a decade, until his wife Hanim gave evidence against him. He was sentenced to twenty-two years in prison. Hanim hoped that her story would encourage other women to refuse to live in violent situations and seek support from the authorities (Bingham, 2009).

There is considerable opposition to this form of violence against women within Muslim communities. Among many others, the Kurdish Women's Rights Organization in the UK, Queen Rania of Jordan, and Musawah ('Equality'), an organization to bring equality and justice into Muslim family law in thirty countries (www.musawah.org), are all working to end such practices.

---

The police initially involved in Tulay Goren's case did not feel pre-pared to deal with the complex family dynamics and cross-cultural tradi-tions involved and went to Turkey to find out about *namus*. As a result, they have now learnt how to intervene more effectively (Bingham, 2009).

This suggests the need for greater training, so that those responsible for upholding the law do not fail in their duty to protect vulnerable young people whose lives are in danger, regardless of cultural traditions. They also need to be able to address issues of racism in ways that encourage them to interrogate the norms of a different culture with sensitivity. It is important that 'culture' is not considered as a unitary entity, so that practitioners can explore cultural differences within and between groups and countries.

Additionally, 'honour killings' may be better described as instances of men's violence against women as they seek to defend patriarchal authority over family members who wish to assert personal autonomy, regardless of age. Violence against women occurs in all societies, and as such is resisted by those who support women's struggles for autonomy. Sometimes these endeavours are high profile, at other times they are not. Moreover, such attacks are opposed by members of the same communities as well as those outside them (*CBC News*, 2008b). Such resistance demonstrates that it is possible to develop alliances that cross social divides if those involved support action that is initiated and controlled by those seeking change.

## International action in the welfare arena integrates the local and the global

International action to address issues of poverty, migratory movements, communicable diseases, and the mobilization of local resources to address local problems has involved social workers, their organizations collaborating with other civil society organizations and governments to change policies and development practices to reflect more closely the views of people on the ground in a wide range of issues. Much of this action was linked to participating in various UN summits, organizing seminars, presenting papers and promoting policy changes. Two important highlights were the Copenhagen Social Development Summit of 1995 and the Beijing Action Platform for Women in the same year.

The Millennium Development Goals (MDGs) formed another UN policy initiative that required intensive involvement by social workers and community workers. The MDGs were formulated in 2000 to carve out a more prosperous future for the most disadvantaged people on the planet and targeted poverty, education and health (www.un.org/millenniumgoals/). Eight goals targeted specific actions and specific groups of people with the aim of setting achievable outcomes. Sadly, this looks unlikely (Correll, 2008). In some respects, the challenges of environmental degradation question the relevance of the MDG targets. The financial crisis that precipitated the virtual collapse of the global banking system has highlighted the weaknesses of international institutions when it comes to handling global problems.

That the heaviest price is exacted from poor people has become abundantly obvious. Public expenditure cuts are taking place in personal social services and welfare provision aimed at providing poor people with education, health and income support in order to bail out the financial sector and bankers. This occurred via the structural adjustment programmes of the 1980s and 1990s in the Global South and the financial crisis of 2007–9 in the Global North. ICSW has engaged in monitoring the developments and is pessimistic about the realisation of the MDGs. Despite the weaknesses in the global economic system, and critiques of their implementation to date (Correll, 2008), the latest UN report predicts that the MDGs could be reached by 2015 if governments put enough resources behind their realization (UNDP, 2009). Monitoring their progress and impact on the ground is something in which social workers can be fully involved.

## The internationalization of social problems

The formation of the MDGs could be considered a response to the internationalization of social problems. The 'internationalization of social problems' (Khan and Dominelli, 2000) is a by-product of globalization processes that encourage people to migrate in response to social problems such as poverty, armed conflict, drought and natural disasters. It is also the result of the growing interdependencies between countries. In other words, the internationalization of social problems provides pivotal points at which the global impacts on the local and the local impacts upon the global. However, social work is usually enacted at the local level because that is where people lead their lives.

Sometimes, what constitutes the local is contested and problems become even more difficult to resolve. This can occur, for example, in cases of child abduction, when a parent takes a child to another country – generally that of the parent's origin. The processes that can be followed to recover the child depend on whether or not the country in question is party to the Hague Convention on the Civil Aspects of International Child Abduction (Hague Convention) of 1980. The UK is a signatory. The return of a child can become very complicated if the country in question has not signed the Hague Convention or is an Islamic country in which sharia law prioritizes the father's rights over those of the mother.

Nations that are party to the convention are called 'contracting states'. A parent who removes a child from another parent living in a 'contracting state' without due process of the law is required to return that child immediately. Regardless of a country's status regarding the Hague Convention, fighting to get a child back can be a costly and painful process for all those concerned. During 2008 in the UK, 336 cases of child abduction involving 470 children were reported to the authorities. This figure may underestimate the numbers involved, as not all instances are reported and most do not make newspaper headlines. In the 336 reported cases, 134 children were taken to countries that had not signed the Hague Convention. Among the children removed from the UK in 2008, thirty were taken to Pakistan, twenty-three to the USA, twenty-two to Ireland and twenty-one to Spain.

In the UK, the Foreign Office deals with cases involving countries that have not signed the Hague Convention. Signatory countries are dealt with by the Ministry of Justice in England and Wales and the Scottish and Northern Irish court services in Scotland and Northern Ireland respectively. The charitable organization International Social Services also assists parents seeking the return of their children, as does Reunite, an agency specializing in international child abduction. Both organizations have reported substantial growth in such actions, with Reunite claiming that international child abduction cases have risen by 93 per cent since 1995. Their spokespersons link the growth in this phenomenon to increasing migration and relationships being formed between those of different cultures (Pidd, 2009).

What may happen in disputed situations is evident in the case study in box 7.2, where a child born in Britain was taken to Libya, a non-signatory to the Hague Convention. Had the convention applied in both countries, the UK would have been treated as the locality with which the child was associated, especially as the mother already had custody. Sharia law is likely to recognize the father's country of origin as the relevant locality. However, this did not occur in this particular situation.

---

*Box 7.2 Case study: Father abducts Nadia Fawzi*

Nadia Fawzi was a four-year-old British child abducted to Libya, where her father's family lived. Following her parents' divorce, she was taken from her home in Wigan by her father, Fawzi Abu Arghub, on the pretext of going to a party. Instead, she was taken to Manchester airport and then on a flight to Libya. Her mother, Sarah Taylor, a white British national, has spent the last two years fighting to get Nadia back. The British courts had already awarded her custody of the child when the marriage broke down. After a year of making no progress, Sarah gave up her job, sold her house and went to Libya to fight her case through the sharia courts. After a lengthy legal struggle in that country, she successfully secured full custody of her daughter in 2008. Unfortunately, her ex-husband refused to comply with the court order and, as his and Nadia's precise whereabouts were not known, the child remained with him in Libya for three years.

Meanwhile, Sarah Taylor's MP, Andy Burnham, had gone to Tripoli to plead on her behalf and to insist that the court's ruling was enforced. In 2009, Gordon Brown asked Colonel Gaddafi to assist in the mother's reunification with her daughter when the two leaders met at an economic summit in Italy. Finally, with the help of Gaddafi and his son Saif, among others, Sarah and Nadia were reunited in December 2009 and the two returned to the UK in February 2010. There are now issues of Nadia's readjustment to being back in the UK and the thorny question of retaining links with her father and his extended family to be addressed. The 'best interests of the child' remain paramount in child abduction cases. However, Nadia's predicament indicates that the matters raised in the interstices between the local and the global cause much pain and are not easy to resolve.

Social workers can support mothers (or fathers) and children through a trying legal process and help with family reunification and/or reconciliation initiatives. They should also be aware that social problems such as these that intersect the local with the global acquire political significance and ramifications as well as causing personal pain and suffering.

Such cases of abduction are fraught regardless of the situation, and often involve children in complex dilemmas not of their making, especially if the parents part on acrimonious terms. It can lead to confused emotions, mixed loyalties, feeling responsible for what has happened and a deep sense of grief and loss (Freeman, 1998). Sometimes the children are denied contact with the absent parent for years – a likely outcome if parents are playing power politics with their children's lives, or if one party moves away, making it difficult to maintain contact (Jenkins, 2006). Social workers may have considerable difficulties in establishing the 'facts' of a situation, even if they achieve contact with both parents, and they may have to ascertain what happened without face-to-face meetings. Additionally, with the internet, new dilemmas may present themselves. For example, an African American woman put her children up for adoption on the internet and sold them to both an American couple, for £4,000, and to a British one, for £9,000 (BBC, 2001). The children ended up in Britain and were taken into care when the American couple complained that they were the first and only legitimate parents. Social services in both England and America had to step in to resolve the matter and consider the relevant local, national and international regulations and legislation. In the end, the children were taken back to America and given to foster parents. The birth mother sought to have them returned to her, but it was not until she had remarried and changed her lifestyle that she was given access to visit their foster home (Langton, 2005). Ironically, the British couple had resorted to the web because they had been unsuccessful in being accepted as adoptive parents. Buying or selling children is illegal in the UK, but the internet allows people to bypass the necessary safeguards for children.

Another problem with international adoption is exemplified by the recent scandal of an American mother sending back a young boy she had adopted from Russia on a flight by himself. She sent a letter with him saying that he had too many problems for her to deal with and that she wanted the adoption annulled. The Russian authorities were incensed because their social workers had approved the adoption, as did those in the USA. The American social workers who undertook follow-up procedures did not detect any problems in the relationship between the mother and child. Consequently, the Russians have called a halt to any further adoptions by Americans for the time being (Stewart, 2010).

The spread of diseases across borders is another instance of an internationalized social problem. Panics have already occurred around this issue in relation to SARS and HIV/AIDS. A more recent example is 'swine flu', or the H1N1 virus, which officially reached pandemic proportions (WHO, 2010). Internationalization is evident not only in the journey that a disease takes in moving from one country to another – a likelihood that occurs more quickly in an era of cheap, rapid airplane travel than at other periods. But speed is also evident in scientific cooperation to trace the movements of the disease, looking for strategies of curtailment and seeking cures. Despite its global dimensions, treatment is administered locally, and the costs of such treatment – whether preventative or curative – are borne locally. This localization makes it difficult for low-income countries or individuals to sustain the costs of treating viruses that can quickly get out of hand, create chaos in everyday routines and cause enormous loss of life. As a result, concerned individuals, including social workers, have:

- highlighted such issues as poor people's lack of access to medicines;
- lobbied large pharmaceutical companies to lower their charges for medicines;
- mounted campaigns both to bring about change in policies and the distribution of medical supplies and equipment, particularly antiviral drugs, to avoid unnecessary loss of life and to encourage the use of local indigenous medical knowledge when this is more effective; and

- offered advice and counselling to people in need, including in rural areas, often using imaginative means of communications such as radio to do so.

The campaign to bring anti-viral drugs to tackle HIV/AIDS in countries in sub-Saharan Africa is indicative of such endeavours.

## Neo-liberal globalization impacts on social work

Neo-liberalism and globalization have impacted on professional social work by making it more complex, increasing connections across borders and introducing problems that have international implications, e.g., international adoptions. Such developments are fuelled by people seeking opportunities to make money, often illegally, and those migrating from one country to another to achieve better standards of living, to escape persecution, and/or to flee armed conflict. Migration and the internationalization of social problems, including human trafficking and the drug trade, complicate local scenarios, as discovered by the social workers who were unable to protect Toni-Ann Byfield.

Toni-Ann was abducted as an infant in Jamaica by her father Bertram Byfield (aka Anthony Pinnock) and brought to England. She was shot at the age of six by Joel Smith in a London bedsit on 14 September 2003 because she saw him murder Byfield, whom she was visiting. Smith, a member of a London street gang, like Byfield, was involved in an international drug ring. Toni-Ann, whose immigration status was in doubt, was under the care of Birmingham City Council's Social Care and Health Directorate and in temporary foster care when she joined her father in London. Her mother, 'Rosyln' Richards, was in Jamaica, but came to England after her daughter's death when questions about the identity of the child's birth father surfaced.

The complex relationships and trends evident in this case simultaneously constitute, expose and magnify the interdependent nature of people's lives as they cross borders. They reveal the impact of global factors on local practice and how local events have a global impact. Social workers also have to respond to the reconfiguration of national boundaries as problems originating elsewhere are brought their way in the interstices of micro-practice – as occurred in Toni-Ann's short life. Other examples can emanate from working with people of diverse ethnic origins, those caught up in wars and intensified armed conflicts, asylum seekers and refugees, and undocumented workers, as well as from diseases that cross borders (e.g., HIV/AIDS, SARS and swine flu), the exploitation of children and women in the drug and sex trade, and transnational adoptions, as is indicated in box 7.3.

---

*Box 7.3 Case study: International trafficking endangers children*

Vladimir had been smuggled into England with the promise of a new life. But unknown to him or his family at the time, he had been trapped by a paedophile crime ring that subjected him to sexual violence and exploited him to make money. He was deprived of his passport and contact with his family, who were in any case being threatened with his death if they did not pay for his passage overseas, and was being coerced into performing for his captors by being told that, if he refused to obey, members of his extended family would be harmed or even murdered. This meant that Vladimir lived in a constant state of fear. The risks would be too great if he were to challenge his situation. However, after several years he developed a relationship with an older man who bought him out of his bondage and with whom he went to live. After what seemed an interminable period, Vladimir had the chance to escape, but he had no money and no friends to turn to. So he walked into a hostel for homeless men to seek help.

---

The case study in box 7.3 exposes the complexities involved in the ways in which the global and the local interact to reshape each domain. Dealing with children and young people in Vladimir's situation is highly skilled, sensitive work and not to be undertaken by those who are newly qualified. There are a number of resources upon which practitioners can draw to help them in the complicated interventions needed to respond to a child's needs. These include psychological support to deal with the emotional trauma and damage caused by being exploited, providing the financial and physical resources required to begin rebuilding their lives, family reunification if appropriate and possible (given the intersection between their existence and that of criminal gangs) and, dependent on age, engaging them in educational programmes and peer interactions. Multi-agency working will be essential in developing the appropriate plan for safeguarding a child such as Vladimir and creating a safe environment in which he can grow. This will involve not only the usual agencies such as psychological services, the NHS, education departments, the criminal justice system and the courts, but also immigration services. Helpful resources to be drawn upon include *Breaking the Wall of Silence* (Pearce et al., 2009), *London Safeguarding Trafficked Children Toolkit* (LSB, 2009) and *Safeguarding Children Who May Have Been Trafficked* (DCSF, 2007).

Regional developments, which are blurring the borders that have been used to articulate the confines of the nation–states, form an important element in models of practice that cross national borders, or even when skilled practitioners do. The European Union, the Association of Southeast Asian Nations, the North American Free Trade Agreement and the Latin American Integration Association provide examples of organizations that have been established to transcend national frontiers. Many of the agencies that enable goods, services and personnel to move across territories are predicated on ideas that valorize market imperatives over people's needs, but the EU, for one, allows its nationals to access welfare rights in other member countries.

The thrust towards market-based developments has been exacerbated by international regulations and multilateral agreements, including those associated with the General Agreement on Trade in Services (GATS), which threatens to undermine the empowering effects of social work education and practice and to promote private or commercial provision in personal social services and social work education in all countries. These establish trends that challenge the idea that social work is a parochial profession dealing only with local issues. Such developments are in addition to the profession's attempts to raise its voice internationally, as described in chapter 1.

Social workers as worker-practitioners are not immune from global processes either. Many may find that, having qualified in one country, they will practise in another (White, 2007). This raises questions about the recognition of qualifications acquired in a country other than the one in which a social worker practises, and what is common in social work training and what is locality specific and different. It also highlights the importance of practitioners learning about local cultures, practice traditions, legislation and policy, and how they are assisted to adjust to the demands of their new positions. Neo-liberal globalization has also brought market discipline into social work at the local level. As a result, it has supported demands for increased professional accountability, client choice (at least in theory), the bureaucratization of 'risk assessments' and managerial control of the labour process.

## Migratory labour forces

Globalization has shrunk the world and made migration an even more widespread phenomenon. The reasons for migration are varied and pose different responsibilities for the nation–states involved. The migration of skilled, professional workers is deemed less problematic than that of unskilled labourers. For example, business people who create jobs are welcomed with open arms in the West (Lester, 2010). Asylum seekers, like unskilled workers, are often defined as economic migrants rather than as fearing for their lives. Thus, they undergo punitive procedures and are often confined in detention centres (Cohen et al., 2004; Briskman, 2007). Migratory movements are also linked to 'terrorism', as individuals move about the world to be 'trained'. Social workers are implicated when called to engage with harsh immigration processes and legislation that excludes a range of migrants from claiming welfare assistance. Racial profiling as a part of border control exacerbates the situation by drawing innocent people into a net intended to capture criminals. The 'Christmas bomber' who attempted to blow up a plane headed for Detroit in December 2009 provides an example of the kind of journeys 'terrorists' take to disguise their objectives and avoid capture. After such people are arrested and have completed their sentences, the question arises of what needs to be done to rehabilitate them and reintegrate them into society. This is an issue in which probation officers can be involved. There are only a few such programmes and what little research there is suggests that these are of limited use (Neumann, 2009; Champion, 2010).

At the same time, the instruments for controlling those who cross borders have become more sophisticated and surveillance-oriented, particularly through the new information technologies. While in the early nineteenth century it was not even necessary to have a passport to travel from one country to another, today's travellers are required to prove that they are entitled to enter a country either by virtue of citizenship or by holding a valid visa. Moreover, machine-readable passports containing detailed personal and biometric information are rapidly becoming the norm. Such instruments of control and surveillance are also 'fixing' identities in a world that would promise personal choice and multiple, fluid identities. As such, the use of these technologies serves to normalize particular attributes associated with specific territories and peoples, making difference less acceptable where migration status and claims to place and space interact. Such trends are particularly evident in discourses around the need for 'homeland security' initiated by the so-called war on terror and the racialized profiling aimed at identifying 'terrorists'.

Moreover, the concern to protect borders and deny access to welfare benefits to those defined as non-citizens or 'other' has resulted in immigration control filtering down to professional practice. Social workers are being asked to check people's passports for their immigration status before giving them help. Immigration control has therefore shifted from being a practice that is enacted by immigration officers at the point of entry to one that can now take place at an 'internal' border that is policed by caring professionals. Moreover, it can be set up at any point where public agencies seek to respond to individual requests for assistance. This creates a fusion of the public and the private that leaves many social workers feeling distinctly uncomfortable, not only because they become involved in a form of surveillance that goes against their professional remit to care but also because they are unable to meet visible need, and they feel constrained by rules and regulations that do not make sense to them as helping practitioners. They feel compromised by having to ration resources in ways that pit the needs of long-standing residents against those of more recent arrivals (Dominelli, 2004a).

Cultural and educational exchanges and the use of the internet and distance learning materials have meant that internationalizing practices are becoming more common and involve a broader range of institutions. Private corporations, such as McDonald's, have established their own 'universities' to ensure that the local people they employ are trained to create their standardized products. Local traditions and expectations about either education or service delivery are rarely accepted, further intensifying the cultural homogeneity that accompanies globalization.

The education of social workers in developing countries retains an element of idealism and the potential for introducing change through social and community development that will enhance the well-being of local people. In industrialized countries, people are more likely to become jaded and simply consider the job as a way of earning money. As a result, migrant workers from the Global South may find their experiences as social workers in industrialized countries are more narrowly focused, and they may become less inclined to think innovatively (Sithole, 2008). The move away from innovating to improve the quality of life for poor and marginalized people in the West suggests that the dynamism reflected in the enormous community work efforts in postwar Europe, the Community Development Projects in the UK and the 'War on Poverty' in the USA (Dominelli, 1997) has been lost, and that social work practice in the Global North has become more bureaucratic and less concerned with social development and change than that in the Global South. Contemporary challenges to the existing configuration of social relations are likely more muted in the Global North. Yet the need for emancipatory changes and action aimed at eradicating structural inequalities and social exclusion may be just as great in both hemispheres.

## Social workers as a mobile, migratory, professional workforce

Professional workers are increasingly likely to acquire qualifications in one country but to work in another, possibly at several different points in their careers (White, 2007; Sithole, 2008). Such movements mean practitioners are part of a transnational phenomenon of people holding allegiance to several locations simultaneously. Moreover, transnational arrangements are likely to augment the potential of social workers both to learn from different cultures and to contribute their own insights and understandings to other practitioners. Such transfers of knowledge should not be assumed to be equal or to indicate parity of exchanges between those involved. Equality has to be worked for and action taken to ensure that it becomes embedded in these relationships rather than being presumed *a priori*.

An interesting feature is that the current trend is primarily one of professional social workers from low-income countries being employed in the West. These workers are highly educated, and in many instances are already familiar with the relevant social work models, language and culture. This is a result of the longstanding tradition of social work being conducted overseas by former colonial powers and the role of the media and globalizing institutions in promoting Western models of professionalism throughout the world. At the same time, the failure of industrialized nations to produce enough qualified social workers to meet their own demands, or to engage in serious workforce planning, challenges employers, educators, practitioners and policy-makers to develop more appropriate approaches to this thorny issue, including compensating sending countries for the loss of their trained personnel. Western governments often utilize agencies for recruitment purposes, ostensibly to reduce employment costs for the state. These agencies can be poorly prepared for the tasks involved and may undermine the well-being of those they encourage to migrate (Devo, 2006).

Specific campaigns aimed at attracting qualified social workers, often at Masters' level, have been mounted by both the state and private recruiting agencies in Canada, India, South Africa and Zimbabwe, among others. These have been crucial in enabling some local authorities to meet their statutory responsibilities towards children and older people. For example, Essex County Council recruited scores of social workers from Canada in the 1990s, and Birmingham City Council brought seventy-two social workers from Zimbabwe. At one point, about 50 per cent of Zimbabwean trained social workers were working outside their own country (Devo, 2006). Some of these workers stayed for several years; others settled permanently in the UK and developed careers in the profession (Sithole, 2008). Several individuals have also applied for posts independently of external recruitment drives (personal communications).

The preparation for these recruits – planned induction programmes and subsequent training – was not always fully thought out. Consequently, many migrants found that they had to rely upon each other, and particularly their fellow nationals already in the country, for assistance. For example, Zimbabweans in Birmingham formed the Zimbabwean Social Workers' Network to help them gain the confidence and support that they needed to make the best use of their skills in an unfamiliar country (Sithole, 2008). The concerns expressed by many in the profession about the failure of the authorities to address these issues at the outset ultimately became incorporated in the government's Social Care Code of Practice for International Recruitment. However, this response is inadequate. Although it addresses some of the concerns about the processes used in recruiting overseas workers, it fails to deal with those linked to career progression and the implications of taking large numbers of trained personnel from countries that are themselves desperately short of skilled professionals. It also begs the question of the chronic under-training of social workers in the UK, which has been evident for decades, but which successive governments have failed to address. Social work is not the only profession that is experiencing these dilemmas. The health professions, particularly nursing and medicine, have a longer history of recruiting overseas professionals without putting in place the necessary infrastructure and mechanisms of support (Buchan and Seccombe, 2006).

Lack of preparation and training for these newly recruited overseas workers to join those already in the imperial heartlands of the West included not welcoming them into their new posts, not finding appropriate housing before their arrival, not holding induction and training classes in agency procedures and cultures, and not ensuring the bases for career progression afterwards. Their absence may be seen as encouraging predatory practices that appropriate the skills and knowledge held by individual professionals who are detached from their social contexts. Each social worker becomes a free-floating agent able to make their own decisions about where they might find employment without the necessary safeguards being in place to facilitate their migratory journey, to handle the transitions involved in becoming settlers, and to promote their development as employees. Sending countries with little control over the export of labour find that they lose considerable numbers of their skilled personnel, as was the case with Zimbabwe, when half of its skilled social workers relocated to one English city (Devo, 2006).

India, South Africa, the Caribbean and Pakistan have similar experiences, with their most skilled workers in a range of professions moving to the West. Silicon Valley in California has benefited enormously from the influx of migrant labour, from India in particular, and companies have been able to augment their own pool of knowledge and skills and maintain a competitive edge in the information technology industry. Remittances sent to countries of origin can be substantial. For example, Sri Lankans overseas contributed £2.9 billion in 2008 and £3.3 billion in 2009 (www.disasporajourney.com). Polish workers in the UK, Sweden and Ireland sent back a total of €6.4 billion, or 2.5 per cent of GDP, in

2004. Most of this money went into consumer spending linked to extended family needs, and led to an 11.9 per cent rise in retail sales (www.workpermit.com), rather than contributing to the wider development of the country's economy (Small, 2007). While this pattern does help lift people out of poverty, it does not compensate for the resulting skewed development or to fill the ensuing gaps in the workforce of the sending country.

A substantial number of continental Europeans have been attracted to work and study in Britain. Since 2004, 380,000 Eastern Europeans have registered for National Insurance numbers (McSmith, 2007). Many of these workers have entered the social care sector. However, the financial recession in the UK and the growth of the Eastern European economies has led to a decline in this source of labour, which threatens the potential of care homes to operate effectively (Kelly, 2008). Eastern European migrants are particularly numerous in residential homes for older people. Addressing the serious shortage of trained staff in the statutory sector has also been helped by Britain's imperial links (Sithole, 2008). It is hard to obtain precise numbers, but estimates suggest that one in ten social workers in the UK is from overseas. This figure may be misleading because it includes people who are British citizens born abroad. Interestingly, the migration of professionals to work in different parts of the world is seldom remarked upon by public commentators.

Ruth White (2007) describes her own personal journey as a transnational social work migrant who has practised in the UK, Canada and the USA. Alongside the issues of meeting immigration requirements – the tediousness and expense of progressing through the formal processes – she highlights the importance of possessing friends with local knowledge and support networks, knowing people who are willing to offer practical help at short notice, and having the ability to work effectively and professionally even while enduring extremely stressful conditions. In some ways, her experience reveals the fragmented nature of the transnational journey for individual migrant workers.

Migratory movements also expose the need for social workers to practise some of their skills on themselves. This could take the form of an international network of social work support for migrant practitioners and academics that could be brought together under the auspices of both IASSW and IFSW. The two organizations could develop high-quality, well-informed services for which individuals might be willing to pay and thus generate income that could be ploughed into further assistance for migrant workers. Such a network could provide help to ensure their well-being by requiring employers to have the appropriate facilities and resources in place when the newcomers arrive; aiding them to settle into local communities by linking them up with social workers already embedded in the community; and supporting them in their career progression. There are instances of local self-help initiatives being taken, such as the Zimbabwean Social Workers' Network in the UK (Devo, 2006), but these local initiatives cater only for the needs of a specific and localized group and do not link up to international organizations to build a wider cache of knowledge. Another difficulty is that local organizations formed spontaneously by migrant workers, such as the network referred to above, are under funded and may not have the capacity to sustain their growth and development over the long term (Sithole, 2008).

The European Union perhaps displays the most organized trends concerning the migration of professionals. As a result of the development of the single market in goods and services, the EU has issued a number of directives based on various agreements and treaties that carry direct implications for professional education and training, including that of social work. Crucial to the EU's deliberations have been the Bologna Process and the Lisbon and Maastricht treaties to bring harmonization in professional qualifications, the recognition of qualifications obtained in one country in another, and the potential for students to begin their studies in one location and complete them elsewhere. What is advocated is a Bachelor's degree of at least three years' duration at undergraduate level, a two-year Master's award at post-graduate level and a three-year PhD at doctoral level. Most EU countries are seeking compliance with these requirements, although there have been criticisms. For example, the Nordic countries, which had four-year undergraduate degrees, have complained that standards will be reduced (Juliusdottir and Petersson, 2003). Portuguese social work educators have made similar claims (personal communications).

Additionally, the Bologna Process has promoted the use of the European Credit Transfer Scheme (ECTS), which has sought to standardize teaching systems. The take-up of ECTS and the use of the Diploma Supplement providing a description of a student's studies has been patchy (Dominelli, 2007b). However, an important aim of these endeavours was to make it easier to have 'portable' qualifications that would be readily accepted in any European country, and in turn to facilitate labour mobility.

The EU has put funding into its drive to harmonize education and ensure that European models acquired currency both within and beyond its borders. For example, the Erasmus programme aims to facilitate staff and student exchanges, while Tempus projects seek to make Western European knowledge readily available to Eastern Europeans, a move that was particularly important for those countries seeking a smooth transition between communist and market-based societies. The EU has cooperation programmes promoting staff and student exchanges in Canada

(TEP), the United States (Atlantis), South Korea, Japan, Aotearoa/New Zealand and Australia (ICI) and funds research involving Asia, Latin America and Africa as well as North America.

All these programmes promote a variety of projects and exchanges. It is usually left to the individual applicant to apply their ingenuity in meeting the relevant funding criteria. Important questions to consider are the following:

- What projects?
- How many projects (per funder and per institution)?
- How many individuals and institutions are to undertake the exchanges?
  - With whom?
  - For how long?
  - Under what conditions?
- Can equality in the relationships between individuals and institutions be maintained?
- What funding is available under what conditions and for whom?
- How can these projects be sustained in the longer term?
- What formal exchange agreements, visa requirements and other preparations are needed?
- How can students be supported when they are overseas so as not to disadvantage them vis-à-vis students who remain at home?

Interestingly, many of these exchanges are being conducted in English, and so the dominance of the language is not being challenged. The EU does fund translation services for some activities, but these are expensive and so often limited in scope, applicability and duration (Dominelli, 2004c).

While these initiatives transcend the borders of the nation–state, they also reinforce national boundaries, as agreements are made between specific institutions and a minimum number of countries have to be included for a project to meet funding requirements. There are also geographical and other anomalies that arise. Countries bordering the Mediterranean have traditionally been less involved in these activities than those in Northern Europe. Additionally, the limited amount of funding provided means that older students with family and caring responsibilities are less likely to participate (Dominelli and Thomas Bernard, 2003). And, because demands for funding outstrip supply, calls for projects have become increasingly competitive, and many good projects, particularly those that are more adventurous, are not funded. There are more projects from the physical and computing sciences that have obtained funding than those in the arts and humanities, for example.

## Conclusions

Globalization has subjected the local to forces that have prised its boundaries open and brought external influences to bear upon it. At the same time, the local has impacted upon the global to alter perceptions of both. The many connections that exist between the two have impacted on social work practice as well as on all other aspects of social, economic, cultural and political life. The profession has become a global one, with tensions between an imperializing mission and that of working with others in egalitarian relationships. The indigenization movement serves as a constant reminder that those from the West have to maintain vigilance over their actions and those of their governments and institutions if they are to become allies in the struggle to maintain locality-specific forms of practice and ways of knowing and doing in the world.

Globalization has opened up opportunities for social workers to train in one country and work in another. While there are issues to be addressed concerning the recognition of qualifications across borders, the preparation that receiving countries need to have in place for overseas recruits, the training and support migrants need to progress in their careers, and reparations to be made to sending countries for the personnel that they have trained, labour mobility among professional groups can enrich the profession.

# 8

# Conclusions

## Introduction

Social work is a profession in flux. In the UK, it has delivered innovative and much needed forms of and reforms in practice to deal with intractable issues such as child abuse, sexual assaults, domestic violence, and deviancy, and it has advocated locally, nationally and internationally for social justice. These endeavours have sought to address both personal and structural inequalities and the failure of social organizations, institutions and governments to respond adequately to people's needs.

At the same time, concerns about individual empowerment, community development, interprofessional collaboration and the nature of links to the international domain continue to be raised, indicating that much remains to be done on all these counts. Knowledge is always limited or partial and particular. Knowledge creation and its distribution is a constantly evolving and unfinished process in social work, as elsewhere. However, the commitment to issues of citizenship, human rights and social justice provide a thread of continuity between past, present and future aspirations for social work to become a profession that is considered relevant and effective in responding to people's needs. Doing so draws on a holistic approach to the world that both encompasses and explores the spiritual, the physical and the social dimensions of human existence at the local, national and international levels (Dominelli, 2002a).

I conclude this book by exploring those elements of theory and practice that can be developed further for social work to continue to make a difference to people's lives, enhance their well-being, and advocate for changes that will promote more egalitarian social relations within and between countries while simultaneously paying attention to environmental considerations. Crucial to promoting such endeavours is finding ways of engaging people fully in the design, delivery and administration of personal social services at the local level and enabling them to take advantage of the opportunities to learn from practice elsewhere. I will argue that community social work, initially supported by Roger Hadley and his colleagues (1987) and the Barclay Report (Barclay, 1981), offers a way forward, despite its failure to gain substantial funds and other forms of government support. Additionally, by describing a community social work initiative that I am supporting in a deprived community in a Northern English city, I suggest that the insights from theories that engage with the concepts of social development and social capital can be useful in adapting Hadley's model of community social work to the realities of contemporary practice.

The education and training of practitioners is another important dimension in the process of developing new theories and forms of practice. I consider the implications for curriculum development, both in the academy and in practice settings, of social work being a professional discipline that is recognized across the world and capable of being a relevant player in policy arenas at the local, national and international levels. This is a demanding task that challenges social work educators and practitioners to think about what they have in common or what they can share with others while ensuring that these commonalities are not being imposed on reluctant peoples; identify what is different among them so that local people can engage with their aspirations, the traditions of their locality, and contexts in which their interventions are embedded; and make links between the structural and personal dimensions of social relations when initiating action to change them. In following this path, I advocate both the eschewing of depictions of reality that separate theory from practice and vice versa and a refocusing on the complexities and uncertainties that arise from constantly evolving outcomes. Additionally, such action has to encompass people acting individually and collectively. I also suggest that facilitating emancipatory change will involve the profession as a whole in contemporaneous processes at both individual and collective levels. These include:

- addressing both the structural and personal dimensions of oppression;
- contextualizing interventions socially, culturally, politically and economically;
- the reclamation of locality-specific knowledge;
- reciprocal knowledge exchanges;

- mutually enhancing learning opportunities;
- multidisciplinary and interdisciplinary working in partnerships of many stakeholders;
- the development of egalitarian social relationships; and
- mobilizing professionals and communities individually and collectively.

## Problematizing knowledges: the search for egalitarian educational processes

Knowledge and education have been and can be used to promote imperialistic ventures (Haig-Brown, 1988). In a globalizing world where internationalizing institutional and professional practices have become a feature of everyday life, education can encompass new forms of exploitation whereby individual institutions, particularly universities in the West, establish 'satellite campuses' to promote their particular brand of teaching and learning and fail to acknowledge local expertise, recognize local resources or respond to local needs. Overseas universities have a choice. They may refuse to engage with locally generated knowledges and curricula and attempt to enforce their own pedagogic processes, or work with local people through egalitarian partnerships to develop an innovative fusion of the two traditions. The development of locality-specific educational processes and practices would necessitate their doing precisely the opposite – that is, treat local actors with respect and dignity and as capable of participating as full partners in knowledge creation and dissemination.

Egalitarian forms of cooperation combine the best from both parties to create reciprocated forms of knowledge that address both structural and personal issues and enable local people to reclaim their own expertise and have it valued by others from overseas. From an emancipatory perspective, social work's response to the issues raised by globalization has been slow. However, there have been authors in various parts of the world – including myself – who, while appreciating its positive contributions, have been critiquing globalization for its deleterious impact on people, especially those who are already marginalized and disenfranchised, and its unhelpful impact on practice.

Indigenous peoples have spent the last 500 years resisting European colonization, with education or knowledge exchange as a potent weapon in this process (Simpson, 2008). Resistance was their way of problematizing the knowledge presented as superior by colonizers (Grande, 2004). The development of alternative ways of being and doing has emerged from such resistance and enabled native peoples to survive, regardless of the coercive and oppressive measures imposed by European rulers (Grande 2004; Siggins, 2005). They responded to imperialistic ventures by retaining, and later reclaiming, local knowledges and establishing 'circles of resistance' (Dominelli, 2006b).

Today, this resistance is aimed at celebrating indigenous knowledges and limiting the homogenizing tendencies of globalization, neo-liberalism and neo-colonialism (Razack, 2002). Responding to local people's agendas enables exchanges of reciprocated knowledge and mutually enhancing learning opportunities to encourage the development of egalitarian partnerships, and the 'indigenization of the social work curriculum' has become a significant trend in the international arena (Grande, 2004). Teaching and learning is collectively passed on through the generations and needs to engage with the spiritual, physical and relational aspects of life. It also has to be mutual and reciprocated learning (Bruyere, 2001, 2009; Green and Thomas, 2007; Cyr, 2007) rather than following the didactic processes espoused in the Western 'banking' system of learning opposed by Paulo Freire (1972) and Alfred North Whitehead (1929), among others. I have been personally aware of and engaged in these struggles since the 1970s.

*Love and Wages*, the first book I wrote – years before it was published – arose from my doctoral studies and encompassed a critique of globalization for the destruction it wrought on industrializing countries. In the 1970s, I used the terminology of the international financial system (Dominelli, 1986) because the term 'globalization' came into popular usage later. *Love and Wages* was an empirical analysis of how poor men and women working in the former settler farms of Algeria were being exploited by a global system that appropriated their lives and resources, in the fullest sense of this word, in exchange for a pittance. Relationships in the extended family and community ties enabled them to survive despite the revolutionary struggle that had led to Algeria's emancipation from French colonial rule (hence the title). The analysis in the book drew on an article that was published in 1974. Since then, the insights that I have gained have been invaluable in helping me understand social work theory and practice from a variety of perspectives. They have also been influential in giving my writings a richness and depth that would otherwise be lacking. Helping to get the Algerians' story known is but a minuscule contribution to the liberation struggles of many of the world's people.

I prefer to continue the practice of problematizing the term 'indigenous'. Thus, I describe indigenous teachings as the celebration and further development of locality-specific knowledges because, although particular groups of people have sought to reclaim the word, 'indigenization' has been and continues to be devalued by being associated with imperialist ventures and white supremacists. Additionally, given the lengthy period of human migration predating written records and the considerable amount of historical interaction among and between peoples, it is no longer clear, in some parts of the world, who or what is 'indigenous' in the sense of being the first group to lay claim to a particular territory. Nor does it accord with scientific findings indicating that all human beings are migrants who descended from common ancestors in Africa (Johanson, 2001; Wolpoff et al., 2001).

Another concern is that 'indigenization' as a term has been appropriated by far-right parties, including the British National Party in the UK, to argue that *they* represent the 'indigenous' people of their lands and to exclude people who are ethnically and culturally different from them (Casciani, 2009). In such disputed contexts, promoting the growth of locality-specific knowledge and developing curricula that are culturally appropriate, create egalitarian and reciprocated learning opportunities (Dominelli, 2007a) and display mutuality in exchanges (Razack, 2002) is both a challenge and a responsibility that ought to involve all social work educators and practitioners.

Moreover, the concept of 'the West' has to be problematized to unpack its heterogeneity and reject the externalization of those deemed 'non-Western' who are already present in the West but are not accepted as equal partners because they do not belong to or form part of the local dominant hegemonic group. This rejection is a reality for increasing numbers of people in today's multicultural Western societies whose origins are non-European. As I put it in a lecture I gave in Ann Arbor, Michigan, in 1998, 'the international is here, and not to be externalized as out there' (Dominelli, 2003).* Interrogating the concept of the West will also identify resistance there to the practices that Said (1978) termed 'Orientalism', or the 'othering' of those who were configured as different from Westerners and the valuing only of Western imperialist ways of thinking.

This involves the emancipation of the West from its own internal forms of structural inequalities. Responding to such challenges will be a substantial undertaking and beyond the capacity of any one profession, including social work. However, as part of the sphere of 'the social', social workers have a role to play in identifying the issues, helping to give problems a name, working with people interested in promoting egalitarian social change, and acting as allies engaged in promoting

---

* This paper, entitled 'Anti-Racist Social Work and International Social Work', was a keynote address that I gave at the conference on Culturally Competent Practice in International Social Work at the University of Michigan and published as Dominelli (2003).

inclusive, citizenship-based forms of practice. Crucial to dealing with the range of inequalities evident in the West itself is confronting those who would maintain the status quo. Such people refuse to eliminate existing inequalities so that they can retain their privileged positions. Becoming professionals who can support indigenization and other movements as trusted allies is important in maintaining social workers' heterogeneous strengths and ethical integrity (Bishop, [1994] 2001).

In a plenary address delivered at the IASSW and IFSW World Congress in Washington, DC, in 1992, I warned about the dangers of the entry of Western educators into Eastern Europe and the tendency to 'McDonaldize' social work by giving rise to a standardized product and assuming that 'one size fits all'. This homogenizing approach is not restricted to universities (Dominelli, 1996a; Ritzer, 2000). Private providers may also thwart the profession's egalitarian aspirations and desire to retain its extensive heterogeneity and pluralistic structures.

While acknowledging the variety of trends in social work, I have challenged the idea that there is an 'international social work' other than as an activity of individuals and information crossing national borders. If international social work is simply doing elsewhere what one does at home, it is unlikely to be appropriate in a new locale (Dominelli, 2000). I also argue that the theories and practices that could effectively explain what *international* social work might be have yet to be developed. I still maintain that position, although there are tentative beginnings in unpacking the term and changing direction. The writings of Lynne Healy (2001) and Karen Lyons and her colleagues (2006) are indicative of such work. Although the concepts of empowerment, social justice and human rights can assist, the task of developing an international social work that is clear on what gives the profession a basis for unity within diversity remains to be achieved.

Abye (2001, 2003) has questioned the unproblematic usage of the term 'international social work' and argues that it is the West that needs to internationalize by learning to appreciate the contributions that other peoples in the world have made to human civilizations, knowledge and learning. Moreover, he has shown that homes in the Global South are being bombarded by the globalized media (Abye, 2007) and has demonstrated that internationalization is a two-way process. People whose origins are in the Global South will impact upon and shape the Global North through their presence, the retention of valued cultural traits from their countries of origin and the maintenance of links with their ancestral lands. At the same time, they draw on social traits and various forms of organization that they have learnt in the West to influence and change behaviour among their extended families and their countries of origin. This interactivity reflects the exercise of agency and reflexivity and the right of people to change their lives on their own terms. Agency is not the prerogative of privileged groups in any society (Dominelli, 2000) and is an essential ingredient in the development of theories aiming to describe and explain what constitutes international social work, as indicated by Healy (2001).

In my view, what has been happening in the international arena is that a number of people are using the opportunities offered by networking to engage in conversations and explore practices that might give the profession the tools for working collaboratively in egalitarian and life-enhancing ways. The IASSW and IFSW have been crucial in facilitating such exchanges in education and practice, primarily through conferences and curriculum development workshops. Those taking part have been acutely aware of the dangers of neo-imperialism, and debates within the organizations have sought to address these within a framework that values equality (Sewpaul and Jones, 2004). This is articulated by Vishanthie Sewpaul, chair of the IASSW Committee on Global Standards: 'The global standards document is characterized by flexibility with an overarching and embedded human rights and social justice emphasis, yet with a simultaneous emphasis on historical, socio-political, economic and cultural context-specific realities' (Sewpaul 2005: 213).

The IASSW–IFSW documents exemplify the potential of such networks to bring together the heterogeneous community of social work educators and practitioners across the world to identify general areas of agreement. Flexible guidelines could be formulated to assist them in promoting the development of locality-specific curricula for both the academy and the field (Sewpaul and Jones, 2004). As these documents are *guidelines*, intended to be used as the actors involved see fit, and as they are *abstract*, their meaning is configured when they are applied in the specific contexts in which they are being considered.

There is no external force imposing its views of what to do upon local actors. The IASSW and IFSW documents can easily be ignored. To assume that people in other countries cannot make decisions for themselves is intellectually arrogant. Such a presumption also ignores the capacities of agency and social capital held by people who, despite being marginalized, resist and challenge oppressive social relations. Dominant groups also configure people with marginalized identities as passive and silent. Those cast in such a light strongly resist such representations in myriad ways (Grande, 2004).

I take issue with Webb's (2003) assertion that there is 'a burgeoning globalization agenda in social work' because it simplifies the existing situation. There is not one overriding agenda in social work. Rather, there are *many* agendas, some of which seek to replace globalization with alternative social arrangements and some which support it. Focusing

only on those that support a homogenizing tendency is somewhat disingenuous and reifies globalization as a unitary phenomenon when this is not the case. Its spread is patchy, and the inequalities it produces are highly differentiated (Cambridge and Thompson, 2001). As chapter 6 demonstrated, some people, particularly in the West, gain more than others from globalization. Moreover, today's patterns are not fixed in stone, but are shifting as the ink dries on this paper. The non-West is already in the West; and the non-West, both within and without, is challenging the West's current supremacy.

Webb (2003) argues that social work is on an imperialist mission. This assertion rests on rocky foundations. He *mis*interprets an article by Khan and Dominelli (2000) based on empirical research conducted in Southern England to explore the failure of the profession to investigate the implications of globalization on practice *in that particular part of the world*. The title, 'The Impact of Globalization on Social Work Practice *in the UK*' (emphasis mine), highlights this point. The article exposed the huge split in how practitioners and managers experienced the impact of globalization on *day-to-day practice in their own localities*. This locality-specific study is not the stuff of which empire-building dreams are made. There are those who would use social work to subjugate other disciplines and peoples, and this has to be guarded against. However, any such charge has to be carefully substantiated and documented in the manner illustrated by a number of authors, including those such as Sarah Grande (2004) writing from an indigenous perspective.

Critiques undertaken across the West reveal a variety of analyses of globalization and heterogeneity in how its hegemonic stance is expressed (Sklair, 1991; Martell, 2010). Globalization's diversity is also reflected in understanding its impact on social work (Ramon and Zaviršek, 2009). Webb (2003), among others, makes several points that are worth reiterating. These are the significance of context in creating the 'situated self', the links between the local and the global, and recognizing the embedded nature of knowledge. These are multi-layered and fluid concepts that cannot be taken as either given or homogeneous, even in a specific locality or within a particular individual. Change occurs at these levels at all points of contact with other people and when individuals reflect upon their own actions. Moreover, this reflective approach is what Schön (1987) argues forms the basis of effective social work education and practice.

The nation–states of the West can no longer assume a continued economic and political dominance (Pramanik, 2000). Dividing this planet into the 'West' and the 'Rest' has become a highly dysfunctional concept that cannot help in finding new solutions to old, intractable problems, including those that the West created in the first instance. Furthermore, this binary belies reality as lived by those designated as 'Other' because they have always retained their own ways of seeing, knowing and doing in and thinking about the world (Collins, 1990), regardless of whether they are accepted by those occupying privileged positions. If an egalitarian world is to be realized, there has to be a decentring of the West (Nayak and Selbin, 2010) that does not create another hegemonic centre.

Some of the earliest critiques of neo-liberal globalization came from scholars, researchers and practitioners in Latin America. Unlike Webb, they did not hold the IASSW responsible for organizing the profession as a monolithic bloc, crushing all before it. Although Webb's allegation is serious, the idea that a loose, under-resourced network of educators with one part-time paid member of staff is capable of dictating an imperializing agenda, and imposing it on a disparate profession, stretches credulity. Latin American scholars did not ignore the many statements and actions made by the IASSW and its sister organisations to denounce unjust policies and promote egalitarian relationships among educators and practitioners across the world. Nor did they discredit their support of the development of locally inspired forms of practice and pedagogic processes.

For example, at the prompting of IASSW colleagues, my first attendance at an IFSW congress was in Stockholm in 1986 to hear Paulo Freire (1972) speak about his energizing conscientization approach to practice, developed in Latin America. Freire had already inspired social work educators in the UK to take it upon themselves, i.e., to exercise agency, to *adapt* (not adopt) his understandings for use. Those of us working with Peter Leonard at Warwick University had been aware of his translated works since the mid-1970s, despite extensive opposition from a range of employers and academics who argued that we had nothing to learn from those outside the British mainstream tradition. Also, in the 1990s the IASSW set up a Task Force on Indigenous Social Work. This never took off as a forum used by indigenous social work educators, but it brought First Nations and Maori social workers together in its conferences, one of which 'Beyond Racial Divides', led to an edited collection of that name. The IASSW also opposed the closure of the Maori social work course at the University of Victoria in Aotearoa/New Zealand. Webb's attack is unfair to those in the West who have struggled to resist attempts to homogenize social work education and practice.

Latin American critics of globalization identified the powerful unaccountable elites and multinational capitalist corporations that exploited workers and appropriated the earth's resources to maximize their own profit-making opportunities, including in the welfare arena (Netto, 2006, 2008). This was unusual at the time, as globalization was seen to be delivering only good things, although this benign view is currently being undermined by the current financial crisis and questioned further by researchers (Vickers, 2009). In addition, the 'West' is not homogeneous, although it is sometimes convenient to treat it as a monolithic entity. Power relations within it are highly differentiated, and there are a variety of positions adopted by the different nation–states, as well as diverse histories, cultures, traditions, political systems and welfare states to be considered. The 'West' is an artefact that has been and is being configured in relation to and in interaction with those that are excluded both from it and by it. As such, it can be constituted in ways that ignore one's own positionality as part of the West (see, for example, Webb, 2003), its plurality and the complex range of responses to globalization that are embedded within it.

Egalitarian educational processes are interactive or negotiated, taking account of where participants are at as a basis for then exploring the wider world from their vantage points. It is used to understand one's own position and that of those being educated, learn from their position and move on to new insights. Social work educators have a responsibility to encourage the development of curricula that focus on interactions between people rather than making assumptions from their own fixed positions about what should happen, often in advance of the contributions of others.

## Community social work: linking a local initiative with the global through holistic practice

As I argued in chapter 7, community social work may provide an interesting way of building on existing theories and the ideas expressed above to bring together understandings of and engagement between the global and the local. I consider how this might be done in the case study in box 8.1 below.

Community social work was advocated by Barclay (1981) and Roger Hadley and his colleagues (1987). It was practised actively in Normanton in West Yorkshire in the early 1980s (Hadley and McGrath, 1980) but did not take off nationally as a model for practice despite its enormous potential to engage practitioners working in disadvantaged areas in supporting people to assume control of their lives and communities. The reasons for this were never fully explored, but I suspect that the Thatcher government's determination to privatize the welfare state was a crucial factor behind it.

The New Labour government followed in the same tracks, as it did not support the idea of autonomous, independent-minded professionals working with residents to enable them to mobilize in pursuit of their own goals. It favoured instead the bureaucratic forms of community involvement (Pattison, 2007; Popple, 2007) that formed part of the New Deal for Communities, set up in 1998, and the Sure Start initiative, begun that same year. Both programmes intervened at the community level, but encouraged top-down forms of intervention that assumed people simply wanted to take as given the terms on which they could become involved. The New Deal also aimed to help unemployed adults get back into paid employment, usually low paid or casual, while Sure Start sought to get children to make better use of the opportunities that the state placed their way. Useful though they were, both emphasized individual self-sufficiency, not structural inequalities.

I suggest that the concepts of social capital, networking and social development that have been popularized since the 1980s offer insights that can be used to revitalize community social work and bring out the enormous potential that the latter holds to re-energize run-down communities and reactivate people in creating their own options in life and to address structural inequalities through collective action. It also draws on some of the partnership ideas of the 1990s to bring different stakeholders together to work for the welfare of everyone in a community, however it is defined – because community is a contested, fluid and constantly changing social construct (Delgado, 2000; Hardcastle et al., 2004; Dominelli, 2006a, 2006b). To involve residents in locality-based collective action that they have initiated, it is important to be context specific and embedded in the complex social relations and geographic or spatial positions within which communities are configured (Naples, 1998).

## Social capital in community social work

Social capital was a concept popularized by Robert Putnam (1993, 2000) to describe the ways in which communities networked with one another – within communities through bonding capital and across communities with bridging capital. Bonding capital was deemed a strength of those who developed connections with others like them within the same family and community. Bridging capital were the ties that people formed with others in the wider community, who could be different but had to share the same geographic space, goals and ambitions. For Putnam, this included membership of civic organizations that promoted democracy. His writings were critiqued for neglecting the multiple dimensions of identity. Edwards (2004), for example, suggested that women accessed social capital differently from men and emphasized its relational basis. Goulbourne and Solomos (2003) felt that Putnam did not see the strengths of people from minority ethnic groups in developing networks that created forms of social capital that often transcended national borders.

Woolcock (1998) developed the idea of linking social capital. This meant extending the concept beyond different communities into the wider world and emphasizing relationships that brought diverse peoples together. In theory, linking capital can be conceptualized as bringing the local, national and global levels of society into interactive tension. These may be creative and positive or negative and frustrating. Others have criticized Putnam for being pessimistic and conservative in his views of what happens in society, ignoring the different ways in which social capital can be created, including through the internet and virtual spaces, and seeing social capital as a fixed entity that bypasses political relationships and the role of power relations in society (Vickers, 2009). By going beyond Putnam, a dynamic, more complex and political understanding of social capital can be useful in enhancing community capacities and mobilizing people at the local, national and international levels.

Social development has been defined by the Brundtland Commission (WCED, 1987) as 'development that meets the need of the present without compromising the needs of future generations to meet their own needs'. This seems a good approach to community development (Midgley et al., [1986] 1996) because it places the onus on communities to formulate their own sustainable solutions to the problems they face. It also expects them to act both collectively and in solidarity with each other in the present and intergenerationally, to link with those who have yet to be born.

Capacity building is another useful concept in developing the idea of community social work (Delgado, 2000) and building on existing strengths. Capacity building refers to the training of individuals to engage in developing organizations to serve their aims and also to grow personally. Planning is essential in building capacity in an empowering and egalitarian manner so that no one person or community exploits another in the process.

## Holistic understandings and interventions

To hold all these threads together, a community social worker who is trying to mobilize a community needs to engage in processes similar to those indicated in the cycle of intervention considered in chapter 3 and do so in a holistic manner, as indicated in figure 8.1. The processes of intervention include investigation, assessment and planning, developing the collective action plan, implementing the action plan, evaluating the action plan, reflecting critically on the action undertaken and the theories

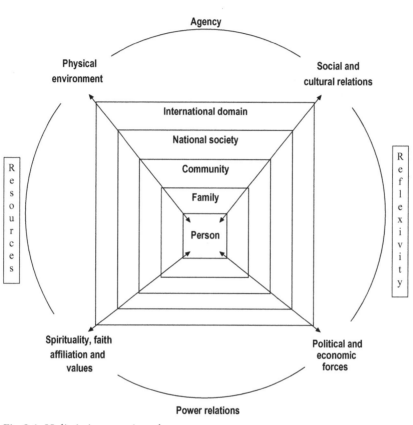

Fig 8.1  Holistic intervention chart
*Source*: Dominelli (2002a).

underpinning it, reassessing the interventions, being accountable to the community for the actions taken (or not taken) and being monitored by its members, and then beginning to rethink the situation to develop further plans and actions.

Empowerment and equality are essential values for social workers interested in co-developing a community with residents. Their interaction is also one that co-creates knowledge. In other words, what is required is the expertise of both the residents, who have expert knowledge of their own community, and the social worker, who is probably better connected and more knowledgeable about formal power structures and the resources that are available and can be channelled to enhance sustainable forms of social and community development.

Figure 8.1 shows the importance of straddling multiple layers and dimensions when engaging in critical, reflective action to bring about transformative social change in a community. It highlights the significance of finding connections while not losing sight of the divisions between different people and systems relevant to any specific situation.

A critical, reflexive, holistic approach to practice enables social workers to become allies in acts of resistance to the logic of the market, which has elevated an economic order managed for the benefit of the few over social life, human need and the planet (Bourdieu, 1998). Coupled with notions of citizenship, social inclusion, empowerment, and social, cultural, political and economic rights vested in all people, holism enables practitioners to keep tabs on the different threads that compose the complex situations in which they are expected to intervene.

The case study in box 8.1 illustrates such a strategic positioning of social work practice. It indicates that it is possible to understand the way in which both local and global relations are connected as part of an integrated whole, and where change in one element can have profound implications for another. It also requires a holistic form of community social work.

---

### Box 8.1 Case study: Community social work transverses the local and the global

Fuel poverty is a big issue in marginalized and deprived communities in the UK. Fuel inequalities in these locations are exacerbated by low incomes, often linked to the loss of blue-collar jobs in heavy manufacturing industries. An initiative in a small part of a city in Northern England drew on the principles of community social work to address inequalities in access to energy by bringing renewable sources of energy within the reach of poor people. The aim was to co-produce knowledge and action by pooling their knowledge with that of experts with the relevant technical skills and to empower local people by acknowledging their expertise, especially in their everyday life practices, and then enable them to take action and solve their problems.

Various local residents had identified fuel poverty and low incomes as issues on this estate. A community social worker who was asked to assist in solving these problems did so by bringing together in a working group a combination of stakeholders – local residents, an interdisciplinary team of academics and students from the local university, practitioners from a range of professions including social work, policy-makers, housing providers, and private businesses investing in micro-generated renewable energy sources. Their aim was fourfold – namely, to reduce levels of fuel poverty and address fuel inequalities, enable local people to access renewable energy sources and thereby reduce their overall carbon footprint, provide sustainable employment opportunities, and, in the process of achieving these goals, become involved in co-producing knowledge and addressing intractable social problems through collective action.

The working group held several public meetings where residents considered the options open to them. These included learning how to reduce the energy they consumed by insulating their properties, using only the energy that they needed for specific purposes; monitoring energy consumption for particular activities; being informed of the range of grants and other forms of assistance available to enable them to access renewable energy technologies that would otherwise be beyond their purchasing power; and linking them to local entrepreneurs and national enterprises that were willing to manufacture renewable energy products locally to provide employment opportunities. They were also offered energy audits and provided with free equipment to reduce energy consumption – low-energy light bulbs, energy monitoring gadgets and renewable energy materials.

This enthused the residents not only to begin adapting their own homes but to convert some of their public buildings to low energy consumption, thereby reducing fuel bills. And they embraced the idea of manufacturing clean technology and green energy products, such as inflector 'curtains', in their local community to reduce their carbon footprint further. Ultimately, it is hoped that this initiative as a whole might lead to a self-sustaining energy community which would be able both to save enough energy to feed back into the national grid and to manufacture green goods for the wider society.

Although the local MP was supportive of the initiative, there was no money or input from government. The project began with only the support of the community social worker, who was central in developing capacity and social capital – bonding, bridging and linking – to form connections between people who normally seldom spoke to one another in order to realize their common objective of 'making a difference' by enhancing community well-being.

## Dialogical interactions between the local and the global

The case study demonstrates how the local and the global interact with each other. A local problem – fuel poverty – can be resolved by being linked to a global issue – reducing greenhouse gas emissions caused by burning fossil fuels. This approach becomes dialogical or interactive through feedback loops that connect structural issues and personal hardship. This example shows how consumer choices in energy consumption are restricted by insufficient levels of income to pay for energy-saving devices and green technologies and how structural inequalities such as unemployment, low benefit levels, low incomes, and tariff structures of higher charges for those on prepayment meters penalize those in disadvantaged communities (CAB, 2005).

Moreover, the interdependence of players and geographic levels can encourage the local production of renewable energy products to contribute to reductions in local carbon emissions. If this local initiative is successful, the community can manufacture clean technology products that can be sold to reduce carbon emissions elsewhere. In doing so, it will demonstrate how the local and the global interact in ways that can produce win–win situations for everyone. The model can be adapted for use elsewhere, as it challenges social workers to think about local social problems in global terms and to try and solve them in ways that do not cost the earth in terms of their demands on the environment.

## International cooperation and reciprocated relationships

Collective action has been a major driver of change within nation–states. The formation of the United Nations was an attempt to create the basis for collective action among what were considered equal sovereign nations. The creation of consensus in securing compromises to reconcile different interests has facilitated the formation of more egalitarian relationships between countries. These have not been easy to achieve and have usually been linked to specific objectives. Agreement over issues is constantly being (re)negotiated. The sovereignty of nations was treated as sacrosanct until recently, when the 'right of humanitarian intervention' was introduced to ensure that countries abided by their duty to uphold the human rights of their nationals (ICISS, 2001). However, intervening is tricky and requires the agreement of the UN Security Council – as occurred in Bosnia and Afghanistan.

Although certain players, particularly those permanent members of the Security Council, may seek to retain dominance, they are constantly being challenged in how they use the power and advantages that accrue to them. Different groups are continuously jockeying for privileged positions. Thus, flux and change are major ingredients in the international sphere. Nonetheless, despite the UN's noble aspirations, many forms of inequality remain. The orgnization has been unable to gain support for or develop mechanisms that would eliminate income inequalities within nation–states, let alone between them, to provide decent living conditions for all of the earth's inhabitants, to protect the physical environment from rapacious exploitation or to enforce the observance of the human rights that have been formally agreed as having universal applicability.

## Global interdependence, universalism and global citizenship

Terms such as 'universalism' and 'citizenship' have had a troubled history in social work. In the UK, they were initially used to signify equality, but this was an equality that neglected the differentiated social relations and the privileging of some people over others. Universalism was therefore subjected to critique for subsuming identities and the privileging of certain groups.

This critique was articulated among those who developed feminist perspectives (Hanmer and Statham, 1988; Dominelli and McLeod, 1989), anti-racist and black perspectives to practice (Dominelli, 1988; Ahmad, 1990: Graham, 2002) and the social model of disability (Oliver, 1990; Barnes et al., 1999). These authors argued for recognition of these differentiated realities and their meanings for the people they affected alongside the elimination of the privileging of the dominant groups. And oppressed groups worked with others for equal opportunities legislation, e.g., the Sex Discrimination Act of 1973, the Race Relations Acts of 1965, 1968, 1975 and Race Relations (Amendment) Act 2000, and the Disability Discrimination Acts of 1996 and 2006.

Those in the new social movements also demanded that people be treated as equals, and that their rights to services should not be withheld simply because they had crossed a national border or resided in a geographic location that divided people into included and excluded groups. A crucial element in their arguments was the view that people also had much in common, and that both commonalities and differences needed to be identified and addressed, rather than be presumed. Their writings did not assume that the commitment to universal principles was a prerogative of the West. Their views were more inclusive and focused on what human beings shared or had in common within and across the borderlands of whatever description, whether imagined or real, while not losing sight of their differences. These borderlands became configured as significant spheres of action for all oppressed people who had been consigned to the margins of society. The spaces that populated the terrain of 'the social' encompassed these borderlands and provided for alternative ways of thinking, knowing, being and acting, to flourish. At the same time, those in the new social movements argued that good practice was ethical practice, without suggesting that only Western ethics prevailed.

*Redefining citizenship*

Citizenship has been defined as the status that accords each individual dignity alongside human, social, political and welfare rights. It is deemed inclusive although it excludes, by definition, those not 'belonging' to a particular territory. Thus, the concept can be both inclusionary and exclusionary. Citizenship practices, or the mechanisms and processes whereby individuals claim their entitlements as citizens, occur within the boundaries of the nation–state. How these are expressed, controlled and accorded to those claiming entitlement depends on the definition a country uses to define its citizens.

The concept of citizenship is extremely problematic because there are various forms of exclusionary practices in nation–states, even within dominant social groups formally considered citizens. For example, in the UK, Dominelli (1991) and Lister (1997) have critiqued the state's inability to provide equal citizenship for women and minority ethnic groups. This concept becomes even more complicated when applied to marginalized groups who are discounted by society, such as the First Nations of Canada, the Maori of Aotearoa/New Zealand, and newly arrived immigrants, for example Iraqi refugees seeking asylum or social workers in the UK recruited from Zimbabwe.

Rooting notions of citizenship within the nation–state also results in its becoming a barrier encountered by growing numbers of people on the move, as they can no longer access services to which they are theoretically entitled in their countries of origin. In short, taking this step results in their being defined as non-citizens or aliens and therefore not the responsibility of the country in which they find themselves. Yet they may have paid taxes and social insurance contributions in their home country. And so the question arises, Why should they lose these rights, especially the social and welfare rights that would enable them to begin life afresh, simply because they have crossed a border? The reply in a globalizing world must be that existing ideas about citizenship need to be problematized and deconstructed so that the concept can be redefined in more inclusionary terms. The UDHR might be one vehicle that can assist in this task.

*Realizing global citizenship*

Despite its shortcomings, the UDHR has been signed and ratified by most countries in the world. It can thus provide a platform from which to reformulate the notion of citizenship. Realizing this objective poses considerable challenges, among which is ensuring that all countries implement the provisions of the UDHR in its entirety. This would necessitate remedying the UN's lack of powers of enforcement. A reformulation of citizenship rights would also require the international community to assume responsibility for enabling all nation–states to implement the provisions of the UDHR, especially Articles 22 to 27 covering income support, the personal social services, health and education. Achieving this goal might also require the transferral of resources from wealthy to low-income countries and could be a major obstacle in itself. Some nation–states might see this suggestion as infringing their rights to national sovereignty.

The UDHR specifies the rights of citizenship – human, civil or political and social – that have been agreed by all members of the United Nations. One major drawback in the UDHR's potential to initiate change is that it currently locates citizenship rights within autonomous nation–states. As a result, citizenship rights may be violated regularly because their realization is fractured along lines of race, ethnicity, gender, ability, class and age and experienced differently by both individuals and social groups within a particular nation–state, and the international community has not acted against such violations. Nor does it enforce their realization when countries plead lack of resources, although each nation–state has power to require individuals to contribute to the funding of these services by paying national insurance contributions, buying private insurance premiums or otherwise being covered by national provisions. Although the UDHR applies human rights to the individual on a universal basis, those that might involve public funding (as do the social and welfare rights covered by Articles 22 to 27) are not portable outside the borders of the particular nation–state that accepts a specific person as its citizen or national. As these rights are lost when an individual crosses those national borders and enters the territory of another country, the current conceptualization legitimates the loss of individual rights rather than deeming them as inalienable, as is suggested in theory by the fine rhetoric contained within the UDHR. This problem is not insurmountable. As the UDHR embeds citizenship rights in individuals, this could become the basis for transcending this limitation. The universalism inherent in the UDHR treats citizenship rights as inalienable rights. Therefore, they should be portable, i.e., go with individuals wherever they go. If these rights can be accepted as inalienable and portable, then it would be possible for an individual to retain them when crossing national borders.

The issue of individuals losing rights simply because they cross national frontiers could be resolved if this particular exclusion could be reworked to enable nation–states to accept the idea that individuals never lose any rights. This would require all UN member countries to accept the portability of rights. Such agreement would be easier to secure if all countries complied with the requirements of the UDHR and the international community ensured that all those living within the borders of any particular nation–state were covered. Under these conditions, vesting these rights in the individual would make portability feasible.

Once the idea of the inalienability and portability of the rights of an individual citizen is accepted, then the issue becomes not one of recognizing an individual's citizenship rights, but one of who pays for the services that are linked to the enjoyment of those rights. To address this problem, I would postulate that the nation–state from which a person originates has the responsibility to ensure that these rights remain inalienable and portable. At the same time, the country that a person visits or where they reside has an obligation to recognize and assist in the realization of these rights, whether or not that person acquires citizenship. If this state provides these services, these could be itemized and an invoice sent to the individual's country of origin for payment. Alternatively, nation–states could agree to recognize the rights of each other's nationals through a set of bilateral or multilateral agreements. In this way, citizenship becomes global and associated with the individual rather than being linked to a nation–state, as has occurred within the European Union.

Citizenship obligations and responsibilities are one side of the coin in universal notions of the rights of citizenship; state duties to meet citizenship entitlements are the other. Both are in tension (Bellamy and Castiglione, 2008). The challenge of a universalism based on realizing the same rights and entitlements for all of the world's peoples without addressing different and often unequal starting points, and with a focus on implementation rather than conception, presents a different conundrum (Abye, 2001).

Another complication is that the Bretton Woods international institutions responsible for facilitating social development through monetary polices – the World Bank and the International Monetary Fund (IMF) – have had a history of endangering social and economic development in many parts of the world by imposing various policies that undermined welfare states and social provision, as did, for example, the structural adjustment programmes of the 1980s. These actions destabilized many regimes, especially in Africa (Hoogvelt, 2007). A similar danger is currently evident in Greece, as it restructures its economy to comply with IMF and European conditions imposed in order to receive funds to refloat its national debt.

The Bretton Woods institutions, initially formed to bring economic stability to the international domain, need to be changed. They had originally pegged currency rates to the price of gold. This practice was ended during the economic crisis of 1967, when the British pound was also replaced by the American dollar as the currency for determining international transactions. Perhaps it is now time for the world to begin to plan for an international currency that all can share – i.e., one that is not linked to any existing nation–state or regional bloc, and one that calculates people's earning power in terms of how long they have to work to purchase a particular commodity. If all economies could be brought into line, the wages for paid work could be set at levels to which all nations could adhere, and the prices for all goods could be standardized across the world, it might make the inalienability and portability of citizenship rights across borders a more attractive proposition. This state of affairs already exists for citizens living in the federal states of Canada and the United States of America.

The social rights specified in Articles 22 to 27 of the UDHR are of specific interest to social workers because they cover education, health and the personal social services. How citizenship is defined is central to social work practice and raises important questions for consideration in an interdependent world where there is constant movement among populations. What are the implications of citizenship status for practice? What knowledge, values and skills do practitioners need to work across the exclusionary boundaries of citizenship as it is currently defined in most nation–states?

If the above proposals were implemented, social workers could play a key role in assessing need, delivering services and seeing that the relevant nation–state is invoiced to ensure payment is obtained. In this way, practice would become more inclusive and the individual citizen would never lose rights to services simply as a result of crossing a border. This could be considered global citizenship in the inclusive sense of the term. It would be embedded within the nation–state, but transcends its borders with ease and ensures that need would be met wherever it occurs. It would also guarantee that social solidarity underpinned considerations about people's welfare, individuals experience their interdependence on each other as a source of support, and reciprocity and mutuality provide the foundation on which nation–states relate to one another. Redefining citizenship in these terms would also mean that universalism would not be about making all people and all societies the same, but about ensuring that every person on the planet had an equal and unquestioned access to the abundance of the earth and the benefits that humanity's organization of social relations can provide.

## Moving social work in new directions

Social workers have an incisive role to play in advocating for a world that is rooted in equality, human rights and all-inclusive forms of citizenship.

They can become allies in various struggles for liberation and the elimination of structural inequalities that impede human growth and development. Such alliances can oppose oppression, be holistic in scope, and act as potent sources of innovation. Social work educators and practitioners can become involved and promote such activities at all levels, from the local to the global. At the international level, they can use existing networks linked to the IASSW, IFSW and ICSW to enable them to be represented in and work with international organizations such as the UN and its associated agencies, which are already working to eradicate inequalities. And they can offer alternative solutions to those problems that have evaded equitable and mutually acceptable solutions for far too long.

## An agenda for social work action

Social workers in a globalizing world have to rise to the challenges of the twenty-first century by becoming involved in a wider range of activities that prevent the undermining of people's well-being. They can do so by being informed about the social, political and economic realities that impact on their practice; widening their understandings of these regardless of the setting or territory in which they are located; and broadening the scope of the curriculum so that it addresses issues that arise in the interstices between the local and the global and supports the development of locality-specific social work. This includes:

- undertaking research to provide the evidence for their practice and the development of existing paradigms of practice;
- exploring both the commonalities and the differences between various groups when working to solve social problems;
- learning from the diversity and variety that exists in social work practice throughout the world;
- bringing marginalized areas of practice into the mainstream, particularly those linked to indigenous knowledges and new areas of endeavour, such as disasters resulting from climate change;
- lobbying for changes in national and international policies that can support human rights and universal citizenship-based entitlements to services; and
- enhancing training to take account of the more complex issues that current practice faces, notably those involving the internationalization of social problems.

This agenda for action is rooted in what I call the 'politics of practice', in which social workers engage with others in activities that will change inegalitarian social relations. The 'politics of practice' involve the 3Rs of recognition, representation, and redistribution of resources. Recognition focuses on the strengths of the people with whom practitioners work. Representation is about helping individuals and communities to represent their views and aspirations to power-holders and decision-makers and lobbying them to eradicate exclusionary practices. The redistribution of resources is about ensuring that the earth's largesse is distributed equitably across all peoples in the world and obtaining the evidence that substantiates the need for this. Social work practitioners and educators can rise to the challenges emanating from the promotion of egalitarian, life-enhancing practices that respond to the needs of a twenty-first century beset with multiple social problems by being innovative, aware of both local and global contexts that impact on their practice and sensitive to the complexities of a world in which mutuality, reciprocity and solidarity with those in need provide the foundation for serving others.

# References

Abhat, D., Dineen, S., Jones, T., Motavalli, J., Sanborn, R., and Slomkowski, K. (2005) 'Cities of the Future: Today's "Mega-Cities" are Overcrowded and Environmentally Stressed', www.emagazine.com/view/?2849 (accessed 2 May 2009).

Abye, T. (2001) 'Universalism and Citizenship in France', in L. Dominelli, W. Lorenz and H. Soydan (eds) *Beyond Racial Divides: Ethnicities in Social Work*. Aldershot: Ashgate.

Abye, T. (2003) 'International Social Work: A Project for Whom?' Paper given at the Council of Social Work Education 49th annual programme meeting, Marriott Hotel, Atlanta, 27 February–2 March.

Abye, T. (2007) 'Ethiopian Migration: Challenging Traditional Explanatory Theories', in L. Dominelli (ed.) *Revitalising Communities in a Globalising World*. Aldershot: Ashgate.

Abye, T. (2009) 'Ethiopian Migration and Social Enterprises', lecture given at the social work seminar in Durham University, School of Applied Social Sciences, 9 March.

ACHSSW (Australian Council of Heads of Schools of Social Work) (2006) *We've Boundless Plains to Share: The First Report of the People's Inquiry into Detention*, www.safecom.org.au/pdfs/peoples-inquiry-first-report.pdf (accessed 21 August 2009).

Adams, R., Dominelli, L., and Payne, M. (2009) 'Introduction', in R. Adams, L. Dominelli and M. Payne (eds) *Critical Practice in Social Work*. 2nd edn, London: Palgrave.

Addams, J. (1914) *Twenty Years at Hull House*. New York: Macmillan.

Agnew, E. (2004) *From Charity to Social Work: Mary E. Richmond and the Creation of an American Profession*. Champaign: University of Illinois Press.

Ahmad, B. (1990) *Black Perspectives in Social Work*. Birmingham: Venture Press.

Allen, V. (2009) 'Boy 16, Arrested after Muslim Woman's Lover is "Forced to Drink Acid"', *Daily Mail*, 24 July; www.dailymail.co.uk/news/ (accessed 21 January 2010).

Amin, S. (2009) 'The Limits of Liberal Orthodoxy: A Critique of the Stiglitz Report', *Pambazuka News*, www.pambazuka.org/en/category/features/58453 (accessed 2 January 2010).

Anti-Globalization (2010) http://en.wikipedia.org/wiki/Anti-globalization_movement.

Appleyard, B. (1993) 'Why Paint So Black a Picture?', *The Independent*, 4 August.

Athwal, H. (2003) 'Close Surveillance of Campsfield Protest', *Institute of Race Relations News*, 3 December; www.irr.org.uk/2003/december/ha000006.html (accessed 2 June 2008).

Attlee, C. R. (1920) *The Social Worker*. London: Library of Social Science.

Axford, Y., and Smol, J. (2009) 'Arctic Lake Sediment Record Shows Warming, Unique Ecological Changes in Recent Decades', http://www.colorado.edu/news/r/fa189a8186a324d8f62b5d55ba4b8969.html (accessed 12 December 2009).

Babington, C. (2010) 'Obama Calls for Tighter Controls of Derivatives', *The Guardian*, 14 April.

Bader, M. (2009) 'The Government's Carbon Off-Set Scheme is a Scam' in *The Vancouver Sun*, 26 October.

Bagnell, K. (2001) *The Little Immigrants: The Orphans who Came to Canada*. Toronto: Dundurn Press.

Bailey, R. (1982) 'Theory and Practice in Social Work: A Kaleidoscope', in R. Bailey and P. Lee (eds) *Theory and Practice in Social Work*. Oxford: Blackwell.

Bailey, R., and Brake, M. (eds) (1975) *Radical Social Work*. London: Edward Arnold.

Barclay, P. M. (1981) *Social Workers: their Role and Tasks*. London: National Institute for Social Work [Barclay Report].

Barker, H. (1986) 'Recapturing Sisterhood: A Critical Look at "Process" in Feminist Organisations and Community Action', *Critical Social Policy*, 16: 80–90.

Barlett, D. I., and Steele, J. B. (1998) 'Corporate Welfare: Special Report', *Time*, 9 November.

Barnard, A., Horner, N., and Wild, J. (eds) (2008) *The Value Base of Social Work and Social Care*. Milton Keynes: Open University Press.

Barne, E. (1999) 'People Smuggling is a Good Business', *Time*, 22 November.

Barnes, C. (2001) ' "Emancipatory" Disability Research: Project or Process?' Paper presented at a public lecture, City Chambers, Glasgow, 21 October.

Barnes, C., Mercer, G., and Shakespeare, T. (1999) *Exploring Disability*. Cambridge: Polity.

Barnes, G. (2009) 'Australia's Harsh Approach to Refugees', *Vancouver Sun*, 3 November, p. A15.

Barretta-Herman, A. (2005) 'A Re-Analysis of the IASSW World Census 2000', *International Social Work*, 48(6): 794–808.

Barretta-Herman, A. (2008) 'Meeting the Expectations of the Global Standards: A Status Report on the IASSW Membership', *International Social Work*, 51(6): 823–34.

Bashir, H. (2009) *Tears in the Desert: A Memoir of Survival in Darfur*. London: One World/Ballantine.

BBC (1999) 'German Opposition Challenges Citizenship Reform', 6 January, http://news.bbc.co.uk/1/hi/world/europe/249541.stm.

BBC (2001) 'Overseas Adoption: Is it Just Children for Sale?' 25 January, http://news.bbc.co.uk/1/hi/talking_point/1122107.stm (accessed 19 June 2009).

BBC (2010) 'History of Immigration', http://news.bbc.co.uk/hi/english/static/in_depth/uk/2002/race/short_history_of_immigration.stm (accessed 20 April 2010).

Beck, U. (1992) *The Risk Society: Towards a New Modernity*. London: Sage.

Beckett, C. (2001) 'The Great Care Proceedings Explosion', *British Journal of Social Work*, 31(3): 493–501.

Bell, S. (2009) 'Cargo Ship Passenger Wanted in Sri Lanka for Terrorism', *Vancouver Sun*, 23 October, p. A8.

Bellamy, R., and Castiglione, D. (2008) 'Beyond Community and Rights: European Citizenship and the Virtues of Republicanism', in P. Mouritsen and K. Jørgensen (eds) *Constituting Communities*. London: Macmillan.

Bent-Goodley, T., and Sarnoff, S. (2008) 'The Role and Status of Women in Social Work Education: Past and Future Considerations', *Journal of Social Work Education*, 44(1).

Beresford, P., and Croft, S. (1993) *Citizenship Involvement: A Practical Guide for Change*. London: Macmillan.

Beveridge, W. (1942) *Social Insurance and Allied Services: Report by Sir William Beveridge*. London: HMSO.

Bingham, J. (2009) 'Honour Killing: Mehmet Goren Tried to Murder his Family Before', *Daily Telegraph*, 18 December; www.telegraph.co.uk/news/ (accessed 21 January 2010).

Bishop, A. ([1994] 2001) *Becoming an Ally: Breaking the Cycle of Oppression*. Halifax, NS: Fernwood.

Blaikie, P., Cannon, T., Davis, I., and Wisner, B. (2004) *At Risk: Natural Hazards, People's Vulnerability and Disasters*. 2nd edn, London: Routledge.

Blair, D. (2009) 'More than a Billion Hungry Worldwide', *Vancouver Sun*, 15 October, p. B5.

Bourdieu, P. (1998) *Acts of Resistance: Against the Tyranny of the Market*. New York: New Press.

Brand, D. (2009) *Nick Stacey and Kent Social Services*. Faversham: privately pubd.

Bridge, A. (1992) 'Britain Attacked for Ignoring Bosnia Refugees', *The Independent*, 17 July.

Briskman, L. (2003) *The Black Grapevine: Aboriginal Activism and the Stolen Generation*. Sydney: Federation Press.

Briskman, L. (2007) 'Research into the Australian Refugee System', paper presented at the IFSW 50th anniversary conference, Munich.

Briskman, L., and Cemlyn, S. (2005) 'Reclaiming Humanity for Asylum-Seekers', *International Social Work*, 48(6): 714–24.

Bruyere, G. (2001) 'Making Circles: Renewing First Nations' Ways of Helping', in L. Dominelli, W. Lorenz and H. Soydan (eds) *Beyond Racial Divides: Ethnicities in Social Work Practice*. Ashgate: Aldershot.

Bruyere, G. (2009) 'Picking up What Was Left by the Trail: The Emerging Spirit of Aboriginal Education in Canada', in M. Gray, J. Coates and M. Yellow Bird (eds) *Indigenous Social Work around the World: Towards Culturally Relevant Education and Practice*. Aldershot: Ashgate.

Buchan, J., and Seccombe, I. (2006) *Worlds Apart? The UK and International Nurses*. London: Royal College of Nursing.

Buchanan, I. (2007) 'The Interpretation of Human Rights in English Social Work: An Exploration in the Context of Services for Children and for Parents with Learning Difficulties', *Ethics and Social Welfare*, 1(2): 147–62.

Buchanan, J. (1968) *The Demand and Supply of Public Goods*. Chicago: Rand McNally.

Bulkeley, H., and Betsill, M. M. (2003) *Cities and Climate Change: Urban Sustainability and Global Environmental Governance*. London: Routledge.

Butler, J. (1990) *Gender Trouble: Feminism and the Subversion of Identity*. London: Routledge.

Butler, P., and Williams, R. (2010) 'Baby P Report on Sharon Shoesmith "was Beefed up to Remove Her"', *The Guardian*, 1 April.

CAB (Citizens Advice Bureau) (2005) *Pre-Payment Meters: Citizens Advice's Response to the OFGEM Consultation on New Powers under the Energy Act 2004 and Update on Recent Developments*. London: CAB.

Callahan, M., Dominelli, L., Rutman, D., and Strega, S. (2002) 'Undeserving Mothers? Practitioners' Experiences Working with Young Mothers in/from Care', *Child and Family Social Work*, 7: 149–59.

Calmfors, L. (2003) *The Role of the Trade Unions in the Twenty-First Century*. Oxford: Oxford University Press.

Cambridge, J., and Thompson, J. (2001) *'A Big Mac and a Coke': Internationalism and Globalisation as Contexts for International Education*. Bath: University of Bath, Centre for the study of Education in an International Context.

Casciani, D. (2009) 'Why Exactly Do People Vote for the BNP?', *BBC News*, 22 October; http://news.bbc.co.uk/1/hi/8319635.stm.

CBC News (2008a) 'Financial Crisis Creating "Perfect Storm" for Organisations', 11 November, www.cbc.ca/canada/story/2008/11/10/charitable-donations.html (accessed 21 March 2010).

CBC News (2008b) 'Muslim, Women's Groups Protest Article on "Honour Killing" of T.O. Girl', 12 November, www.cbc.c/arts/media/story/2008/11/12/parvez-magazine.html (accessed 12 April 2010).

CDP (Community Development Projects) (1977) *Gilding the Ghetto*. London: CDP.

CEUC (Commission of the European Communities) (2000) *Community Institutions and Policies for Roma Inclusion*. Brussels: CEUC.

Chadwick, E. (1842) *The Report on the Sanitary Conditions of the Labouring Population*. Edinburgh: Edinburgh University Press.

Challis, D., Chessum, R., Chestermen, J., Luckett, R., and Woods, B. (1987) 'Community Care for the Frail Elderly: An Urban Experiment', *British Journal of Social Work*, 18: 13–42.

Champion, G. (2010) 'Prison is "Not Taming" Islamist Radicals', *BBC News*, 13 April, http://news.bbc.co.uk/1/hi/uk/8615390.stm (accessed 20 April 2010).

Chan, M. (2009) *The World Health Organisation Health Report, 2008: Primary Care: Now More Than Ever*. Geneva: WHO.

Chen, M. A. (2001) 'Women in the Informal Sector: A Global Picture, the Global Movement', SAIS Review, 21(1): 71–82.

Chepstow-Lusty, A. J., and Beresford-Jones, D. (2009) 'The Nazca People of Peru Doomed by Cutting Down Trees', *Latin American Antiquity*, 20(3).

Chomsky, N. (1980) *Rules and Representation*. New York: Columbia University Press.

Chrisjohn, R. D., Young, S. L., and Maraun, M. (2006) *The Circle Game: Shadows and Substance in the Indian Residential School Experience in Canada*. Penticton, BC: Theytus Books.

Clarke, J., and Newman, J. (1997) *The Managerialist State*. London: Sage.

Cohen, S., Hayes, D., and Humphries, B. (2004) *Social Work, Immigration and Asylum: Debates, Dilemmas and Ethical Issues for Social Work and Social Care Practice*. London: Jessica Kingsley.

Collins, P. H. (1990) *Black Feminist Thought: Knowledge, Consciousness and the Politics of Empowerment*. London: Routledge.

Compton, B., and Galaway, B. (2005) *Social Work Processes*. 7th edn, Homewood, IL: Dorsey Press.

Conn, D. (2010) 'A Sadistic Attack on the Jobless', *The Guardian*, 27 January.

Conservative Manifesto (2010) *Invitation to Join the Government of Britain*. London: Conservative Campaign Headquarters.

Correll, D. (2008) 'The Politics of Poverty and Social Development', *International Social Work*, 51(4): 453–66.

Corrigan, P., and Leonard, P. (1978) *Social Work under Capitalism*. London: Macmillan.

Coulshed, V., and Orme, J. (2006) *Social Work Practice*. 4th edn, London: Palgrave Macmillan.

Cox, R. (1981) 'Social Forces, States, and World Orders: Beyond International Relations Theory', *Millenium*, 12(2): 146–57.

Coyle, A. (1989) 'Women in Management: A Suitable Case for Treatment', *Feminist Review*, 31: 117–25.

Craig, G. (2001) 'Social Exclusion: Is Labour Working?', *Community Care*, 27 September–3 October.

Craig, G., and Mayo, M. (eds) (1995) *Community Empowerment: A Reader in Participation and Development*. London: Zed Books.

Culpitt, I. (1992) *Welfare and Citizenship: The Crisis of the Welfare State*. London: Sage.

Cyr, G. (2007) 'An Indigenist and Anti-Colonialist Framework for Practice', in L. Dominelli (ed.) *Revitalising Communities in a Globalising World*. Aldershot: Ashgate.

*Daily Telegraph* (2008) 'Sharon Shoesmith Sacked after Baby P Scandal', 8 December.

Davies, M. (1985) *The Essential Social Worker*. Aldershot: Gower.

DBERR (Department for Business, Enterprise and Regulatory Reform) (2007) *The State Aid Guide: Guidance for state Aid Practitioners*. London: DBERR.

DCSF (Department of Children, Schools and Families) (2007) *Safeguarding Children who May Have Been Trafficked*. London: DCSF.

Deacon, B., Hulse, M., and Stubbs, P. (1997) *Global Social Policy: International Organisations and the Future of Welfare*. London: Sage.

Delgado, M. (2000) *Community Social Work Practice in an Urban Context: The Potential of a Capacity Enhancement Perspective*. Oxford: Oxford University Press.

Denzin, N., Lincoln, Y., and Smith, L. T. (2008) *The Handbook of Critical and Indigenous Methodologies*. London: Sage.

Devo, J. (2006) 'Out of Africa, into Birmingham: Zimbabwean Social Workers Talk to Professional Social Work', *Professional Social Work*, 1 August, pp. 12–13.

Diamond, J. (1995) 'Easter Island's End', *Discover Magazine*, 16(8): 63–9.

Di Palma, S., Topper, G. G., and Cruz, M. (1999) 'Women's Attainment of Leadership Positions in Social Work Academia: The Impact of Region', http://rutgersscholar.rutgers.edu/volume01/dipacruz/dipacruz.htm (accessed 20 April 2010).

Doel, M., and Marsh, P. (1992) *Task-Centred Social Work*. Aldershot: Ashgate.

Dominelli, L. (1986) *Love and Wages: The Impact of Imperialism, State Intervention and Women's Domestic Labour on Workers' Control in Algeria, 1962–1972*. Norwich: Novata Press.

Dominelli, L. (1988) *Anti-Racist Social Work*. Basingstoke: Macmillan.

Dominelli, L. (1990) *Women and Community Action*. Birmingham: Venture Press.

Dominelli, L. (1991) *Women across Continents: Feminist Comparative Social Policy*. Hemel Hempstead: Harvester Wheatsheaf.

Dominelli, L. (1992) 'European Unity: Opportunities or Opportunism?', address for the closing plenary at the Congress for the International Association of Schools of Social Work, Howard University, Washington, DC, 20 July.

Dominelli, L. (1996a) 'European Unity: Opportunity or Opportunism?', in L. Healy (ed.) *Realities of Global Interdependence: Challenges to Social Work Education*. Alexandra, VA: Council on Social Work Education, pp. 31–9.

Dominelli, L. (1996b) 'Deprofessionalising Social Work: Competencies, Postmodernism and Equal Opportunities', *British Journal of Social Work*, 26: 153–75.

Dominelli, L. (1997) *Sociology for Social Work*. London: Macmillan.

Dominelli, L. (1999) 'Neo-Liberalism, Social Exclusion and Welfare Clients in a Global Economy', *Journal of International Social Welfare*, 8(1): 1–15.

Dominelli, L. (2000) 'International Comparisons in Social Work', in R. Pearce and J. Weinstein (eds) *Innovative Education and Training for Care Professionals: A Providers' Guide*. London: Jessica Kingsley, pp. 25–42.

Dominelli, L. (2002a) *Anti-Oppressive Social Work Theory and Practice*. London: Palgrave Macmillan.

Dominelli, L. (2002b) *Feminist Social Work Theory and Practice*. London: Palgrave Macmillan.

Dominelli, L. (2002c) 'Values: Continuities and Discontinuities', in R. Adams, L. Dominelli and M. Payne (eds) *Social Work: Current Themes, Issues and Debates*. London: Palgrave Macmillan.

Dominelli, L. (2003) 'Culturally Competent Social Work: A Way Towards International Anti-Racist Social Work?' in L. Gutiérrez, M. Zuñiga and D. Lum, D (eds.) *Education for Multicultural Social Work Practice: Critical Viewpoints and Future Directions*. Alexandria, VA: Council on Social Work Education, pp. 281–94.

Dominelli, L. (2004a) 'Practising Social Work in a Globalising World', in N. T. Tan and A. Rowlands (eds) *Social Work around the World III*. Berne: International Federation of Social Workers.

Dominelli, L. (2004b) *Social Work: Theory and Practice for a Changing Profession*. Cambridge: Polity.

Dominelli, L. (2004c) 'Crossing International Divides: Language and Communication within International Settings', *Social Work Education*, 23(5): 515–25.

Dominelli, L. (2006a) *Women and Community Action*. 2nd edn, Bristol: Policy Press.

Dominelli, L. (2006b) 'Circles of Resistance: The Development of Empowering Practice', paper presented at the Student Conference, La Catolica University, Santiago, Chile, 15 July.

Dominelli, L. (2007a) 'Challenges in Internationalising Social Work Curricula', in L. Dominelli (ed.) *Revitalising Communities in a Globalising World*. Aldershot: Ashgate.

Dominelli, L. (2007b) 'Contemporary Challenges to Social Work Education in the United Kingdom', *Australian Social Work*, 60(1): 29–45.

Dominelli, L. (2009) *Introducing Social Work*. Cambridge: Polity.

Dominelli, L., and Hoogvelt, A. (1996) 'Globalisation and the Technocratisation of Social Work', *Critical Social Policy*, 16(2): 45–62.

Dominelli, L., and McLeod, E. (1989) *Feminist Social Work*. London: Macmillan.

Dominelli, L., and Thomas Bernard, W. (eds) (2003) *Broadening Horizons: International Exchanges in Social Work*. Aldershot: Ashgate.

Dominelli, L., Strega, S., Callahan, C., and Rutman, D. (2005) 'Endangered Children: The State as Parent and Grandparent', *British Journal of Social Work*, 35(7): 1123–44.

Donzelot, J. (1982) *The Policing of Families*. London: Hutchinson.

Douglas, N. (1983) *Old Calabria*. London: Century Books.

Duffield, M. (1996) 'The Symphony of the Damned: Racial Discourse, Complex Political Emergencies and Humanitarian Aid', *Disasters*, 20(3): 173–93.

Edwards, R. (2004) *Social Capital in the Field: The Researchers' Tales*. London: London Southbank University.

Ehrenreich, B. (2002) *Nickel and Dimed: On (Not) Getting by in America*. London: Granta.

Ehrenreich, B., and English, B. (1979) *For her own Good: 150 Years of the Experts' Advice to Women*. London: Pluto Press.

Ehrkamp, P. (2005) 'Placing Identities: Transnational Practices and Local Attachments of Turkish Immigrants in Germany', *Journal of Ethnic and Migration Studies*, 31(2): 345–64.

Engels, F. ([1844] 2009) *The Condition of the Working Class in England*, ed. D. McLellan. Oxford: Oxford University Press.

EPI (Economic Policy Institute) (2007) *Health Care for America*, EPI Briefing Paper no.180; http://usgovinfo.about.com/gi/o.htm?zi=1/XJ&zTi=1&sdn=usg ovinfo&cdn=newsissues&tm=46&gps=454_329_1004_610&f=00&tt=2&bt =0&bts=0&st=23&zu=http%3A//www.sharedprosperity.org/bp180.html (accessed 20 April 2010).

Esping-Andersen, G. (1990) *The Three Worlds of Welfare Capitalism*. Princeton, NJ: Princeton University Press.

Esping-Andersen, G. (2009) *The Incomplete Revolution: Adapting to Women's New Roles*. Cambridge: Polity.

Fanon, F. (1968a) *The Wretched of the Earth*. Boston: Grove Press.

Fanon, F. (1968b) *Black Skin, White Masks*. London: MacGibbon & Kee.

Ferguson, H., Jones, K., and Cooper, P. (2007) *Best Practice in Social Work: Critical Perspectives*. Basingstoke: Palgrave Macmillan.

Ferree, M. M., and Tripp, A. M. (ed.) (2006) *Global Feminism: Transnational Women's Activism, Organizing, and Human Rights*. New York: New York University Press.

Field, M. (1989) *Success and Crisis in National Health Systems: A Comparative Approach*. London: Routledge.

Fillion, R. (2008) 'Donations to Charities Decline', *Rocky Mountain News*, 9 October; www.rockymountainnews.com/news/2008/oct/09/donations-to-charities-decline/ (accessed 21 March 2010).

Finn, D. (1985) *The Community Programme and the Long Term Unemployed*. London: Unemployment Unit.

Finn, D. (2009a) ' "The Welfare Market": The Role of the Private Sector in the Delivery of Benefits and Employment Services', in J. Millar (ed.) *Understanding Social Security: Issues for Policies and Practice*. 2nd edn, Bristol: Policy Press.

Finn, D. (2009b) ' "The Welfare Market" and the Flexible New Deal: Lessons from Other Countries', *Local Economy*, 24(1): 51–8.

Fitzhugh, W., and Ward, E. (2000) *Vikings: The North Atlantic Saga*. Washington, DC: Smithsonian Institution Press.

Flexner, A. ([1915] 2001) 'Is Social Work a Profession?', repr. in *Research on Social Work Practice*, 11(2): 152–65.

Folgeraiter, F. (2004) *Relational Social Work: Toward Network and Societal Practices*. London: Jessica Kingsley.

Fook, J. (2002) *Social Work: Critical Theory and Practice*. London: Sage.

Foster, P. (2009) 'Beijing's Early Snowfall Made in China', *Vancouver Sun*, 3 November, p. B5.

Foucault, M. (1977) *Discipline and Punish*. London: Allen Lane.

Foucault, M. (1979) 'Truth and Power', in M. Morris and P. Patton (eds) *Michel Foucault: Power, Truth, Strategy*. Sydney: Feral.

Foucault, M. (1991) 'Governmentality', in G. Burchell, C. Gordon and P. Miller (eds) *The Faucault Effect: Studies in Governmentality*. Hemel Hempstead: Harvester Wheatsheaf.

Frankfort, E. (1972) *Vaginal Politics*. New York: Quadrangle Books.

Freeman, M. (1998) 'The Effects and Consequences of International Child Abductions', *Family Law Quarterly*, 38: 603–12.

Freire, P. (1972) *The Pedagogy of the Oppressed*. Harmondsworth: Penguin.

Freitag, C. N. (2009) 'Charitable Contributions Decline as Economic Crisis Continues', 8 January, www.associatedcontent.com/article/1353398/charitable_contributions_decline_as.html?cat=48 (accessed 20 April 2010).

Friedlander, W., and Apte, R. (1974) *Introduction to Social Welfare*. London: Prentice-Hall.

Fromm, E. (1941) *Escape from Freedom*. New York: Henry Holt.

Fromm, E. (2002) *Beyond the Chains of Illusion: My Encounter with Marx and Freud*. New York: Continuum.

Fulcher, L. (1999) 'The Cultural Origins of the Contemporary Family Group Conference', *Child Care in Practice*, 5(4): 328–39.

Furniss, E. (1995) *Victims of Benevolence: The Dark Legacy of the Williams Lake Residential School*. Vancouver: Arsenal Pulp Press.

Garber, R. (2000) 'Social Work and Globalization', *Canadian Social Work*. 2(1): 198–215 [special issue].

GCC (Gloucestershire County Council) (2007) 'Summer 2007 Floods', www.gloucestershire.gov.uk/index.cfm?articleid=19561 (accessed 10 July 2008).

George, S. (2003) 'Globalizing Rights?', in M. J. Gibney (ed.) *Globalizing Rights*. Oxford: Oxford University Press.

George, S. (2008) 'Talking Telephone Numbers', *The Guardian*, Supplement on Development, 22 November, p. 2.

Giangreco, D., and Moore, K. (1999) *Dear Harry: Truman's Mailroom, 1945–1953*. Mechanicsburg, PA: Stackpole Books.

Giddens, A. (2009) *The Politics of Climate Change*. Cambridge: Polity.

Gilchrist, R., and Jeffs, T. (2001) *Settlements, Social Change and Community Action*. London: Jessica Kingsley.

Gill, A. (2009) 'No Honour in "Honour" Killings', www.roehampton.ac.uk/news/tulaygoren.html (accessed 20 April 2010).

Gitterman, A. (2009) *Vulnerability, Resilience and Social Work Practice*, presentation at the Buffalo School of Social Work Alumni Day, 16 September.

Glendinning, C., Arksey, H., Jones, K., Moran, N., Nethen, A., and Rabiee, P. (2009) *The Individual Budgets Pilot Projects: Impact and Outcomes for Carers*. York: University of York, Social Policy Research Unit; Canterbury: University of Kent, Personal Social Services Research Unit.

Goffman, E. (1961) *Asylums: Essays on the Social Situation of Mental Health Patients and Other Inmates*. Harmondsworth: Penguin.

Gordon, L. (1988) *Heroes of their own Lives: The Politics and History of Family Violence*. Harmondsworth: Penguin.

Goulbourne, H., and Solomos, J. (2003) 'Families, Ethnicity, and Social Capital', *Social Policy and Society*, 2: 329–38.

Graham, M. (2002) *Social Work and African-Centred Worldviews*. Birmingham: Venture Press.

Grande, S. (2004) *Red Pedagogy: Native American and Political Thought*. Lanham, MD: Rowman & Littlefield.

Gray, M., and Mitchell, B. (2007) 'The Road Less Travelled: Reconstruction, Welfare and Social Development in South Africa', in L. Dominelli (ed.) *Revitalising Communities in a Globalising World*. Aldershot: Ashgate.

Gray, M., Coates, J., and Yellow Bird, M. (2009) *Indigenous Social Work around the World: Towards Culturally Relevant Education and Practice*. Aldershot: Ashgate.

Green, J., and Thomas, R. (2007) 'Learning through our Children, Healing for our Children: Best Practice in First Nations Communities', in L. Dominelli (ed.) *Revitalising Communities in a Globalising World*. Aldershot: Ashgate.

Greenaway, N. (2009) 'Deportation Order Ended in Death', *Vancouver Sun*, 26 October, p. B2.

Greer, P. (1994) *Transforming Central Government: The Next Steps Initiative*. Buckingham: Open University Press.

Griffiths, R. (1988) *Community Care Agenda for Action: The Griffiths Report*. London: HMSO.

GSCC (General Social Care Council) (2009) *Raising Standards in Social Work Conduct in England, 2003–2008*. London: GSCC.

Guevara, C. (1969) *Che: Selected Works of Ernesto Guevara*, trans. R. Bonachea and P. V. Nelson. Cambridge, MA: MIT Press.

Guterres, A. (2009) 'World Refugee Day: 42 million Uprooted People Waiting to Go Home', www.unhcr.org/4a3b98706.html (accessed 20 April 2010).

Hadley, R., Cooper, M., Dale, P., and Stacey, G. (1987) *A Community Social Worker's Handbook*. London: Tavistock.

Hadley, R., and McGrath, M. (eds) (1980) *Going Local: Neighbourhood and Social Services*. London: Bedford Square Press.

Haig-Brown, C. (1988) *Resistance and Renewal: Surviving the Indian Residential School*. Vancouver: Arsenal Pulp Press.

Hamburger, F., Sander, G., and Wöbcke, M. (n.d.) 'Social Work Education in Europe', www.certs-europe.com/SITE_ANGLAIS/papers/swed-eur.pdf (accessed 18 April 2010).

Hancock, G. (1991) *Lords of Poverty: The Power, Prestige, and Corruption of the International Aid Business*. New York: Atlantic Monthly Press.

Hanmer, J., and Statham, D. (1988) *Women and Social Work: Towards a Woman-Centred Practice*. Basingstoke: Macmillan.

Hardcastle, D., Powers, P., and Wenour, S. (2004) *Community Practice: Theories and Skills for Social Workers*. Oxford: Oxford University Press.

Harrison, P., and Grajewski, M. (2009) 'EU Agrees Final Stance for Copenhagen Climate Talks', 30 October, http://uk.reuters.com/article/idUKTRE59S2XK20091030 (accessed 2 January 2010).

Harten, A. (2009) 'More Help on the Way for British Pensioners in Spain', *Spanish News*, 17 September.

Haski-Leventhal, D. (2005) *The Professionalisation Process of Volunteer Management in Australia*, CSI Issues Paper no. 2. Sydney: University of New

South Wales, Centre for Social Impact; www.csi.edu.au (accessed 20 April 2010).

Healy, K. (2005) *Social Work Theories in Context: Creating Frameworks for Practice*. Basingstoke: Palgrave Macmillan.

Healy, L. (2001) *International Social Work: Professional Action in an Interdependent World*. Oxford: Oxford University Press.

Hepworth, D. H., Rooney, R. H., Rooney, G. D., Strom-Gottfried, K., and Larsen, J. A. (2010) *Direct Social Work Practice: Theory and Skills*. 8th edn, Belmont, CA: Brooks/Cole.

Heraud, J. (1981) *Training for Uncertainty: A Sociological Approach to Social Work Education*. London: Routledge & Kegan Paul.

Herdman, R. (1994) *International Comparisons of Administrative Costs in Health Care*. Washington, DC: Government Printing Office.

Hering, S., and Waaldijk, B. (eds) (2003) *History of Social Work in Europe (1900–1960): Female Pioneers and their Influence on the Development of International Social Organisations*. Opladen: Leske & Budrich.

Hewitt, K. (1997) *Regions of Risk: A Geographical Introduction to Disasters*. Harlow: Longman.

Hier, S. P., and Bolaria, S. B. (eds) (2006) *Identity and Belonging: Rethinking Race and Ethnicity in Canadian Society*. Toronto: Canadian Scholars' Press.

Higham, P. (2006) *Social Work: Introducing Professional Practice*. London: Sage.

Hill, L. (2007) *The Book of Negroes*. Toronto: HarperCollins.

Hill, M. F. (2009) 'UBC Engineers Prepare VW Bug for Future, Not for Hanging About', *Vancouver Sun*, 26 October, p. A11.

Hirst, P., Thompson, G., and Bromley, S. (2009) *Globalization in Question*. 3rd edn, Cambridge: Polity.

Hogan, M. J. (1987) *The Marshall Plan: America, Britain, and the Reconstruction of Western Europe, 1947–1952*. Cambridge: Cambridge University Press.

Hogan, M. J. (1991) *Informal Entente: The Private Structure of Cooperation in Anglo-American Economic Diplomacy, 1918–1928*. Chicago: Imprint.

Holden, J. (2008) 'On the Right Side of the Law', *The Guardian*, Special Supplement on Development, 22 November, p. 7.

Hollingsworth, L., and Tyyska, V. (1988) 'The Hidden Producers: Women's Household Production during the Great Depression', *Critical Sociology*, 15: 3–27.

Hoogvelt, A. (2001) *Globalization and the Postcolonial World: The New Political Economy of Development*. Baltimore: Johns Hopkins University Press.

Hoogvelt, A. (2007) 'Globalisation and Imperialism: Wars and Humanitarian Intervention', in L. Dominelli (ed.) *Revitalising Communities in a Globalising World*. Aldershot: Ashgate.

Hopkins, K. (2009) 'G8's Promise to Africa Likely to be Broken', *The Guardian*, 11 June.

Howe, D. (1986) 'The Segregation of Women and their Work in the Personal Social Services', *Critical Social Policy*, 15: 21–36.

HREOC (Human Rights and Equal Opportunity Commission) (2005) *Bringing Them Home: Report of the National Inquiry into the Separation of Aboriginal and Torres Strait Islander Children from their Families*. Sydney: HREOC; www.hreoc.gov.au/social_justice/bth_report/index.html (accessed 18 April 2010).

HRM (2010) 'UK Unemployment', *Human Resource Management Guide*, 17 March; www.hrmguide.co.uk/jobmarket/unemployment.htm (accessed 20 April 2010).

HSRP (Human Security Research Project) (2009) *Human Security Report 2009*. Vancouver: Simon Fraser University, School for International Studies; www.hsrgroup.org (accessed 20 April 2010).

Huber, E., and Stephens, I. (2001) *Development and Crisis of the Welfare State: Parties and Policies in Global Markets*. Chicago: University of Chicago Press.

Hugman, R. (1991) 'Organisation and Professionalism: The Social Work Agenda in the 1990s', *British Journal of Social Work*, 21: 199–216.

Hume, S. (2009a) 'Chill Out, and Let the Refugee Claim Process Do its Work', *Vancouver Sun*, 20 October, pp. A1–A3.

Hume, S. (2009b) 'Let's Get a Grip and Let the Refugee Process Unfold', *Vancouver Sun*, 26 October, p. A6.

Humphreys, M. (1996) *Empty Cradles*. London: Corgi.

ICISS (International Commission on Intervention and State Sovereignty) (2001) *Responsibility to Protect: Report of the International Commission on Intervention and State Sovereignty*. Ottawa: ICISS; www.iciss.ca/menu-en.asp (accessed 20 March 2010).

Ife, J. (2001a) *Human Rights and Social Work: Towards Rights-Based Practice*. Cambridge: Cambridge University Press.

Ife, J. (2001b) 'Local and Global Practice: Relocating Social Work as a Human Rights Profession in a New Global Order', *European Journal of Social Work*, 4(1): 515–21.

IPCC (Intergovernmental Panel on Climate Change) (2007) *The Fourth Assessment on Climate Change*. New York: IPCC.

Jackson, S., and Nixon, P. (1999) 'Family Group Conferences: A Challenge to the Old Order?', in L. Dominelli, L (ed.) *Community Approaches to Child Welfare: International Perspectives*. Aldershot: Ashgate.

Jansen, B. (2008) 'Between Vulnerability and Assertiveness: Negotiating Resettlement in Kakuma Refugee Camp, Kenya', *African Affairs*, 10: 569–87.

Jenkins, J. (2006) 'Non-Resident Fathers' Engagement with their Children: The Salience of Leisure', *Australian Journal of Social Issues*, 41(2): 183–93.

Jha, M. K. (2008) 'Liquid Disaster and Frigid Response: Disaster and Social Exclusion', paper given at the conference 'Social Work in Times of Disaster' St Aidan's College, Durham University, 24 April.

Johanson, D. (2001) 'Origins of Modern Humans: Multiregional or Out of Africa?', www.actionbioscience.org/evolution/johanson.html (accessed 20 April 2010).

Johnson, E. (2006) 'Tsunami: Two Year Update', www.unicef.org/emerg/disasterinasia/index_37954.html (accessed 18 April 2010).

Johnston, D. (2006) 'Tax Cheats Called Out of Control', *New York Times*, 1 August.

Jones, C., and Novak, T. (1993) 'Social Work Today', *British Journal of Social Work*, 23(3): 195–212.

Jones, P. d'A. (1968) *The Christian Socialist Revival, 1877–1914: Religion, Class, and Social Conscience in Late-Victorian England*. Princeton, NJ: Princeton University Press.

Joyner, J. (2007) 'New Generation of American Deserters in Canada', www.outsidethebeltway.com (accessed 1 February 2009).

Juliusdottir, S., and Petersson, J. (2003) 'Common Social Work Education Standards in the Nordic Countries: Opening an Issue', *Social Work & Society*, 1(1): www.socwork.net/2003/1/articles/398.

Kee, R. (2000) *The Green Flag*. Harmondsworth: Penguin.

Kelly, C. (2008) 'Home Office Figures Confirm Migration from Eastern Europe Falls to New Low', *Immigration Matters*, 25 August; www.immigrationmatters.co.uk/home-office-figures-confirm-migration-from-eastern-europe-falls-to-new-low.html (accessed 20 April 2010).

Kendall, K. (1991) *IASSW: The First Fifty Years, 1928–1978*. Washington, DC: CSWE-IASSW.

Kendall, K. (2000) *Social Work Education: Its Origins in Europe*. Alexandra, VA: CSWE.

Keynes, J. M. (1989) *The Collected Writings*, Vol. 26. London: Macmillan.

Khan, P., and Dominelli, L. (2000) 'The Impact of Globalization on Social Work in the UK', *European Journal of Social Work*, 3(2): 95–108.

Kincaid, J. (1973) *Poverty and Equality in Britain*. Harmondsworth: Penguin.

Kirkup, J. (2009) '50 Per Cent Tax Rate for Higher Income Earners in Budget 2009', *Daily Telegraph*, 22 April.

Knijn, T., and Ungerson, C. (1997) 'Introduction: Gender and Care Work in Welfare Regimes', *Social Politics*, 4(fall): 323–7.

Krieger, L. (1963) *The Idea of the Welfare State in Europe and the United States*. Philadelphia: University of Philadelphia Press.

Kroll, L. (2008) 'The World's Billionaires', *Forbes Magazine, Special Report*, 5 March.

Kroll, L., and Fass, A. (2007) 'The World's Billionaires', *Forbes Magazine, Special Report*, 8 March.

Kroll, L., and Miller (2010) 'The World's Billionaires', *Forbes Magazine, Special Report*, 3 March.

Kroll, L., Miller, M., and Serafin, T. (2009) 'The World's Billionaires', *Forbes Magazine, Special Report*, 11 March.

Laing, R. D. (1969) *Intervention in Social Situations*. London: Association of Family Caseworkers.

Laming, H. (2003) *The Victoria Climbié Inquiry*. CM 5730. London: HMSO.

Laming, H. (2009) *The Protection of Children in England: A Progress Report*. London: HMSO.

Lampton, D. M. (1977) *The Politics of Medicine in China: The Policy Process, 1949–1977*. Boulder, CO: Westview Press.

Langton, M. (2005) 'Court Gives Mother Access to Twins She Sold on Internet', *Daily Telegraph*, 26 March.

Lappin, B. (1965) 'Stages in the Development of Community Organisation Work as a Social Work Method', PhD thesis, University of Toronto.

Laxer, G. (1989) *Open for Business: The Roots of Foreign Ownership in Canada.* Oxford: Oxford University Press.

Layton-Henry, Z. (1984) *The Politics of Race in Britain.* London: Allen & Unwin.

Leighninger, L. (1998) 'Social Workers Anticipate the Marshall Plan', *Journal of Progressive Human Services*, 9(1): 63–73.

Lenin, V. (1961) *Collected Works*, Vol. 5. Moscow: Progress Publishers.

Leonard, P. (1975) *The Sociology of Community Action*, Sociological Review Monograph 21. Keele: University of Keele.

Leonard, P. (1997) *Postmodern Welfare: Reconstructing an Emancipatory Project.* London: Sage.

Leopold, L. (2009) *The Looting of America: How Wall Street's Game of Fantasy Finance Destroyed our Jobs, Pensions and Prosperity – and What You Can Do about It.* White River Junction, VT: Chelsea Green.

Lester, M. (2010) 'When Immigration and Job Creation Collide', *Carrboro Citizen* [Carrboro, NC], 18 March.

Lister, R. (1997) *Citizenship: Feminist Perspectives.* London: Macmillan.

Loney, M. (1986) *The Politics of Greed: The New Right and the Welfare State.* London: Pluto Press.

Long, S., and Clark, S. (1997) *The New Child Care Block Grant: State Funding Choices and the Implications.* Washington, DC: Urban Institute.

Lorenz, W. (1994) *Social Work in a Changing Europe.* London: Routledge.

Löscher, P. (2009) 'Preface', *Pictures of the Future: The Magazine for Research and Innovation, Special Edition: Green Technologies.* Munich: Siemens.

LSB (London Safeguarding Board) (2009) *London Safeguarding Trafficked Children Toolkit.* London: LSB.

Luxton, M. (1997) 'The UN, Women, and Household Labour: Measuring and Valuing Unpaid Work', *Women's Studies International Forum*, 20(3): 431–9.

Lyons, K., Manion, K., and Carlsen, M. (2006) *International Perspectives on Social Work.* Basingstoke: Palgrave Macmillan.

McDougall, G. (2009) *United Nations Country Reports on the Status of Ethnic Minorities.* New York: UN Committee on the Elimination of Racial Discrimination.

Mackenzie, D. (2008) 'The Use of Knowledge about Society', *Journal of Economic Behaviour and Organization*, 67(3-4): 676–88.

Mackenzie, H., and Shillington, R. (2009) *Canada's Quiet Bargain: The Benefits of Public Spending.* Ottawa: Canadian Centre for Policy Alternatives.

McLuhan, M. (1995) 'The Mechanical Bride', in *The Essential McLuhan*, ed. E. McLuhan and F. Zingrone. London: Routledge.

Macpherson, C. B. (1964) *The Political Theory of Possessive Individualism: From Hobbes to Locke.* Oxford: Oxford University Press.

McSmith, C. (2007) 'Figures Show Number of Eastern Europeans in Britain Exaggerated', *The Independent*, 20 June.

Manthorpe, J. (2009) 'Indonesia a Hub for Human-Trafficking Gang Bosses', *Vancouver Sun*, 23 October, p. A8.

Mao Zedong (1966) 'The Little Red Book', or Quotations from Chairman Mao Tse Tung. Beijing: Foreign Languages Press.

Marsh, L. (1943) Report on Social Security for Canada: The Requirements for Post-War Planning. Ottawa: n.p.

Marshall, T. H. (1970) Social Policy in the Twentieth Century. London: Hutchinson.

Martell, L. (2010) The Sociology of Globalization. Cambridge: Polity.

Marx, K. (1965) Capital: A Critical Analysis of Capitalist Production, 3 vols. Moscow: Progress.

Mathbor, G. M. (2008) Effective Community Participation in Coastal Development. Chicago: Lyceum Books.

Mayeda, A. (2009) 'Canada Falling Behind in Global Clean-Tech Boom', Vancouver Sun, 26 October, p. B4.

Meo, N. (2009) Ethiopia on Brink of Famine Again as Midge Ure Returns 25 Years After Band Aid', Daily Telegraph, 31 October; www.telegraph.co.uk/news/worldnews/africaandindianocean/ethiopia/6473368/Ethiopia-on-brink-of-famine-again-as-Midge-Ure-returns-25-years-after-Band-Aid.html (accessed 2 January 2010).

Metro (2008) 'Darling Hails £50bn Bank Aid Plan', Metro, 21 April.

Metro (2009) 'Decline in Donations to Oxfam Shops', Metro, 8 May.

Midgley, J. (1995) Social Development: The Developmental Perspective in Social Welfare. Thousand Oaks, CA: Sage.

Midgley, J., with A. Hall, M. Hardiman and D. Narine ([1986] 1996) Community Participation, Social Developments and the State. London: Methuen.

Milner, J. (2002) Women and Social Work: Narrative Approaches. Basingstoke: Palgrave.

Mishra, R. (2005) 'Social Rights as Human Rights: Globalising Social Protection', International Social Work, 48(1): 9–20.

Mohanty, C. (1992) 'Feminist Encounters: Locating the Politics of Experience', in M. Barrett and A. Phillips (eds) Destabilizing Theory. Cambridge: Polity.

Moosa-Mitha, M. (2002) 'Rights Discourses and Child Sex Trade Workers', PhD thesis, Southampton University.

MSNBC (2006) '1 Million March for Immigrants across US', NBC News, 1 May; www.msnbc.msn.com/id/12573992/ (accessed 25 August 2008).

Munasinghe, M., and Swart, R. (2005) Primer on Climate Change and Social Development: Facts, Policy Analysis, and Applications. Cambridge: Cambridge University Press.

Munnion, C. (2008) 'South Africa Violence: Death Toll Mounts', Daily Telegraph, 20 May; www.telegraph.co.uk/news/1993949/South-Africa-violence-Death-toll-mounts.html.

Muñoz, M. (2007) 'Peru Earthquake', Vancouver Sun, 16 August, p. A14.

Myers, N. (2005) 'Environmental Refugees: An Emergent Security Issue', paper delivered at the 13th Economic Forum, Prague, 23–7 May.

Naples, N. (1998) Community Activism and Feminist Politics: Organizing across Race, Class and Gender. New York: Routledge.

Nayak, M., and Selbin, E. (2010) Decentering International Relations. London: Zed Books.

Netto, P. (2006) 'The Challenges and Opportunities of Neo-Liberalism: A Marxist Perspective', paper given at the IASSW Biannual Conference, Santiago, Chile, July.

Netto, P. (2008) 'La instumentalidad del servicio social en Latinoamérica: desafíos', *Revista Trabjo Social*, 44: 99–106.

Neumann, P. (2009) *Old and New Terrorism*. Cambridge: Polity.

Nussbaum, M. (1999) *Sex and Social Justice*. Oxford: Oxford University Press.

Nussbaum, M. (2000) *Women and Human Development: The Capabilities Approach*. Cambridge: Cambridge University Press.

OECD (2005) *Ensuring Quality Care for Older People*, Policy Brief, March; www.oecd.org/publications/policybriefs.

Oliver, M. (1990) *The Politics of Disablement*. London: Macmillan.

O'Malley, P. (2004) *Risk, Uncertainty and Government*. London: Glasshouse.

ONS (Office for National Statistics) (2008) 'Working Lives: Focus on Gender', www.statistics.gov.uk/cci/nugget.asp?id=1654 (accessed 15 April 2009).

ONS (Office for National Statistics) (2010) 'UK Government Debt and Deficit', 31 March, www.statistics.gov.uk/cci/nugget.asp?id=277 (accessed 21 April 2010).

Osterhammel, J. (2005) *Colonialism: A Theoretical Overview*. Princeton, NJ: Markus Wiener.

Parker, J. (2007) *Disability and Stigma by Association*. Basingstoke: Palgrave Macmillan.

Parsons, T. (1957) *Essays in Sociological Theory*. New York: Free Press.

Parton, N. (1991) *Governing the Family: Child Care, Child Protection and the State*. London: Macmillan.

Parton, N., and O'Byrne, P. (2000) *Constructive Social Work: Towards a New Practice*. Basingstoke: Palgrave.

Patterson, M., and Cochrane, L. (2008) 'Emerging Markets Take Record Share of World Equity', www.bloomberg.com/apps/news?pid=20601087&sid=aqO3hUtyjtuw (accessed 2 December 2009).

Pattison, G. (2007) 'Community Participation: A Critical Appraisal of the Role of Community in Urban Policy', in L. Dominelli (ed.) *Revitalising Communities in a Globalising World*. Aldershot: Ashgate.

Payne, M. (2005) *Modern Social Work Theory*. Basingstoke: Palgrave Macmillan.

Payne, M. (2009) 'Understanding Social Work Processes', in R. Adams, L. Dominelli and M. Payne (eds) *Social Work: Themes, Issues and Critical Debates*. 3rd edn, London: Palgrave Macmillan.

Payne, M., and Askeland, G. (2008) *Globalization and International Social Work*. Aldershot: Ashgate.

Payne, S. G. (1975) *Basque Nationalism*. Reno: University of Nevada Press.

Pearce, J. J., Hynes, P., and Bovarnick, S. (2009) *Breaking the Wall of Silence: Practitioners' Responses to Trafficked Children and Young People*, www.nspcc.org.uk/Inform/research/Findings/breaking_the_wall_of_silence_report_wdf66135.pdf (accessed 20 April 2010).

Pease, B., and Fook, J. (eds) (1999) *Transforming Social Work Practice: Postmodern Critical Perspectives*. London: Routledge.

Phillips, M. (1993) 'An Oppressive Urge to End Oppression', *The Observer*, 1 August.

Phillips, T. (2008) 'People on the Move: More Different, More Unequal', address to the Commonwealth meeting, 15 January; www.equalityhumanrights.com (accessed 21 March 2009).

Pidd, H. (2009) '500 Children a Year Abducted from UK', *The Guardian*, 9 August.

Pincus, A., and Minahan, A. (1973) *Social Work Practice: Model and Method*. Itasca, IL: F. E. Peacock.

Pinker, R. (1993) 'A Lethal Kind of Looniness', *Times Higher Educational Supplement*, 10 September.

Pittaway, E., Bartolomei, L., and Rees, S. (2007) 'Gendered Dimensions of the 2004 Tsunami and a Potential Social Work Response in Post-Disaster Situations', *International Social Work*, 50(3): 307–19.

Piven, F., and Cloward, R. (1971) *Regulating the Poor*. New York: Pantheon Books.

Pope, J. (2008) 'Decline in Charitable Giving Hits Nonprofits', www.nola.com/news/index.ssf/2008/07/decline_in_charitable_giving_h.html (accessed 21 March 2010).

Popple, K. (2007) 'Community Development Strategies in the UK', in L. Dominelli (ed.) *Revitalising Communities in a Globalising World*. Aldershot: Ashgate.

Pramanik, A. H. (2000) 'Whither Welfare States? The Lessons from Fast-Growing East Asian Emerging Economies and the Grameen Bank Model', *Humanomics*, 16(2): 3–18.

Prospects (2009) 'Social Workers Salaries and Conditions', www.prospects.ac.uk/p/types_of_job/social_worker_salary.jsp (accessed 20 April 2010).

PSW (2008) 'New Migrant List Threat to Social Care Recruitment', *Professional Social Work*, October, p. 9.

Putnam, R. (1993) *Making Democracy Work: Civic Traditions in Modern Italy*. Princeton, NJ: Princeton University Press.

Putnam, R. (2000) *Bowling Alone: The Collapse and Revival of American Community*. New York: Simon & Schuster.

Quinsey, V. L. (1995) 'Predicting Sexual Offences: Assessing Dangerousness', in J. C. Campbell (ed.) *Violence by Sexual Offenders: Batterers and Child Abusers*. London: Sage.

Ramesh, R. (2009) 'Billionaire Club Doubles in Year as India's Rich Stay Immune to Recession', *The Guardian*, 20 November, p. 31.

Ramon, S., and Zaviršek, D. (2009) *Critical Edge Issues in Social Work and Social Policy: Comparative Research Perspectives*. Ljubljana: University of Ljubljana, Faculty of Social Work.

Rangihua, John Te Rangi-Aniwaniwa and Maori Perspective Advisory Committee (1990) *Puao-te-ata-tu (Day Break): The Report of the Ministerial Advisory Committee on a Maori Perspective for the Department of Social Welfare*. Wellington: New Zealand Government.

Rapport, M. (2009) *1848: Year of Revolution*. New York: Basic Books.

Rawls, J. (1973) *A Theory of Justice*. Oxford: Oxford University Press.

Razack, N. (2002) 'Imagining the International: Contesting and Complicating Race, Space, Postcoloniality, and Helping in International Exchanges', paper given at the Congress of the International Association of Schools of Social Work, Montpelier, France, 15–18 July.

Read, P. (1981) *The Stolen Generation: The Removal of Aboriginal Children in New South Wales, 1883–1969*. Sydney: Department of Aboriginal Affairs.

Refugee Council (2010) 'Protests at Yarl's Wood: Refugee Council Response', *Refugee Council News*. London: Refugee Council. www.refugeecouncil.org.uk/news/archive/news/2010/March/040310_newsyarlswood (accessed 30 March 2010).

Reichert, E. (2007) *Challenges in Human Rights: A Social Work Perspective*. New York: Columbia University Press.

Reid, W., and Epstein, L. (1972) *Task-Centered Casework*. New York: Columbia University Press.

Reid, W., and Shyne, W. (1969) *Brief and Extended Casework*. New York: Columbia University Press.

Rink, H. J. (2004) Danish Greenland: Its Peoples and its Products. Chestnut Hill, MA: Adamant Media Corporation.

Ritzer, G. (2000) *The McDonaldization of Society*. Thousand Oaks, CA, and London: Pine Forge Press.

Roberts, J. (1994) *Athens on Trial: The Antidemocratic Tradition in Western Thought*. Princeton, NJ: Princeton University Press.

Robinson, E. (2001) *Monkey Beach*. Toronto: Knopf Canada.

Robinson, J. (2009) *Bluestockings*. London: Viking.

Rollston, B., and Smyth, M. (1982) 'The Spaces between Cases: Radical Social Work in Northern Ireland', in R. Bailey and P. Lee (eds) *Theory and Practice in Social Work*. Oxford: Blackwell.

Rose, N. (1996) 'The Death of the Social? Reconfiguring the Territory of Government', *Economy and Society*, 25(3): 327–56.

Ross, T. (2008) 'Ofsted Knew of Baby P Tragedy When it Gave Council Glowing Report', *Evening Standard*, 14 November.

Roy, A. (1999) 'Lies, Damned Lies and Statistics', *The Guardian*, 5 June.

Roy, M. N. (2004) *M. N. Roy, Radical Humanist: Selected Writings*. Amherst, NY: Prometheus Books.

Rudra, N. (2005) 'Welfare States in Developing Countries: Unique or Universal?', www.princeton.edu/~pcglobal/conferences/IPES/papers/rudra_F1100_2.pdf.

Sachs, J. (2010) 'Robin Hood Tax's Time Has Come', *The Guardian*, 18 March.

Said, E. (1978) *Orientalism*. New York: Pantheon Books.

Saleeby, D. (2002) *The Strengths Perspective in Social Work Practice*. Boston: Allyn & Bacon.

Salomon, A. (2004) *Character is Destiny: The Autobiography of Alice Salomon*. Ann Arbor: University of Michigan Press.

Sanders, E. (2009) 'Climate Change Creates Refugees', *Vancouver Sun*, 26 October, p. B5.

Sapsted, D. (2009) 'Europe Waking up to Honour Killings after Turkish Kurd Jailed in UK', www.ekurd.net/mismas/articles/misc2009/12/kurdsworldwide422.htm (accessed 20 April 2010).

Scarpino, S. (1992) *Tutti a casa, terroni*. Milan: Leonardo.

Schmidt, G., Westhues, A., Lafrance, J., and Knowles, A. (2001) 'Social Work in Canada: Results from the National Sector Survey', *Canadian Social Work*, 3(2): 83–92.

Schneider, K. (2009) 'Climate Deal Not Accepted by All, but Copenhagen Conference Makes it "Operational"', www.grist.org/article/late-night-agreement-not-accepted-by-all-parties-at-copenhagen-climate-conf/ (accessed 20 January 2010).

Schön, D. A. (1987) *Educating the Reflective Practitioner: Toward a New Design for Teaching and Learning in the Professions*. San Francisco: Jossey-Bass.

Seldman, B. F., and Murphy, N. J. (2004) *Toward a New Political Humanism*. Amherst, NY: Prometheus Books.

Sen, A. (1999) *Development as Freedom*. Oxford: Oxford University Press.

Sewpaul, V. (2005) 'Global Standards: Promises and Pitfalls for Re-Inscribing Social Work into Civil Society', *International Journal of Social Welfare*, 14: 210–17.

Sewpaul, V., and Hölscher, D. (2004) *Social Work in Times of Neoliberalism*. Pretoria: Van Schaik.

Sewpaul, V., and Hölscher, D. (2007) 'Against the Odds: Community-Based Interventions for Children in Difficult Circumstances in Post-Apartheid South Africa', in L. Dominelli (ed.) *Revitalising Communities in a Globalising World*. Aldershot: Ashgate.

Sewpaul, V., and Jones, D. (2004) 'Global Standards for Social Work Education and Training', *Social Work Education*, 23(5): 493–513.

Shekarau, M. I. (2007) 'Private Entrepreneurs to be Promoted in Power Sector', *Press Trust of India*, 29 July.

Sheldon, B. (1995) *Cognitive Behavioural Therapy: Research, Practice and Philosophy*. London: Routledge.

Sherlock, P., and Bennett, H. (2006) *The Story of the Jamaican People*. Kingston: Ian Randle.

Shiva, V. (2003) 'Food Rights, Free Trade and Fascism', in M. Gibney (ed.) *Globalizing Rights*. Oxford: Oxford University Press.

Shore, R. (2009) '10 Years After: BC's Chinese Boat Migrants', *Vancouver Sun*, 20 October, p. A4.

Sidel, R. (1986) *Women and Children Last: The Plight of Poor Women in Affluent America*. New York: Viking Books.

Siggins, M. (2005) *Bitter Embrace: White Society's Assault on the Woodland Cree*. Toronto: McClelland & Stewart.

Simons, K., and Jankowski, T. (2007) 'Factors Influencing Nursing Home Social Workers Intending to Quit Employment', *Administration in Social Work*, 32(1): 5–21.

Simpkin, M. (1979) *Trapped within Welfare: Surviving Social Work*. London: Macmillan.

Simpson, L. (ed.) (2008) *Lighting the Eighth Fire: The Liberation, Resurgence, and Protection of Indigenous Nations*. Winnipeg: Arbeiter Ring.

Simpson, S. (2009) 'Haida Turn to Wind and Water for New Power', *Vancouver Sun*, 14 August, p. C1.

Sinclair, M. (2010) *How to Cut Public Spending (and Still Win an Election)*. London: Biteback.

Sithole, M. (2008) 'Zimbabwean Social Workers in Birmingham City Council', PhD research paper, Durham University, School of Applied Social Sciences.

Sklair, L. (1991) *Sociology of the Global System*. London: Harvester Wheatsheaf.

Small, J. (2007) 'Rethinking and Unravelling the Interlocking Dynamics of Caribbean Emigration and Return', in L. Dominelli (ed.) *Revitalising Communities in a Globalising World*. Aldershot: Ashgate.

Smith, G., and Corden, J. (1981) 'The Introduction of Contracts in a Family Service Unit', *British Journal of Social Work*, 11(1): 289–313.

Smith, M. K. (2006) 'Community Work', www.infed.org/community/b-comwrk. htm (accessed 27 May 2007).

Social Work Task Force (2009) *Facing up to the Task: The Interim Report of the Social Work Task Force, July 2009*. London: Department of Health and Department for Children, Schools and Families.

Soete, L. (2010) 'Science and Technology Policy Challenges in the Green Economy', paper presented at the GRIPS symposium, UNU-MERIT, Maastricht, 22 February.

Stedman Jones, G. (1971) *Outcast London*. Oxford: Clarendon Press.

Stewart, W. (2010) 'Fury as US Woman Adopts Russian Boy, 7, then Sends Him Back Alone with Note Saying, "I Don't Want Him Anymore"', *Daily Mail*, 10 April.

Stiglitz, J., Sean, A., and Fitoussi, J.-P. (2009) *Report of the Commission on the Measurement of Economic Performance and Social Progress*, http://media. ft.com/cms/f3b4c24a-a-141-11de-a88d-00144feabdc0.pdf.

Stott, K. (2009) 'Remote Village Turns to the Sun for Power', *Vancouver Sun*, 26 October, p. B4.

Strega, S., Brown, L., Callahan, M. L., Dominelli, L., and Walmsley, C. (2009) 'Engaging Fathers in Child Welfare Practice', in S. Strega and J. Carrière (eds) *Walking This Path Together: Anti-Racist and Anti-Oppressive Child Welfare Practice*. Halifax, NS: Fernwood, pp. 238–56.

Stubbs, P. (2007) 'Community Development in Contemporary Croatia: Globalisation, Neoliberalism and NG0-isation', in L. Dominelli (ed.) *Revitalising Communities in a Globalising World*. Aldershot: Ashgate.

Swift, K., and Callahan, M. (2009) *At Risk: Social Justice in Child Welfare and Other Human Services*. Toronto: University of Toronto Press.

Tait-Rolleston, W., and Pehi-Barlow, S. (2001) 'A Maori Social Work Construct', in L. Dominelli, W. Lorenz and H. Soydan (eds) *Beyond Racial Divides: Ethnicities in Social Work*. Aldershot: Ashgate.

Tennant, P. (1990) *Aboriginal People and Politics: The Indian Land Question in British Columbia, 1849–1989*. Vancouver: University of British Columbia Press.

Tetrault, M. (2009) 'Island Coal Operation Would Supply Asian Steel Mills', *Vancouver Sun*, 31 October, p. F4.

Thompson, E. P. (2002) *The Making of the English Working Class*. Harmondsworth: Penguin.

Timmins, N. (2010) 'Private Providers Face NHS Setback', *Financial Times*, 4 April.

Travis, A. (2010) 'Charitable Giving and Volunteering in Decline, Survey Finds', *The Guardian*, 29 April; www.guardian.co.uk/society/2010/apr/29/donations-charity-volunteering-decline.

Trotsky, L. (2007) *The History of the Russian Revolution*. London: Haymarket Books.

UNDP (United Nations Development Programme) (2008) *Climate Change: Scaling up to Meet the Challenge*. New York: UNDP.

UNDP (United Nations Development Programme) (2009) *Overcoming Barriers: Human Mobility and Development: Human Development Report*. New York: UNDP.

United Nations (2005) 'World Population to Reach 9.1 billion in 2050, UN Projects', www.un.org/apps/news/story.asp?NewsID=13451&Cr=population&Cr1 (accessed 12 April 2009).

United Nations (2009) *The Millennium Development Goals Report 2009*. New York: United Nations.

Ungar, M. (2002) 'A Deeper, More Social Ecological Social Work Practice', *Social Services Review*, 76: 480–97.

Van Ewijk, H. (2009) 'Citizenship-Based Social Work', *International Social Work*, 52(2): 167–79.

Van Opstal, W., and Gijselinckx, C. (2008) *The Cooperative Provision of Public Services in an Evolving Welfare State*, http://ssrn.com/abstract=1330425 (accessed 19 April 2010).

Vermeer, E. B. (1979) *Social Welfare Provisions and the Limits of Inequality in Contemporary China*. Berkeley: University of California Press.

Vickers, T. (2009) 'Social Capital Think Piece for PhD Thesis', Durham University.

Wallerstein, I. (2005) 'After Developmentalism and Globalization, What?' *Social Forces*, 83(3): 1263–78.

Walton, R. (1975) *Women in Social Work*. London: Routledge & Kegan Paul.

Ward, D. (2009) 'Canadian Critics Slam Obamacare in the US', *Vancouver Sun*, 10 October, p. A6.

Waterson, J. (1993) 'Balancing Research and Action: Reflection on an Action-Research Project in a Social Services Department', in C. Jones Finer and G. Lewando Hundt (eds) *The Business of Research: Issues of Policy and Practice*. Oxford: Blackwell.

Watson, M., and Lee, P. (1982) 'Baptism of Fire: Some Dilemmas in Becoming a Social Worker', in R. Bailey and P. Lee (eds) *Theory and Practice in Social Work*. Oxford: Blackwell.

WCED (World Commission on Environment and Development) (1987) *Our Common Future*. Oxford: Oxford University Press [Brundtland Commission report].

Webb, S. (2003) 'Local Orders and Global Chaos in Social Work', *European Journal of Social Work*, 6(2): 191–204.

Weber, M. (1978) *Max Weber: Selections in Translation*, ed. W. G. Runciman, trans. E. Matthews. Cambridge: Cambridge University Press.

Wernham, M. (2004) *An Outside Chance: Street Children and Juvenile Justice: An International Perspective*. London: Consortium for Street Children.

White, R. (2007) 'Challenges and Opportunities for Social Workers in the Trans-national Labour Force', in L. Dominelli (ed.) *Revitalising Communities in a Globalising World*. Aldershot: Ashgate.

Whitehead, A. N. (1929) *The Aims of Education and Other Essays*. London: Macmillan.

Whitmore, E., Muñoz, M., Calhoun, A., and Wilson, M. (2008) 'Advocacy in a Neoliberal World: Effectiveness in Social Action', paper presented at the Social Work National Conference, Toronto.

WHO (World Health Organization) (2010) 'Pandemic (H1N1) 2009', www.who.int/csr/disease/swineflu/en/ (accessed 19 April 2010).

WHO and UNICEF Joint Monitoring Programme (2009) *Progress on Drinking Water and Sanitation: Special Focus on Sanitation*. Geneva: WHO; New York: UNICEF.

Whynes, D. (1994) 'The Growth of UK Health Expenditure', *Social Policy and Social Administration*, 26(4): 285–95.

Wichterich, C. (2000) *The Globalized Woman: Reports from a Future of Inequality*. London: Zed Books.

Williams, J. (2001) 'The 1998 Human Rights Act: Social Work's New Benchmark', *British Journal of Social Work*, 31(6): 831–44.

Wilson, E. (1977) *Women and the Welfare State*. London: Tavistock.

Wolpoff, M. H., Hawks, J., Frayer, D. W., and Hunley, K. (2001) 'Modern Human Ancestry at the Peripheries: A Test of Replacement Theory', *Science*, 291: 293–7.

Wood, G. (2009) 'Thousands Rally for Action on Climate Change', *Vancouver Sun*, 26 October, p. A13.

Woolcock, M. (1998) 'Social Capital and Economic Development: Toward a Theoretical Synthesis and Policy Framework', *Theory and Society*, 27(2): 151–208.

Woolhandler, S., Campbell, T., and Himmelstein, D. (2003) 'Costs of Health Care Administration in the United States and Canada', *New England Journal of Medicine*, 349(8): 768–75.

World Bank (2008) *World Development Indicators, 2008*. Washington, DC: World Bank.

World News (2010) 'Haiti Charges US Missionaries with Child Kidnapping', 5 February, http://article.wn.com/view/2010/02/05/Haiti_charges_US_missionaries_with_child_kidnapping_x/ (accessed 18 April 2010).

Worsley, P. (1964) *The Third World*. Chicago: University of Chicago Press.

Yang, J. M. (2009) 'Community Development in South Korea', PhD thesis, Durham University, School of Applied Social Sciences.

Yip, K.-S. (2005) 'A Dynamic Asian Response to Globalization in Cross-Cultural Social Work', *International Social Work*, 48(5): 593–607.

Younghusband, E. (1978) *Social Work in Britain, 1950–1978*. London: Allen & Unwin.

Zaviršek, D. (2008) 'Engendering Social Work under State Socialism in Yugoslavia', *British Journal of Social Work*, 38(4): 734–50.

Zhang, N., Gammonley, D., Pack, S., and Frahm, K. (2008) 'Facility, Service, Environment, Staffing and Psychosocial Care in Nursing Homes', *Health Care Financing Review*, 30(2): 5–17.

# Author Index

# Subject Index

Lightning Source UK Ltd.
Milton Keynes UK
UKOW06f2214250116

267070UK00010B/446/P